THE EXCLUSIVE SOCIETY

*Social Exclusion, Crime and
Difference in Late Modernity*

JOCK YOUNG

SAGE Publications
London · Thousand Oaks · New Delhi

For
JESSE, JOSEPH and FINTAN

First published 1999
Reprinted 1999

SAGE Publications Ltd
6 Bonhill Street
London EC2A 4PU

SAGE Publications Inc
2455 Teller Road
Thousand Oaks, California 91320

SAGE Publications India Pvt Ltd
32, M-Block Market
Greater Kailash - I
New Delhi 110 048

British Library Cataloguing in Publication data

A catalogue record for this book is
available from the British Library

ISBN 0 8039 8150 3
ISBN 0 8039 8151 1 (pbk)

Library of Congress catalog record available

Typeset by Type Study, Scarborough, North Yorkshire
Printed in Great Britain by Redwood Books, Trowbridge, Wiltshire

CONTENTS

FIGURES AND TABLES

Figures

Tables

ACKNOWLEDGEMENTS

This book started off as one on criminology and ended up as one on cultural studies and political philosophy. Many people influenced me on the way: Zygmunt Bauman was kind enough to read the manuscript and his work remains a constant inspiration; my colleagues at Middlesex University were, as always, supportive and generous in their help. John Lea and Roger Matthews provided invaluable intellectual companionship throughout. Paul Corrigan, Trevor Jones and John Lloyd will recognize some of the ideas about radical meritocracy from the series of mini-seminars which we ran at my house several years ago. Stan Cohen, Ian Taylor, Nigel South, Vincenzo Ruggiero, Kev Stenson, Ken Plummer, Ruth Jamieson, Lynne Segal, Rene van Swaaningen, Michael Jacobson, Lynn Chancer, Tim Hope, John Pitts, Richard Kinsey, Keir Sothcott, Malcolm Read, Ralf Steinkamp, David Garland, Marc Mauer and Elliott Currie – in no particular order – all variously aided and abetted my endeavour. Albert Ross loafed around as usual.

Gillian Stern has been the most patient and sympathetic editor, thankfully this book was delivered way ahead of Ben's Bar Mitzvah. Catriona Woolner worked heroically on the manuscript. My partner Jayne Mooney remains my best critic and my staunchest support.

Jock Young
Stoke Newington, London

INTRODUCTION

This book is about difficulty and it is about difference. It traces the rapid unravelling of the social fabric of the industrialized world in the last third of the twentieth century, charting the rise of individualism and of demands for social equality which emerged on the back of the market forces that have permeated and transformed every nook and cranny of social life. It notes the slow but steady erosion of deference whether it is in politics, in public life, in the classroom or in the family. It is a movement from an inclusive society of stability and homogeneity to an exclusive society of change and division. In this late modern world exclusion occurs on three levels: economic exclusion from labour markets, social exclusion between people in civil society and the ever-expanding exclusionary activities of the criminal justice system and private security.

We live in a time where there has been massive structural change: where there have been fundamental changes in the primary and secondary labour markets; where the employment patterns of women have radically changed; where structural unemployment has been created on a vast scale; where communities have disintegrated; where new communities have emerged in a multicultural context; where patterns of leisure have been manifestly restructured; where patterns of social space have undergone redefinition; where the agencies of the state have undergone systematic transformations and reappraisal by the public. And these structural changes have been accompanied by cultural changes no less dramatic: patterns of desire have been transformed; the global village engendered by the mass media has become an ever-present reality; the old patterns of reward and effort have been redefined; institutionalized individualism has permeated areas of social life hitherto sacrosanct; the naturalistic language of the market place has challenged and threatened the metanarrative of social democracy and modernity. And all of this – the wider structural and cultural changes – must be related to the quantum leap in crime and incivilities and to the debate over rules and standards which we now experience.

We live now in a much more difficult world: we face a greater range in life choices than ever before, our lives are less firmly embedded in work and relationships, our everyday existence is experienced as a series of encounters with risk either in actuality or in the shape of fears and apprehensions. We feel both materially insecure and ontologically precarious. Furthermore, we have come to inhabit a world of greater difference: rules change from year to year and rules vary between groups throughout society. The mass media has become a key element in our lives: mediated relationships become as important as face to face encounters. We spend an inordinate amount of time, perhaps between 30 and 40 hours a week, in front of televisions, listening to the radio, reading newspapers. Both difficulty and difference, risk and the debate about rules are central staples of the media. Each day the normative contours of our society, in chat show, soap opera, news item or sport, are discussed in intimate detail. At no time in human history has so much time been spent in public self-reflection, at no other time have so many people gazed at so many others and has every normative nuance been so measuredly scrutinized.

In such an urban existence the tendency is for attitudes to become wary and calculating, blasé and actuarial. Difficulties are to be avoided, differences to be accepted yet kept at a distance, not allowed to affect one's security or composure. Yet at the same time as such a withdrawal of judgement another contradictory attitude occurs. For material and ontological precariousness is a fertile soil for projection and moralism. Social blame and recrimination ricochets throughout the social structure: single mothers, the underclass, blacks, new age travellers, junkies, crackheads – the needle spins and points to some vulnerable section of the community to whom we can apportion blame, and who can be demonized. In this new world of exclusion any radical politics must tackle the basic problems of justice and community which are the root causes of the material and ontological insecurity experienced throughout the population. The ever-present temptation, politically, is that of nostalgia to attempt to retreat to the inclusive world of the 1950s and 1960s. But the terrain has changed irretrievably and the opportunities in front of us are to be welcomed rather than faced with dread. It is the charting of such a terrain, and the route through it, that is the aim of this book.

1 FROM INCLUSIVE TO EXCLUSIVE SOCIETY

My task in this chapter is threefold: firstly to trace the transition which has occurred between the Golden Age of the post-war period within the First World to the crisis years of the late 1960s onwards. It is a movement from modernity to late modernity, from a world whose accent was on assimilation and incorporation to one which separates and excludes. It is a world where, I will argue, the market forces which transformed the spheres of production and consumption relentlessly challenged our notions of material certainty and uncontested values, replacing them with a world of risk and uncertainty, of individual choice and pluralism and of a deep-seated precariousness both economic and ontological. And it is a world where the steady increment of justice unfolding began to falter: the march of progress seemed to halt. But it is a society propelled not merely by rising uncertainty but also by rising demand. For the same market forces which have made precarious our identity and unsure our future have generated a constant rise in our expectations of citizenship and, most importantly, have engendered a widespread sense of demands frustrated and desires unmet.

Secondly I wish to ground the dramatic changes that occurred in levels of crime and in the nature of deviance and disorder in the material changes which occurred within both the spheres of production and consumption, or the transition which, metaphorically at least, has come to be seen as the movement from Fordism to post-Fordism (see Lea, 1997). It is important that the lines of causality between changes in work and leisure, the levels and nature of crime, the impact on the crime control apparatus and eventually criminology are made clear, at very least for the reason that criminologists persistently attempt to disassemble them. Thus those of the right frequently attempt to suggest that levels of crime have no relationship to the changes in work and leisure but are rooted in the supposedly autonomous areas of child rearing, drug use or a free-floating world of moral values. Whereas, those on the left repeatedly attempt to suggest that changes in imprisonment, patterns of social control, the emerging actuarialism, etc. are political or managerial decisions unrelated to the problem of crime. Indeed, their critical edge is often based on an overt denial of a relationship. And both left and right tend to downplay the level to which *their* criminology, at least, is affected by the external world outside of the academy.

Lastly, I want to stress how such changes, although arising throughout the developed world, occur in specific circumstances. The contrast I want to make here is between the material and cultural situation in Western Europe and that in the United States: between the European Dream and the American Dream.

The compass fails

Eric Hobsbawm, in *The Age of Extremes* (1994), pinpoints the extraordinary changes which developed in the last third of the twentieth century. The Golden Age of post-war Europe and North America was a world of full employment and steadily rising affluence, it witnessed the gradual incorporation of the working class into at least the trappings of full citizenship, the entry of women more fully into public life and the labour market, the attempt in the United States to create political equality for African-Americans. It was an era of inclusion, of affluence and of conformity. But, as Hobsbawm wryly delineates it, the Golden Age was followed by the cultural revolution of the late 1960s and 1970s, with the rise of individualism, of diversity, of a vast, wide scale deconstruction of accepted values. A world of seeming certainty was replaced by one of pluralism, debate, controversy and ambiguity. And whereas social commentators of the early 1960s had bemoaned the conformity of the age, the subsequent years experienced widespread disorder, rebellion and rising crime, despite the continuing increase in average incomes and the most committed attempts to socially engineer a satisfied and orderly society. It was a world where commentators of all political persuasions talk of 'the compass' failing, where each of the seeming certainties of society – the family, work, the nation, and even affluence itself – became questioned.

But let us look for a moment at the post-war world, the world before the great transition. I take two books off my shelf, both rather yellowed Penguins, both redolent of certainty and security, the first published in 1962, the second in 1967. The first is by Ronald Fletcher on the family, the famous *Britain in the Sixties: The Family and Marriage*. He writes:

> Frequently . . . it is said that divorce has been continually increasing during the past few decades. This statement is simply not true . . . the figures of divorce do not show that there is *in fact* any decline in the stability of the family. Actually something like 93% of marriages do not end in the divorce court. In 1950 the estimated percentage of marriages terminated by divorce was 7.3. Indeed the 'cohort analysis' of divorce recently presented by Griselda Rowntree and Norman Carier seems to suggest . . . that the rate of divorce may well decline still further in the future. (1962, pp. 136, 142)

He speculates on a figure of 3%. So passionate is his belief in stability, he later cites Geoffrey Gorer's findings that:

> the younger generation – those under 24 – are just as strict in their views of

desirable and undesirable sexual behaviour as their elders. There seems every reason to believe that the social morals of the English have changed very little in the present century. (1955, p. 82)

The second book is Michael Stewart's *Keynes and After*. At that time Stewart was Reader in Political Economy at University College London, Adviser to the Treasury and Cabinet Office and Senior Economic Adviser at 10 Downing Street:

Some . . . predicted that the Second World War, just like the First, would be followed by a temporary boom which gave way to a prolonged depression. But such worries and sceptics were proved totally wrong. Full employment has been maintained year in and year out. Since the War unemployment has averaged $1^3/_4\%$. This is a good performance even by the apparently optimistic standards laid down during the War by Beveridge, who said that if unemployment could be kept down to 3% the country would be doing very well. By the standards of the inter-War period, when unemployment averaged about 13%, the achievement is monumental. Moreover this achievement has not been confined to Britain. . . . In fact in no highly developed country has there been anything remotely like a recurrence of the unemployment of the 1930s. (1967, pp. 186–7)

He concluded:

Whatever the qualifications, the basic fact is that . . . the days of uncontrollable mass unemployment in advanced industrial countries are over. Other economic problems may threaten; this one, at least, has passed into history. (1967, p. 299)

The Golden Age was one where the twin sectors of society, work and the family, fitted together like a functionalist dream: the site of production and the site of consumption, a Keynesian duality of supply and demand each necessary for the other, but underscored by an accepted division of labour between sexes and all heavily underwritten by the ever-increasing collateral of affluence. The cars got larger and larger as, indeed, did the kitchens. It was an era of inclusion, of affluence and of conformity. Rebels were without causes, teenagers cut their hair shorter and shorter and dreamt of dating and high school: the Everly Brothers were on the radio. Social commentators of the time did not complain of crime and delinquency but of conformity and acceptance, Galbraith lampooned *The Affluent Society* (1962), Vance Packard pilloried *The Status Seekers* (1960), Riesman (1950) talked of the 'other-directed American' while William Whyte charted the careful suburban lives of *The Organisation Man* (1960) and his wife and family. It was a time when Betty Friedan (1960) dared to think '*is this all there is?*' (emphasis in original), as she ferried the kids from home to school to Guides and back again.

It was a consensual world with core values centring around work and the family. It was an inclusive world; a world at one with itself, where the accent was on assimilation whether of wider and wider swathes of society (lower working class, women or youth), or immigrants entering into a monocultural society. It was a world where the modernist project was deemed within a breath of success.

The modernist paradigm: a world at one with itself

The modernist project has, over the century, involved the greater and greater incorporation of the population into full citizenship. Such a social contract is based on the notion of a citizenship, not merely of formal rights, but of substantive incorporation into society. In the terms of T.H. Marshall's famous essay (1950), citizenship should bestow not only legal and political rights, but social rights: a minimum of employment, income, education, health and housing. In these terms, the full employment, high income, economies of the Western world in the post-war period up to the recession were well on the way to achieving full citizenship for the mass of the population. I am well aware that, in reality, there were considerable pockets of extreme poverty, of the continuing existence of massive social inequalities and of the contradictions that such a welfare society engendered (see Offe, 1984) and of the fact that it was *male* full employment that was actually being referred to, but this does not concern us here. What is of importance is that the consensual politics of the period quite clearly, and on a bipartisan level, saw society in terms of a social contract enveloping the vast majority of adults. Let us examine the major premises of the modernist paradigm as a discourse relating crime and deviancy to the normal citizenry.

1 **Citizenship resolved:** The long march of citizenship is either resolved or is on the brink of resolution. The incorporation of blacks and women into full citizenship in the formal sense of legal and political equality is accompanied by the achievement of social equality for the vast majority of citizens.
2 **The interventionist state:** The role of the state is to intervene in order to achieve in a piecemeal fashion social justice as a part of a metanarrative of progress. It is Keynesian in economics and Fabian in its social policy. The twin pillars of modernity are the Rule of Law and the welfare state as represented by neo-classicist legal theory and social positivist notions of planning. The State protects and the state delivers.
3 **Absolutist social order:** The vast number of citizens accept the given social order as the best of all possible worlds. Unemployment is low, the level of wealth is the highest in the history of humanity and the average income has annually increased since the war. The social order is viewed not only as just but as obviously in the interests of all: the major institutions of work, the family, democratic politics, the legal system, and the mixed economy are accepted without much question. The rules are seen in absolute terms: they are obvious, clear cut and uncontested. The end

of ideology is at hand and Western values represent the end point of human progress.

4 **The rational conforming citizen and the determined deviant:** The vast majority of people are rational and freely embrace the consensus of values. The exceptions are a tiny minority of professional criminals and a larger, but still small, number of criminals and deviants who are determined by psychological and social circumstances. The large scale rational criminality and dissent possible prior to the modern advances in citizenship ceases to exist. No longer is the rational criminal, the spectre which haunts the work of Beccaria, a major threat or possibility. People by and large do not choose deviance – they are propelled into it.

5 **The narrow conduit of causality:** Causality is reserved for those who deviate; explanation for or conformity to absolute rules is, of course, unproblematic – aetiology is after all only necessary when things go wrong. Deviance occurs because of problems located not so much in the present as in the past: the conduit of causality is individualized and sited frequently in the family. The notion of sizeable, socially distinguishable groups occupying identifiable space is replaced by the atomistic individual, a random product of some unusual family background. The dangerous classes of pre-modernity become the individual deviant in modernity; it is not till late modernity that the spatial and social pariah recurs with a vengeance in the concept of the underclass.

6 **The assimilative state:** The role of the welfare state is to assimilate the deviant from the margins into the main body of society. To this end a corpus of experts builds up, skilled in the use of the therapeutic language of social work, of counselling, of clinical psychology and allied positivistic disciplines.

Nowhere was such an inclusive society embracing the citizen from cradle to grave, insisting on full social as well as legal and political citizenship, so developed as in the welfare states of Western Europe: in Germany, France, Scandinavia and the Benelux countries. If the coming decades made the American dreamer fitful and listless, in Europe the events conjured up the beginnings of a nightmare.

The deviant other in the inclusive society

It is a society which does not abhor 'the other', nor regard him or her as an external enemy so much as someone who must be socialized, rehabilitated, cured until he or she is like 'us'. The modernist gaze views the other not as something alien, but as something or somebody who lacks the attributes of the viewer. It is lacking in civilization, or socialization or sensibilities. It is a camera which is so strangely constituted that it can only take negatives of the photographer.

The deviant 'other' is thus:

- a minority;
- distinct and objective;
- constituted as a lacking in values which are absolute and uncontested. Indeed, contesting itself is usually a sign of lack of maturity or sensibility;
- ontologically confirming rather than threatening. Our own certainty of values is confirmed by seeing the precariousness of those who lack our standards;
- subject to the goal of assimilation and inclusion. The discourses both penal and therapeutic are, therefore, of integration. Criminals 'pay their debt to society' and then re-enter, the drug addict is cured of his or her sickness, the aberrant teenager is taught to adjust to a welcoming society;
- confronts barriers to outsiders which are permeable: they encourage a cultural osmosis of the less socialized towards the well socialized.

From inclusive to exclusive society

The cultural revolution was followed by the economic crisis: 'The history of the twenty years after 1973,' Hobsbawm writes, 'is that of a world which lost its bearings and slid into instability and crisis' (1994, p. 403). The two processes, the cultural revolution of individualism and the economic crisis and restructuring of the labour markets of the advanced industrial world, are often conflated but they are distinct. Thus, those on the left such as David Harvey (1989) tend to stress the economic crisis and use 1973 as the turning point, whereas those on the right, such as James Q. Wilson, stress cultural change and date the turning point earlier.

Other commentators, such as Eric Hobsbawm himself, solve the problem by consigning each process to a separate chapter without intellectually connecting them. And separate they are, representing radical changes in each of the two spheres of order: that of work and community yet, as we shall see, also connected in that the changes in each are the responses to the same market forces which transformed the First World in the latter part of the twentieth century. The cultural revolution, of course, preceded the economic crisis, as indeed did the rise in the crime rate, which began in most advanced industrial countries before the early 1970s and then continued to rise, often at a greatly augmented rate, as the economic recession began to bite.

If the first moment in the 1960s and 1970s was that of the rise of individualism, the creation, if you like, of zones of personal exclusiveness, the unravelling of traditionalities of community and family, then the second lasting through the 1980s and 1990s, and involved a process of social exclusion. This is a two-part process, involving firstly the transformation and separation of the labour markets and a massive rise in structural unemployment, and secondly the exclusion arising from attempts to control the crime which arises out of such changed circumstances and the excluding nature of anti-social behaviour itself.

The transition from modernity to late modernity can be seen as a movement from an *inclusive* to an *exclusive* society.[1] That is from a society whose accent was on assimilation and incorporation to one that separates and excludes. This erosion of the inclusive world of the modernist period, what Hobsbawm calls 'The Golden Age', involved processes of disaggregation both in the sphere of community (the rise of individualism) and the sphere of work (transformation of the labour markets). Both processes are the result of market forces and their transformation by the human actors involved. It behoves us here, however schematically, to attempt to spell out the links between the changes in market relationships which bring about this shift and ultimately underscore the changes, conceptions and expectations of citizenship which, in turn, have transformed contemporary developments of criminality and its control.

The most fundamental undercurrent is the familiar, although hotly debated, movement between Fordist and post-Fordist modes of production. Fordism in the post-war period involves mass standardized production, near total male employment, a considerable manufacturing sector, massive hierarchical bureaucracies, a sizeable primary labour market of secure jobs and standardized career prospects, clearly demarcated jobs, corporatist government policies and mass consumption of fairly uniform products. The world of work is paralleled by the sphere of leisure and the family; underwritten by the division of labour between the sexes, the family becomes the site of consumption, the celebration of an affluent lifestyle, the essential demand side of Keynsianism, and is presented with an ever-expanding array of standardized consumer goods by which to measure individual success and to mark out the steady economic progress of an expanding economy. Such is the consensual world where the core values centring around work and the family present themselves like absolutes . . . a social order which abhors 'the other' not as an external enemy so much as something or someone who must be transformed, socialized, rehabilitated and made into 'one of us'.

All of this interwoven and buttressed structure was to unfold. If we start with a structure seemingly monolithic and all embracing, its basic elements undergirding and stoutly maintaining the weight of the absolute certainties of biography and aspiration of its members, we end with a world which is more chaotic; its structure begins to unravel, its constituents fragment and the everyday world of its members seems problematic, blurred and uncertain. The major institutions of work and the family no longer provide the cradle to grave trajectories which embrace, engulf and insure. The strains, always there, between for example inherited wealth and merit, equality of citizenship and inequality of gender, formal and substantial equality, were contained for a while by the sheer success of the 'never had it so good' societies. The seeds of change were already present in the contrast between the primary and secondary labour markets (Harvey, 1989) while the rise of individualism heightened demands for fuller and more developed citizenship as well as registering protest at the lack of equality in the system. That is a movement both of rising aspiration and thwarted expectation.

The market economy emerging in post-Fordism involved a qualitative leap in the levels of exclusion. The downsizing of the economy has involved the reduction of the primary labour market, the expansion of the second-ary market and the creation of an underclass of structurally unemployed. Will Hutton in *The State We're In* (1995) describes this as the 40:30:30 society. Forty per cent of the population in tenured secure employment, 30% in insecure employment, 30% marginalized, idle or working for poverty wages. We may quarrel with his proportions but the percentage of the population who are part of J.K. Galbraith's 'constituency of content-ment' (1992) is a minority and ever shrinking. Indeed, the middle classes, once contented, have found their world rendered precarious and transient. The downsizing of the economy involves 'lean production' in manufactur-ing industry with the de-skilling of labour and the stress on the flexibility of the workforce. Secure, skilled work with steady salaries is thus reduced within a firm, while at the same time a considerable proportion of labour is 'outsourced' in terms of short contracts to small firms or to freelance per-sonnel. Despite a general shift from manufacturing to service industries, the latter are scarcely exempt from automation. The 're-engineering' of service industries such as banking, communications and insurance involves the use of more and more sophisticated computer software which allows firms to eliminate whole layers of low-level managers and white collar jobs (see Head, 1996). The resulting effect of lean production and re-engineering is to remove a sizeable proportion of middle income jobs and to engender a feeling of *precariousness* in those previously secure.

If we picture contemporary meritocracy as a racetrack where merit is rewarded according to talent and effort, we find a situation of two tracks and a motley of spectators: a primary labour market where rewards are apportioned according to plan but where there is always the chance of demotion to the second track where rewards are substantially inferior, only small proportions of the track are open to competitors and there is always the chance of being demoted to the role of spectator. As for the spectators, their exclusion is made evident by barriers and heavy policing: they are denied real access to the race but are the perpetual viewers of the glittering prizes on offer.

Yet it is not only that opportunities to the race are available with no more than a contingent relationship to talent; the prizes have also become more unequal. For in the recent period income inequalities have widened. (Joseph Rowntree Foundation, 1995; Hills, 1996). Such a gradient of inclusion and exclusion engenders, according to Edward Luttwak (1995), both chronic relative deprivation amongst the poor which gives rise to crime and a precarious anxiety amongst those better off which breeds intolerance and punitiveness towards the law-breaker. Like pincers on our society, crime and punishment stem from the same source. What I am suggesting is that both the causes of criminal violence and the punitive response towards it spring from the same source. The obsessive violence of the macho street gang and the punitive obsession of the respectable citizen are similar not only in their nature but in their origin. Both stem from dislocations in the labour market: the one from a market which excludes participation as a worker but encourages voraciousness as a consumer, the other from a market which includes, but only in a precarious fashion. That is, from tantalizing exclusion and precarious inclusion. Both frustrations are consciously articulated in the form of relative deprivation. The first is fairly obvious: here not only economic but social citizenship is denied and the comparison is with those within the labour market. But the second is less obvious.

Relative deprivation is conventionally thought of as a gaze upwards: it is the frustration of those denied equality in the market place to those of equal merit and application. But deprivation is also a gaze downwards: it is dismay at the relative well-being of those who although below one on the social hierarchy are perceived as unfairly advantaged: they make too easy a living even if it is not as good as one's own. This is all the more so when rewards are accrued illicitly, particularly where the respectable citizen is also a victim of crime. It is the way in which cities are constituted that the respectable poor and the ne'er-do-well live close at hand: those least able to withstand the impact of crime are the most victimized; those whose working hours are longest and most poorly paid who live adjacent to those who are without work and live in idleness. The regentrification which has occurred in many European cities has added a further twist to this, for 'chic' by jowl, the wealthy middle class live, in many cases, across the street from the structurally unemployed.

The hard-pressed taxpayer views with alacrity the bottom and top of our class structure. For whereas at the bottom there is perceived scrounging, at the top there is sleaze and seemingly unbelievable bonuses/payoffs to top managers and industrialists. For if the spectators are seen to consume free handouts without competing, the privileged are seen as part of a 'winner takes all' culture where prizes are doled out without thought of justification or merit. What a recipe for dissatisfaction! (see Frank and Cook, 1996).

In the large scale Fordist bureaucracies rewards were fairly standardized between firms and across the nation. Meet a manager with a certain level of responsibility or a skilled electrician at a given level of proficiency and one could guess their income even if they came from the opposite part of the country. The decline in the primary labour market, the rise in outsourcing and consultancy work, the development of a massive and variegated service industry makes the development of a genuinely agreed scale of merit difficult. It also makes more mysterious the always occluded sense of why and how anyone is particularly wealthy. The seemingly arbitrary distribution of reward is compounded by this lack of standardization to produce what one might call a *chaos of reward*. Thus this recipe for dissatisfaction is given a further stir of disequilibrium. To precariousness is added a sense of unfairness and a feeling of the arbitrary. In the Fordist period we had relative deprivation, to be sure, but this involved serried ranks of the incorporated casting envious glances at those across the visible division of reward. But now this fixed infantry of conflict is substituted by the loose cannons of discontent.

The sphere of distributive justice, of merit and reward is thus transformed by the rise of the exclusive society. But let us now turn to the other sphere of order, that of community, and trace how the personal exclusiveness of individualism has its roots in post-Fordism. Here we are concerned more with the arena of consumption than production. David Harvey begins his treatise on post-modernity (1989) with a discussion of Jonathan Raban's *Soft City* published in 1974. As in so many other interesting works at this point of change, Raban overturns the conventional depiction of the city as the epitome of rationalized mass planning and consumption; the iron cage where human behaviour is programmed, where the mass of humanity is channelled and pummelled through the urban grid of suburbs, downtown, offices, factories, shopping zones and leisure facilities. Rather than being the site of determinacy, Raban sees the city as the arena of choice. It is an emporium where all sorts of possibilities are on offer, a theatre where a multiplicity of roles can be played, a labyrinth of potential social interactions, an encyclopaedia of subculture and style.

What interests David Harvey about *Soft City* is that the book is:

> a historical marker, because it was written at a moment when a certain shifting can be detected in the way in which problems of urban life were being talked about in both popular and academic circles. . . . It was also written at that cusp in intellectual and cultural history when something called 'post-modernism' emerged from its chrysalis . . . (1989, p. 3)

Urban life was changing, carried on a market-driven current of consumerism: the emerging consumer society, with its multiplicity of choices, promised not merely the satisfaction of immediate desires but also the generation of that characteristic word of the late twentieth century – *lifestyles*.

The shift from the stolid mass consumption and leisure of Fordism to the diversity of choice and a culture of individualism involving a stress on immediacy, hedonism and self-actualization has profound effects on late modern sensibilities. The Keynesian balance between hard work and hard play, so characteristic of the Fordist period (see Young, 1971b) becomes tipped towards the subterranean world of leisure. 'Modern capitalism', as Paul Willis nicely puts it, 'is not only parasitic upon the puritan ethic, but also upon its instability and even its subversion' (1990, p. 19). Out of such a world of choice, whether it is in the urban emporium or the wider world of cultural communities, people are able to construct identities: although springing from commercial, market forces they are transformed by the human actors. Thus Ian Chambers' (1986) work on working class youth shows how the consumer culture of the late twentieth century allowed young people to create a series of subcultures and styles. And, of course, it was a changing and dynamic youth culture which, in turn, generated of its own accord a constantly new swathe of consumer demands.

Such a transition can be seen reflected in the subcultural theory of the academics. The wooden actors of American subcultural theorization of the 1950s and early 1960s who passively pursued conventional ends by unconventional means or as rebels without causes merely invented middle standards, became active and creative. Subculture becomes now a site of imagination, of innovation and resistance, and the subcultural theory of the Birmingham school, in particular, fixes on and gladly celebrates this (see, e.g., Hall and Jefferson, 1976 and the commentary in Walton and Young, 1998). Similarly, in cultural studies, Stuart Hall and Paddy Whannel in their survey of *The Popular Arts* written in 1964 present a popular culture which is commercialized, a mass commodity impressed upon the people yet hinting in footnotes and half-realized paragraphs that something seemed to be changing: the Beatles, the pop group explosion which transformed world music. Yet they evocatively quote C. Wright Mills' image of the consumer society:

> In its benevolence, the Big Bazaar has built the rhythmic worship of fashion into the habits and looks and feelings of the urban mass: it has organised the imagination itself. (1964: 151)

By the 1970s the Big Bazaar had become the urban emporium: the new individualism which emerges on the back of the consumer society is concerned with pluralistic choice (it creates freely new subcultural styles bricollaging both from the present and the past), it is concerned with self-actualization (the individual creates a lifestyle and a personal identity through choice), it is hedonistic and immediate (the old Keynesian personality involving a balance between work and leisure, production and consumption, deferred gratification and immediacy becomes tipped towards the latter) and it is, above all, voluntaristic (choice is valued, freedom is seen to be possible, tradition is devalued) (see Campbell, 1987; Featherstone, 1985). Such expressive demands augment the instrumental demands for monetary success and status which are the staple of the modern period. By late modernity the frustration of expressive demands becomes a source of strain in the system and, together with relative deprivation in the material world, a potent source of deviance. (For early sightings of this phenomenon see Downes, 1966; Young, 1971b.) What is without doubt is the rise of a culture of high expectations both materially and in terms of self-fulfilment, one which sees success in these terms and one which is far less willing to be put upon by authority, tradition or community if these ideals are frustrated.

Out of such frustrations arise both positive and negative consequences. *The Soft City* of Jonathan Raban is soft more in its plasticity than in its kindness:

> The city, our great modern form, is soft, amenable to a dazzling and libidinous variety of lives, dreams and interpretations. But the very plastic qualities which made the city the great liberator of human identity also cause it to be especially

vulnerable to psychosis. . . . If it can, in the Platonic ideal, be the highest expression of man's reason and sense of his own community with other men, the city can
also be a violent . . . expression of his panic, his envy, his hatred of strangers, his
callousness. (1974, pp. 15–16)

There is, as one writer remarked, room for the flâneur but not for the
flâneuse (Woolf, 1985). Here we have the paradox of the new individualism.
The demise of consumer conformity gives rise to a dynamic, diverse, pluralism of lifestyles. Such a release of human creativity has clearly liberative and
progressive possibilities yet each diverse project has the potentiality to contradict and impede the others. Subcultures are frequently in collision: diversity may impede diversity. Discontent about one's social predicament, the
frustration of aspiration and desire may give rise to a variety of political,
religious and cultural responses which may open up the possibilities for
those around one but they may well, often purposively, close up and restrict
the possibilities of others. They may also create criminal responses and
these very frequently bear the currency of restricting others. Let me give a
couple of examples. The downsizing of the manufacturing base, discussed
in the last section, generates relative deprivation throughout the class structure but, in particular, amongst those unskilled workers clustered around
the empty factories, on the desolate estates. Although the young women in
these areas can find a role for themselves in child rearing and, very often,
work in the service sector, young men are bereft of social position and
destiny. They are cast adrift; a discarded irrelevance locked in a situation of
structural employment not even available to offer the stability of 'marriageable' partners (see W.J. Wilson, 1987). They are barred from the racetrack of the meritocratic society yet remain glued to the television sets and
media which alluringly portray the glittering prizes of a wealthy society.
Young men facing such a denial of recognition turn, everywhere in the
world, in what must be almost a universal criminological law, to the creation
of cultures of machismo, to the mobilization of one of their only resources,
physical strength, to the formation of gangs and to the defence of their own
'turf'. Being denied the respect of others they create a subculture that
revolves around masculine powers and 'respect'.

Paul Willis, in his classic *Learning to Labour* (1977), traces the way in
which 'the lads', seeing through the irrelevance of their schooling for the
labouring jobs to which they are heading, construct a subculture of resistance against the school and the wider middle class world. But their reaction
to being excluded from the primary labour market, from career, good
prospects and a promising future, is to rubber stamp their own exclusion,
which serves to exclude equally vulnerable others. Thus their subculture or
resistance elevates toughness and physical strength to a prime virtue: it is
sexist, frequently racist and avowedly anti-intellectual.

So the excluded create divisions amongst themselves, frequently on
ethnic lines, often merely on the part of the city you live in, or, more pro-
saically (yet to some profoundly), what football team you support. Most

importantly, as Willis points out, this creates problems of safety and security for other members of the community, particularly women. They are excluded, they create an identity which is rejecting and exclusive, they exclude others by aggression and dismissal, and they are, in turn, excluded and dismissed by others, whether school managers, shopping mall security guards, the 'honest' citizen, or the police officer on the beat. *The dialectics of exclusion* is in process, a deviancy amplification which progressively accentuates marginality, a Pyrrhic process involving both wider society and, crucially, the actors themselves which traps them in, at best, a series of dead-end jobs and at worst, an underclass of idleness and desperation.

As our second example, let me turn from a situation where exclusion creates crimes to one where attempts at inclusion are met by violence and aggression. The entry of women into the labour market and their fuller participation in public life, whether leisure, politics or the arts, is perhaps the most profound structural change of the post-war period. Yet this process of inclusion involves, as Ulrich Beck puts it, 'erupting discrepancies between women's expectations of equality and the realm of inequality in occupations and the family', which 'it is not difficult to predict . . . will amount to an externally induced amplification of conflicts in personal relationships' (1992, p. 120). It is not, however, merely the increasing expectations of women but the challenge of these expectations to male preconceptions and the resistance to them which encapsulates the rising conflict. Here, surely, Giddens is right to point out that violence is a more frequent occurrence in the family, *as in politics*, where hegemony is threatened not where patriarchal, or state domination is accepted. Widespread violence is the currency of hegemony *breaking down* not of hegemony *in control* (see Giddens, 1992, pp. 121–2). In the case of patriarchy it is where the ability of the man to dictate, without question, the unequal and marginal status of the women-folk within his family is challenged and severely weakened. Thus domestic violence increases whilst simultaneously, as Sandra Walklate argues, 'women are less likely to tolerate violent relationships . . . than they once were' (1995, p. 99). Thus the violence which has always occurred in domestic relationships is tolerated less while the amount of conflict increases.

It is commonplace to think of violent crime as the product of exclusion, the young men of my first example, but it is important to stress that much violence occurs because of conflicts over inclusion (i.e. of equality and modernity against subordination and tradition, see Table 1.1). The case of violence against women is a key example, although racist violence is a close parallel. Indeed, Jayne Mooney (1996) in her research on the social and spatial parameters of violence, points out that 40% of all violence in a North London district is domestic and against women. Violence in these two examples can occur, therefore, as a result of exclusion and inclusion, and it can be caused by relative deprivation and by clashes among individuals demanding equality and others resisting them. Of course, where both relative deprivation and individualism occur together as in the macho-culture of lower class, young unemployed males when confronting the demands for

TABLE 1.1   *The vicissitudes of masculinity: two paths to violence*

Source	Economic precariousness	Ontological threat
Role	Male role diminished	Female role equalized
Crisis	Crisis in masculinity	Crisis in masculine hegemony
Typical victimization	Male to male	Male to female
Typical scenario	Gang violence	Domestic violence
Occurrence	Low in class structure	Throughout class structure

equality of women, often in poorly paid yet steady employment, one would expect a particularly high rate of conflict, often resulting in the preference for setting up home separately and the preponderance of single mothers. Indeed this latter group have the highest rates of violence against them, usually from ex-partners (see Mooney, 1997). It is ironic to note that a major source of violence in our society stems from an attempt to maintain traditional relationships and occurs within the family, rather than being alleviated by the 'back to basics' philosophy beloved by Conservative politicians.

Pluralism and ontological insecurity

Up till now I have traced how changes in the economy have given rise on one hand to increased relative deprivation and economic precariousness and on the other hand to a more rampant individualism. But there is a further force for destabilization and that is the emergence of a more pluralistic society, one in which people's sense of personal security, the stability of their being, becomes more insecure.

As Anthony Giddens graphically delineates, the situation of late modern life is characterized by heightened choice (stemming both from the opportunities of consumption and the flexible demands of work), by a constant questioning of established beliefs and certainties, a raised level of self-reflexivity, a lack of embedded biography and life trajectory and the constant confrontation with a plurality of social worlds and beliefs (1991, pp. 70–88). Such a situation breeds ontological insecurity, that is where self-identity is not embedded in our sense of biographical continuity, where the protective cocoon which filters out challenges and risks to our sense of certainty becomes weakened and where an absolute sense of one's normality becomes disoriented by the surrounding relativism of value. Individualism, with its emphasis on existential choice and self-creation, contributes significantly to such insecurity, while the pressing nature of a plurality of alternative social worlds, some the result of such incipient individuality, manifestly undermines any easy acceptance of unquestioned value.

The pluralism which the actor encounters can be seen as stemming from three major sources: (1) the *diversification* of lifestyles which are a result of growing individualism; (2) the closer *integration* of society, including the narrowing of travelling times through physical space and the implosion of glimpses of other societies and cultures provided by a growing and ever-proliferating mass media. Business, tourism, television, all bring us together; (3) the *immigration* of people from other societies.[2] In Europe, in the last 20 years, such a pluralism has been pronounced on all three levels: mass immigration has occurred, increased European integration is a palpable fact, however disorganized the political process and limited nature of a common identity (see Melossi, 1996), while the diversification characteristic of advanced industrial societies has proceeded apace.

Such a situation has considerable effect on our perception of and reaction to deviance. In modernity, as we have seen, the deviant other appears as a distinct, minority phenomenon in contrast to the vast majority consensus of absolute values which it lacks and, thus, by its very existence conforms rather than threatens. In late modernity the deviant other is everywhere. In the city, as Richard Sennett writes in *The Conscience of the Eye*, everyone is a potential deviant. The distinct other is no longer present, cultures not only appear plural but they blur, overlap and cross over. Youth cultures, for example, do not form distinct ethnic groupings but are hybrids constituted by bricolage rather than by ethnic absolutism (see Gilroy, 1993; Back, 1996).

Because of ontological insecurity there are repeated attempts to create a secure base. That is, to reassert one's values as moral absolutes, to declare other groups as lacking in value, to draw distinct lines of virtue and vice, to be rigid rather than flexible in one's judgements, to be punitive and excluding rather than permeable and assimilative. This can be seen in various guises in different parts of the social structure. The most publicized attempt at redrawing moral lines more rigorously is the 'back to basics' initiative of the British Conservatives in 1995, which was a replay of the Back to Family Values campaign of the Bush administration. Lower in the structure this can be seen in the attempt by the socially excluded to create core and distinct identities. Part of the process of social exclusion, as Jimmy Feys argues, is: the inability 'to cast their anchor in a sea of structure prescribed by society' (1996, p. 7). That is, social exclusion produces a crisis of identity. And one could point to the policies of such groups as Black Muslims, fundamentalists in émigré communities, and perhaps even the tawdry traditionalism of supporters of the far right, as an indication of this. A reaction to exclusion is heightened commitment to past values: to create imaginary nationalisms where the present precariousness is absent, and, often, to ape the conventional or, at least, some imagined image of it. Lastly, amongst the intelligentsia, an aspect of political correctness involves a decline in tolerance of deviance, an obsession with correct behaviour and speech, and an insistence on strict policing of moral boundaries (see Moynihan, 1993; Krauthammer, 1993). Whatever the rights and wrongs of such pronouncements – and there is undoubtedly much that is genuinely progressive in such debates – it is remarkable that the selfsame strata who expanded tolerance of deviance to the point of recklessness in the 1960s now restrict it like characters from a Victorian etiquette book in the 1990s. In Table 1.2 below I contrast the dramatic changes in social attitudes to the deviant other which have occurred in late modernity.

TABLE 1.2   *The deviant other in late modernity*

	Modernity	Late modernity
Society	Inclusive	Exclusive
Size	Minority	Majority
Values	Absolutism	Relativism
Adherence	Consensus	Pluralism
Distinctiveness	Distinct	Blurred/continuum/ overlap/crossover
Constituted barriers	Permeable	Restricting
Threshold	Tolerant	Intolerant

The dyad of crime

The changes, then, in the sphere of production and consumption and their development and reinterpretation by the actors involved have effects both on the causes of crime and deviance and the reactions against it. That is, on both sides of the dyad of crime. (See Table 1.3).

The combination of relative deprivation and individualism is a potent cause of crime in situations where no political solution is possible: it generates crime but it also generates crime of a more internecine and conflictive nature. The working class area, for example, implodes upon itself: neighbours burglarize neighbours, incivilities abound, aggression is widespread. The old-style crime of the 1950s, which was to a large extent directed at commercial targets and involved the judicious use of violence to control the 'manors' of each 'firm', becomes replaced with a more Hobbesian spread of incivilities. 'We never harmed members of the public', muttered one of the Kray gang, lamenting the decline in civilized values in the East End of London. Some index of this is that in the Metropolitan district of London, from 1950 to 1990, burglary and robbery rose from 6% of all crime to 14%, and domestic burglary in 1950 was 40% of all burglary (domestic and commercial), whereas by 1990 it was 66% (Harper et al., 1995).

The contribution of economic precariousness and ontological insecurity is an extremely inflammable mixture in terms of punitive responses to crime and the possibility of scapegoating. We have already seen, in Luttwak's discussion of the likely impact of economic precariousness alone, these tenuously included those in the job market set against those transparently out of it. Ontological insecurity adds to this combustive situation the need to

TABLE 1.3   *The spheres of justice and community*

The dyad of crime	Sphere of justice	Sphere of community
Causes of crime and deviance	Relative deprivation	Individualism
Reaction to crime and deviance	Material precariousness	Ontological insecurity

redefine less tolerant definitions of deviance and to reaffirm the virtues of the in-group. It is important, however, to distinguish tendencies from necessities and to specify the precise social scenario where such dynamics will be played out. I will return to this at the end of this chapter, but first of all I will document the impact of crime on patterns of exclusion within our society.

Rising crime and social exclusion

In Chapter 2 I will detail the rise in crime which occurred in the latter part of the twentieth century in most advanced industrial nations and its impact both on the public and on criminological theory itself.

The major motor in the transformation of public behaviour and attitudes, in the development of the crime control apparatus and in criminology, is the rapid rise in the crime rate. This has had profound effects from the perspective of exclusion:

1 **On public avoidance behaviour**
  Rising crime rates fuel public fear of crime and generate elaborate patterns of avoidance behaviour, particularly for urban women. The isolated problem area of modernity becomes an intricate map of no-go zones, of subways and parks to be avoided, of car parks to be navigated and of public space to be manoeuvred. And for many women these possibilities of the day become a curfew at night (see, e.g., Painter et al., 1989). This is not the place to enter into the 'reality' of such fears, let alone to explore what 'realistic' risk calculations might look like; suffice it to point to the exclusion which crime generates and that its impact varies greatly by age, class, gender and ethnicity.
2 **On penal exclusion**
  The rise in crime results in an increase in those incarcerated. Of course there is no linear relationship, but the absence of such does not obviate the fact that in the long run prison populations have in most countries risen in a response, perhaps mistakenly, to the need for crime control.[3] Indeed, the seemingly large differences between US and European imprisonment rates are less a matter of politics than the result of actual differences in the crime rates. The frequent mistake here is to simply look at rates per population: thus James Lynch found that, when levels of crime

and seriousness were controlled for, 'the extreme differences in incarceration between the United States and several other Western democracies are lessened considerably and in some cases disappear. To a large extent differences in ... incarceration rates cross-nationally are due to differences in the types and levels of crime across countries' (1988, p. 196). Significant differences do remain, however, particularly between Germany and the United States, although somewhat less between the latter and England and Wales, and these are due to differences in the administration of justice together with the extraordinary intensity of the 'war against drugs' being conducted in the United States.

In the United States those in prison constitute a significant excluded population in their own right: approaching 1.6 million people are imprisoned – a city which would be as large as Philadelphia if all were brought together in one place. Furthermore, 5.1 million adults are under correctional supervision (prison, parole or probation), one in 37 of the adult residential population (Bureau of Justice Statistics, 1996). Indeed, the American gulag is now the same size as the Russian gulag and both contrast with the situation in Western Europe, where the total prison population is in the region of 200,000 (Council of Europe, 1995).

3 On exclusion from public space

The rise in crime generates a whole series of barriers to prevent or manage crime. Thus we have a privatization of public space in terms of shopping malls, private parks, leisure facilities, railways, airports, together with the gating of private residential property. These now commonplace precautions are backed by stronger outside fortification, security patrols and surveillance cameras. The security industry, whose very job is exclusion, becomes one of the major growth areas (South, 1994). The city, then, becomes one of barriers, excluding and filtering, although it must be stressed that such barriers are not merely an imposition of the powerful; systems of exclusion, visible and invisible, are created by both the wealthy and the dispossessed. Some of the latter can be as discriminatory as the powerful (Ruggiero and South, 1997) but much can be seen as *defensive exclusion*. For example, within Stoke Newington, the area of London that I live in, one finds gated communities of Kurds who live in constant threat of violence, of Hasidic Jews who face widespread anti-Semitism, there are women-only leisure centres, schools with intensive precautions against vandalism, etc. Furthermore, we must remember that the most commonplace barriers and by far the most costly are those that we are forced to erect to protect our own houses.

Towards an exclusive dystopia?

We cannot imagine a Europe that continues to be divided, not by the Iron Curtain this time, but economically, into a part that is prosperous and increasingly united, and another part that is less stable, less prosperous and disunited. Just as one half of a room cannot remain forever warm whilst the other half is cold, it is equally unthinkable that two different Europes could forever live side by side without detriment to both. (Havel, 1996, p. 40)

Are we heading towards a dystopia of exclusion, where divisions occur not only between the nations of Europe, as Havel suggests, but within the nations themselves? Can one part of a room remain forever warm whilst the other half is perpetually closed off and cold? For many authors such a division between worlds has its own inevitability and forms a functioning, if oppressive, whole. Let us look at its components:

A central core

A sizeable section of the population are in full-time work, with career structures and biographies which are secure and embedded. Here is the realm of meritocracy, of equality between the sexes (both partners work), of the stable nuclear family, of a working week which gets longer just as joint salaries get higher. It is here that neo-classicism operates within the criminal justice system just as meritocracy occurs within work and school. It is a world graded by credit ratings and consumer profiling (it is *the* prime market place, after all) but it is, on the face of it, kind and gentle in its relationships where social control increasingly, both in work and leisure, takes on a casual, almost Disney-like aspect (see Ericson and Carriere, 1994). It is a world where the exigencies of biography are covered fully comprehensively by insurance, whether it is for ill health, accident, job loss or, indeed, criminal victimization. It is a world which holidays in the Third World outside its customs barriers whilst shunning the Third World enclaves within it.

But it is an ever-shrinking core. The largest-growing part of the labour market becomes that of the secondary market where job security is much less secure, where career structures are absent and where life is experienced as precarious.

The cordon sanitaire

A clear line is created between the core group and those outside by a whole series of measures: by town planning, by road networks which divide cities, by the gating of private estates, by the blocking off of areas from easy access, but above all by money: the cost of public transport downtown, the price of goods in the shops, the policing of the core areas, whether suburban shopping mall or inner-city development, and whether it involves private or public police, is aimed at removing uncertainties, of sweeping the streets clean of alcoholics, beggars, the mentally ill and those who congregate in groups. It is an actuarial police calculating what is likely to cause disorder and discontent, and moving on the inappropriate rather than arresting the criminal. It is aided by the widespread introduction of CCTV (which in fact is more effective in dealing with incivilities than with serious, planned, crime) and by the enforcement of numerous pieces of legislation to control disorderly behaviour.

The outgroup

The outgroup becomes a scapegoat for the troubles of the wider society: they are the underclass, who live in idleness and crime. Their areas are the abode of single mothers and feckless fathers, their economics that of drugs, prostitution and trafficking in stolen goods. They are the social impurities of the late modern world, whom David Sibley, in his eloquent *Geographies of Exclusion* (1995), sees as victims of sanitizing and moralizing geographies reminiscent of the nineteenth-century reformers. But unlike the reformers from the late nineteenth century, up until the 1960s the goal is not to physically eliminate their areas and integrate their members into the body politic; it is to hold at bay and exclude.

Up until the 1980s the word 'marginalization' is used for such an outgroup: they are the people that modernity has left behind, pockets of poverty and deprivation in the affluent society, but from then on 'social exclusion' becomes the phrase (see Feys, 1996), encompassing as it does a more dynamic expulsion from society and, most importantly, a decline in the motivation to integrate the poor into society. The neo-liberalism of the late 1980s and 1990s not only attempts to draw back the limits of the state, it (perhaps more successfully) allows the limits of civil society to recede. It is not public policy but the market which is seen as their only possible salvation, yet the chances of such an increased labour market are extremely unlikely. This section of the population has a large ethnic minority constitution, creating the possibility of easy scapegoating and of confusing the vicissitudes of class with those of race.

The future of exclusion

Of course, all this talk of exclusion might be easily dismissed as a temporary problem. The hopes of politicians of both the left and the right often hinge on a return to full employment, to the inclusionist societies of the 1950s. Unfortunately this nostalgia, however bipartisan, is likely to be temporary rather than bringing about any long-run change in reality. The future does not augur well for two reasons that I have already touched upon. Firstly, the demand for unskilled and semi-skilled manual labour has contracted in all the countries of the First World. The globalization of capital has meant that the factories of South East Asia can compete much more cheaply than can those of Europe and North America. The poor are isolated in inner-city ghettos, in orbital estates, and in ghost towns where capital originally led them then left them stranded as it winged its way elsewhere, where labour was cheaper and expectations lower. This exclusion is on a large scale – in Will Hutton's (1995) estimation it is perhaps 30% of the population – and is a radically different problem from the marginalized pockets of poverty characteristic of the immediate post-war period. Furthermore, the full entry of China into the world economy will create reverberations which will vastly eclipse that of the Asian tigers. Secondly, the introduction of more and more sophisticated computer software will eliminate many lower middle class jobs as well as making many lower-rung professional jobs more precarious. The successful company nowadays is one that increases productivity whilst losing workers, not one which increases the size of its personnel. As James Fallows puts it:

> The most important fact about these layoffs is that they result not from corpor-ate failures but from what is defined as success – progress toward a 'friction-free' world of the most efficient production and distribution. But they create a society of winners and losers that is unpleasant even for the winners to live in. (1996, p. 18)

Yet, on the face of it, it is difficult to understand how such a dystopian society could maintain itself. How is it possible to contain within its fron-tiers a permanently dispossessed minority, particularly one which views citizenship, in the broadest sense of social as well as political equality, as a right rather than as something which is achieved? That is, a society which holds firm to the values of meritocracy yet denies to so many participation in the race. The actuarial cordon sanitaire which separates the world of the losers from that of the winners is an attempt to achieve this: to make life more tolerable for the winners while scapegoating the losers.

To some extent the dangers and disruptions created by the excluded are delimited. Most significant is the sporadic rioting which takes place across the First World. In London, Birmingham, Paris and Marseilles they repre-sent riots of citizenship. They occur constantly with the same pattern: a section of people who are economically marginalized are subject, over time, to stereotypical suspicion and harassment by the police. That is, not only are they denied their social rights, as citizens, of access to the labour market on fair terms, they are treated on the streets in a manner which palpably denies their legal rights (see Lea and Young, 1993). Interestingly, the exclu-sion of the market place is matched by the actuarial exclusion of policing which I described earlier. A single incident of prejudiced policing usually provides the trigger for the riot itself: this represents quite clearly a *riot of inclusion*, compared to race riots, which are of an exclusionary nature, or insurrections where the fundamental aim is to redraw the nature of citizen-ship.

In terms of targets, such riots are invariably contained: they involve the destruction of the local community, the rage is directed implosively rather than explosively. The poor no longer threaten the gentlemen's clubs of St James's; they terrorize the small shopkeepers of Brixton and Handsworth. Meanwhile, those areas are consumed by what one might call *the slow riots* of crime, incivilities and vandalism – a world turned in upon itself and, at times, each person against the other. And the actuarial line of differential policing, zoning and crime prevention helps maintain this; indeed, to the extent that it *displaces* crime from well protected middle class to less protected lower working class areas, it actually increases the problem (see Hope, 1995, 1996; Trickett et al., 1995). There are limits, however, to such an exclusionary project. This involves a package with two components: material and cultural. It is an actuarial process of exclusion and risk management coupled with a cultural mechanism of scapegoating: the creation of a spatially and socially segregated deviant other.

But let me first make the distinction between the material and cultural situation in Western Europe and in the United States, because there are important differences.

The American Dream and the European Dream

The American Dream has very specific notions both of community and of opportunity. Although the process of exclusion occurs in all developed industrial countries, it is important to stress the exclusionary nature of American ideology when compared to European ideals. In the American Dream the ideal is equality of opportunity: all get a chance to compete in the meritocratic race, but it is the winners who get the prizes and the losers who naturally do not. And losers fail because of individual qualities, it is *their* fault that they have lost (see Merton, 1938). The notion of citizenship has, therefore, a strong stress on legal and political equality and much less on social equality. It is a cocktail glass society where social and cultural focus is on the successful and where winners, more and more, take all (see Frank and Cook, 1996). In a way, then, social citizenship is something to be earned by hard work and forthrightness ('the American way'): it is not a right of citizenship.

In the European Dream, in contrast, there is much greater stress on rights of inclusion. In the post-war settlement the welfare state stresses that social citizenship is as important as legal or political citizenship. In this race all are rewarded commensurate to their merit, and even those at the end of the race get compensation prizes to allow themselves the basic necessities of life. Failure is seen less as an individual fault than as a fault of the system.

The readier acceptance of economic exclusion in the United States is backed up by a far greater social and spatial exclusion. The famous 'concentric rings' of the Chicago School are a symbol of this symmetry between economic and social exclusion. And such a vertical segregation is reinforced by a much greater horizontal segregation between different communities even when at the same level of affluence.

The United States is a quite exceptionally exclusionary society. The notion of the ethnic segregation of suburban development scarcely causes criticism. Indeed the word 'community' comes to be used as the singular form of a plural entity and even Amitai Etzioni's (1993) much vaunted 'communitarianism' is not one of integration but of overarching values and shared sentiments (see also J.Q. Wilson, 1985). Ironically, Marcus Felson (1994), with rather amusing ethnocentricity, sees the 'divergent' cities of suburban sprawl and segregation of North America as the future when compared to the 'convergent' cities of urban villages and downtown heterogeneity of Europe and the American past (including Manhattan). Indeed he instructs his students to compare Los Angeles with the 'old convergent cities of Europe – for example Paris, Amsterdam, Brussels, Copenhagen and Stockholm' (p. 171). It takes a radical critic such as William Julius Wilson (1996) to point to the need to reverse the levels of suburbanization and to repair the neglected city centres characteristic of American cities in order to emulate those of Europe, to obviate the fashion in which deprived groups are spatially isolated.[4]

The public and social policies which in the United States have allowed unrestricted suburbanization, the flight from the city and the deterioration of city centres have not, on the whole, been present in Europe. Without such segregation, the ability to give spatial bearings to a distinct underclass is absent as, indeed, is the social setting on a large scale where there is a lack of any reference points to the workaday world. Overall, spatial and social exclusion has not occurred on anything like the scale in Europe that it has done in the United States.

With these caveats in mind, let us turn now to the general problems which limit material and cultural exclusion.

The cordon sanitaire

The heterogeneity of the city, both in urban dwelling but also in the need to transmit the urban sprawl for reasons of work and leisure, makes it very difficult to isolate different populations. Indeed the city, whether Manhattan, Paris, Barcelona or Rome, is something which is attractive in its own right, where the *frisson* of difference constantly amazes, bemuses and sometimes alarms: 'The rapid crowding of changing images, the sharp discontinuity in the grasp of a single glance, and the unexpectedness of onrushing impressions', as George Simmel put it in 'The Metropolis and Mental Life' (1950), and the emporium of roles and possibilities is a key attraction of the 'soft city'. The actuarial line, the cordon sanitaire of control, is, therefore, difficult to achieve and perhaps more so in a world which emphasizes diversity, pluralism and choice.

But there is another important reason why the cordon sanitaire is unable to protect the 'honest' citizen from crime and disorder. The notion that the criminal is an external enemy out there is fundamentally flawed. Relative deprivation and individualism occurs through the class structure: the existence of widespread white collar crime (see Lea, 1992) and crimes amongst the 'respectable' working class scarcely allows us to cordon off the criminal from the non-criminal. And in terms of violence, as Jayne Mooney has shown (1996), not only is it widely distributed throughout the class structure, but one half of all violence against men and women occurs in the home.

The cordon sanitaire must, therefore, fail because the fifth column of offenders is in the suburbs, at work, or in one's local streets; indeed, the chances of violence are greater from a close friend or member of the family than from a stranger.

The scapegoating function

It might appear that this problem, the subject of this book, has been largely eclipsed by forces which have breached old boundaries and created a world of fractured, hybridised and fused identities. For example, the end of the cold war has rendered a particularly powerful rhetoric which supported a boundary between 'good' and 'evil' redundant. Migrations of peoples and cultures have given the South a much more influential presence in the North than in the past and not just in established cosmopolitan centres like London, Paris or New York. In the academy, post-modern texts have blurred previous subject identities.

I doubt, however, whether these cultural, political and social transformations have really made people less fearful, less concerned about keeping a distance from others, less exclusionary in their behaviour. The world political map in 1994 is replete with new, strong boundaries which are designed to secure cultural homogeneity, and, at the local level, hostility towards outsider groups like New Age Travellers in England and Wales and ethnic minorities in much of Europe is no less acute than it was before 'the passing of the modern world'. The desire for a purified identity, which requires the distant presence of a bad object, a discrepant other, seems to be unaffected by cross-currents of culture which are characteristic of recent global change. (1995, pp. 183–4)

David Sibley, in the above quote, makes, I believe, the error of believing the rhetoric of the time for the reality. It is easy to mistake the siren voices of basic values for current melody, but they are singing songs that have long been out of fashion, they celebrate a world which will never return, their very insistence is because of incipient failure, they are signs of a world being lost rather than a hegemony triumphant. It is an irony that it is at the point when widespread exclusion occurs and when the existing system needs to justify itself more that traditional ideology begins to lose its currency.

The ideas become all the more necessary precisely when they become all the more implausible. It is difficult to create the notion of a deviant other where:

- crime is so 'normal and extensive that it is *implausible* to assume that it is all or largely due to an underclass or to immigrants or to a special group of people called 'criminals';
- the mass media are only too ready to focus not only on fecklessness at the bottom of the social structure but on sleaze at the top. It would be a naive citizen today who believed that crime and deviance were a monopoly of the lower classes;
- the causes are too widespread to be allocated to a particular outgroup.

Who does not know a family that has broken up, a single mother bringing up her children, a friend who has become unemployed? In a precarious world it would be a foolhardy person who could not see the possibility that there but for fortune they might be in the same predicament;
- the relative lack of segregation in Europe compared to the United States makes it much more difficult to spatially locate an isolated deviant other.

A clear sign of this collapsing hegemony is the phenomenon of moral panics: Angie McRobbie and Sarah Thornton (1995) have discussed the transformation of moral panics in the late modern period. They highlight the following features:

- *frequency*   Moral panics increase in frequency.
- *contest*   They are contested: experts and pressure groups disagree both as to the nature of the panic and, more importantly, if there is a basis of a 'panic' at all, e.g. the moral panic about single mothers is strongly contested.
- *reflexivity*   The notion of moral panics has now entered the vocabulary so that it is common for politicians, journalists and promoters to attempt to set off moral panics.
- *difficulty*   Moral panics become more difficult to set off, not only that they are contested, but that 'the hard and fast boundaries between "normal" and "deviant" would seem to be less common' (1995, pp. 572–3).
- *rebound*   Moral panics can easily rebound: even a Conservative press has an avid, commercial interest in examining the credentials of those who claim the moral high ground. Attempts, for example, to go back to the inclusive world of the 1950s lamentably failed. Prime Minister John Major's cabinet, government and then backbenchers were ruthlessly examined by the mass media for basic values and found to be lamentable failures. Mistresses abounded, broken families were commonplace, sexual peccadilloes were scrutinized, the moral panic rebounded back upon itself.

McRobbie and Thornton pinpoint such changes as being the result of the vast expansion and diversification of the mass media. There is no doubt that such a competition for audience has vastly increased the rate at which attempts at panic are made, but we must look to demand as well as supply if we are to understand this proliferation. The level of ontological insecurity of audiences in a pluralistic society makes such revelation of deviance followed by reassurance of the limits of normality extremely attractive. Indeed, a plethora of chat shows, from Oprah Winfrey to Ricki Lake, tackle daily a host of problems. They attempt to firm up normality in a world which is, as McRobbie and Thornton point out, increasingly uncertain. The revelation industry is thus coupled with a personal advice and therapy service (see Giddens, 1992).

The centre cannot hold: the periphery fragments

Jimmy Feys talks of the process of exclusion resulting in a crisis of identity for the excluded. This is certainly true, but the crisis is not only of those on the edge of society, but those at its core. The ontological insecurity of a plural world, where biographies no longer carry the actors on time-honoured tracks and where reflexivity is a virtue, does not allow for any self-satisfaction of place or smugness of being. Nor is there a fixed deviant other out there who grants one certainty by being the reverse of all that is absolutely correct and virtuous. The gaze of late modernity looks at the world seeking the firm and reassuring contours of the other but the gaze wavers, the camera is supposed to produce hard focus but the pictures of the other come out blurred and mosaic, at times some fragments look like pictures of one's own friends and family; the hand steadies resolutely, but the pictures keep on blurring.

Conclusion: the news from Gent

I have in this chapter traced the transition from an inclusive to an exclusive society. That is, from a society which both materially and ontologically incorporated its members and which attempted to assimilate deviance and disorder to one which involves a great deal of both material and ontological precariousness and which responds to deviance by separation and exclusion. Such a process is driven by changes in the material basis of advanced industrial societies, from Fordism to post-Fordism and represents the movement into late modernity.

My second task was to root changes in crime and disorder to changes in the material base. The fundamental dynamic of exclusion is a result of market forces which exclude vast sections of the population from the primary labour market and of market values which help generate a climate of individualism. Such a situation has an effect both on the causes of crime (through relative deprivation and individualism) and on the reactions against crime (through economic precariousness and ontological insecurity). The exclusions which occur on top of this primary process are an attempt to deal with the problem of crime and disorder which it engenders. *They are often based on misperception but they are a misperception of a real not an imaginary problem.* Crime itself is an exclusion as are the attempts to control it by barriers, incarceration and stigmatization. Such processes often exacerbate the problem in a dialectic of exclusion: but the changes which occur in the burgeoning apparatus of crime control are in the long run a response to this predicament. So too are the theories of crime which evolve during this period: the new administrative criminology with its actuarial stance which reflects the rise of risk management as a solution to the crime problem. James Q. Wilson's popular zero-tolerance theory of eliminating incivilities in selected areas, Charles Murray's notion of an underclass of single mothers and feckless fathers which gives an ideological basis to exclusion. Thus exclusionist theories occur at times of social exclusion. None of this suggests reductionism but it insists that there is a strong continuity of influence between the material basis of society, levels of crime, the crime control apparatus and criminology itself.

Lastly, I have heeded the demands of specificity and contrasted the material and cultural situations in Western Europe and the United States. No doubt such contrast is over-schematic, for the differences within Western Europe are immense, but the constant tendency to generalize from the United States to Europe, without acknowledging the profound cultural differences, has to be resisted.

As to the future, the scenario presented by Edward Luttwak is clear: the combination of increased lawlessness and economic precariousness is a formula which could lead to ever-increasing punitiveness and scapegoating, probably with a strong racist undercurrent. The pre-war history of Europe is a grim portent for such a scenario. I have suggested, in this chapter, that there is certainly no inevitability in this process, indeed, that there are strong forces which undermine the delivery of a 'successful' exclusionary policy whether actuarial or cultural. It is on these that a progressive politics must be based. In a world where more and more jobs are precarious, where families are frequently unstable, and where there is widespread knowledge of those from other cultures, it is surely not difficult to understand the predicament of the unemployed, to sympathize with the single mother, to empathize with and, indeed, enjoy cultural differences. The creation of folk devils is not facilitated by the late modern world. But what is necessary is a politics which embraces the excluded and those whose positions are precarious. We need a politics which starts at the edges and goes in as far as is palatable (which is a long way) rather than that which starts at the centre and goes out as far as is charitable (which is not very far). The social democratic nostalgia for the inclusionist world of the 1950s with full (male) employment, the nuclear family, and the organic community is an impossible dream. As our friends from Gent have pointed out (Hofman, 1993, 1996; Lippens 1994, 1996) any realism which has as its fundamental agenda the reduction of crime by a return to those times is doomed to failure. The task of devising new forms of community, employment which is not totally dependent on the whims of the market place and new and emerging family structures is a matter which is paramount.

Notes

1. Zygmunt Bauman has argued that the most exclusionary episode of modern European history, the Holocaust, is a direct product of modernity: 'I propose to treat

the Holocaust as a rare, yet significant and reliable test of the hidden possibilities of modern society' (1989, p. 12). The bureaucratic efficiency of the operation, the industrialization of the slaughter, even the eugenic ideas which underpinned the travesty were part and parcel of modern ideas detachable from the specific circumstances of Adolf Hitler and the Third Reich. In terms of more recent history, Nils Christie (1993) argued that the prison gulag of the present period, particularly in the United States, represents a contemporary manifestation of such tendencies inherent in modernity. Bauman himself is perhaps less sure of this linkage, talking of a 'totalitarian solution without a totalitarian state' (1995, p. 205) with regard to the present period and of Hitler's camps as 'a modern invention even when used in the service of anti-modern movements' (ibid., p. 206). Clearly the distinction between Fascism and liberal democracy has to be reiterated, as has the link between Enlightenment values and the industrial and organizational structures concomitant, although not coincident, with modernity. The ideals of the Enlightenment were radically inclusivist. Moreover, as Todd Gitlin (1995) has strenuously indicated, they were intended to ensure inclusion and equality despite difference.

The exclusions of Fascism (and Stalinism) and of present-day liberal democracies are thus of a different nature. The inclusive post-war period discussed in this chapter points to what was to some extent a historical high point of liberal democracy: involving the widening political and economic base of citizenship. But it was an inclusion which did not recognize difference; difference became deviance from absolute standards. It managed to achieve a high degree of inclusion but at the expense of diversity. Exclusion, when it occurred, was at a very high threshold, the 'totalitarianism' of the post-war period was in conformity: in 'the other directedness' of each and every one. The exclusive society that follows it is much more ready to both accept differences *and* exclude. Diversity of 'lifestyle' is an ideal, cultural pluralism a cherished value: exclusion is based not on difference but on risk. Acceptable society is thus differentiated and unacceptable society excluded in an actuarial gradient. We have, if you wish, a littoral society stretching from differences in credit rating to differences of assessed dangerousness.

The modern period saw itself as on the road to solving the problem of communality of interests but could not cope with difference of identity; the late modern period exalts differences but cannot cope with the differences of material interest which exist between citizens. The problem lies in the fundamental contradiction of liberal democracy between a system which legitimizes itself in terms of equality of opportunity and reward by merit but which is unequal and grossly unmeritocratic in its structure. In the United States, for example, 1% of individuals own one-third of the wealth and large segments of the population are denied access to the primary labour market. It is such a criminogenic situation which generates the possibility of mass imprisonment. The present increase in the prison population builds on the basis of the chronic rise in crime that occurred throughout the Western world in the late modern period. It is a direct result of the rising rate of relative deprivation coupled with increasing individualism which present-day market economies engender. Thus it is, at core, the result of the *detraditionalization* of modern societies (see Beck, 1992; Giddens, 1991). People are no longer willing to accept their place in the hierarchy or to unthinkingly place collective over individual interests. The glue that stuck together an unfair and oppressive situation has begun to lose its powers of adhesion. The process of exclusion, which has reached its epitome in the American gulag, is therefore very much a product of the present moment of liberal democracy and the contemporary development of late modernity. It is a grossly misappropriate reaction to a very real problem: crime. It is qualitatively different in both its origins and nature from anything that happened in the exclusionary regimes of Hitler and Stalin.

2. Although it is commonplace to see immigration as the key factor in the formation of more pluralistic societies in the West, I do not think that this is the major

influence on the level of pluralistic debate or on ontological insecurity. Indeed many of the values of immigrant cultures are traditional and pose little challenge to the diverse values of late modernity. Rather it is the indigenously generated process of diversification which has been at the cutting edge of the new pluralism: witness the debates around women's role, violence, sexual orientation, the environment, animal rights, etc. The debate is as acute in Dublin with little immigration as it is in London or Paris. The role of the immigrant is, as argued in this chapter, more as a scapegoat, an outgroup set up to assuage ontological insecurity rather than a cause of such (see Vidali, 1996).

3. The mistake here, surely, is that reacting against the empirical fact that there is no simple linear relationship between level of recorded crime and imprisonment, fear of crime and risk of crime, etc. we assert that imprisonment, fear and crime prevention measures are autonomous of crime rates and, hence, caused by other factors (e.g. displaced anxiety about economic security, urban development, race). Undoubtedly such displacement occurs (indeed is described in detail in this chapter) but this certainly does not allow us to eliminate crime itself from the equation. It must be remembered that human actors (whether manning the social control apparatus or as citizens walking the streets) are not positivistic creatures who are simply reflexes of risk rates or crime levels. The human capacity is to assess and make sense of the social world. It would be surprising, therefore, if one ever found a simple linear relationship or the high correlations typical of the natural sciences. Let me give two examples:

(a) *Imprisonment*: the response to an increase in crime might be to bemoan the high cost of imprisonment and its ineffectiveness and to enter into a period of decarceration (perhaps involving the diversion of juvenile offenders and a plethora of alternative schemes). This might be followed by a period of punitiveness and increased incarceration as a reaction to the fact that reported crime continues to increase. Such a change of policy would ensure that there is no linear relationship between crime rates and imprisonment but the shifts in policy, the diversion schemes, the number and nature of the alternatives, and the scale and nature of the subsequent prison building programme could not be understood without acknowledging the major influence of the problem of crime.

(b) *Fear of crime*: one response by lower working class men in cities to social exclusion is to create a machismo-based culture. This involves, as a matter of manliness, a low fear of crime despite a climate of mutual hostility which spills over frequently into crime. Thus a high risk rate is combined with a low fear of crime. Urban women, on the other hand, in the same environment, may become less tolerant of crime, may actively disdain violence, and may demand a better quality of life. This will manifest itself in higher 'fear' (or at least annoyance, indignation, etc.). Thus two urban groups will develop diametrically opposite reactions to the risk of crime. To complicate matters further, the elaborate avoidance behaviour developed by sections of urban women to tackle crime may lower risks and allow criminologists to comment that they have unnaturally high levels of anxiety about crime given that their actual risk is low. There is no conceivable way that one could expect a linear relationship between crime and fear of crime in a survey of such an urban population.

4. Loic Wacquant (1996) in his incisive comparison of Woodlawn on the south side of Chicago and La Courneuve in the outer ring of Paris points to the crucial role of the state in the process of exclusion. The semi-welfare state of the US props up rather than deflects market society. In Chicago 'state abandonment' and withdrawal of public institutions occurs in this spatially segregated 'racial reservation'. In Paris, if anything, La Courneuve suffers from an 'over penetration' of state agencies and public organizations. It is, furthermore, mixed ethnically and socially. 'Racial enclaves such as Chicago's South Side', are, he notes, 'unknown in France – and in all of Europe for that matter' (1996, p. 560).

2 CRIME AND DISCORD IN AN AGE OF LATE MODERNITY

It is my belief that the last 20 years has witnessed the most profound transformation in criminology. Heralded by the new deviancy 'explosion' of theory in the late 1960s and early 1970s and with *The New Criminology* (Taylor et al., 1973) as a convenient marker, we have experienced the shattering of the seemingly monolithic world of modernity associated with the post-war period and the emergence of a late modernity where the ground rules of certainty undergirding our subject have become blurred, contested, ambiguous and perpetually debatable. The changes have occurred at the level of crime, of crime control and of criminology itself.

They are certainly not merely an intellectual product – perhaps the reverse; real changes have occurred in the world both in the quantity and quality of crime and this has shaped public discourse on crime, whether in the mass media, in fiction, or at the doorstep. Nor, of course, is such a transformation limited to crime and criminology; it is part of a wider movement into late modernity which has resonances in every sphere of life whether cultural, architectural, sexual, biographical or economic (see Harvey, 1989). Indeed, making the connection between the wide ranging changes that have occurred within the labour market, in leisure, within the family, in changing usage of public and private space, in relationships of gender, and the newly emerging patterns of crime and victimization must be top of our agenda. But let us, for the moment, note that the vast majority of advanced industrial countries have experienced a dramatic rise in crime and disorder. Victimization has become more common in the public sphere and, at least on the level of revelation, apparently widespread within the private sphere. Crime has moved from the rare, the abnormal, the offence of the marginal and the stranger, to a commonplace part of the texture of everyday life: it occupies the family, the heartland of liberal democratic society as well as extending its anxiety into all areas of the city. It is revealed in the highest echelons of our economy and politics as well as in the urban impasses of the underclass. At times, it seems as frequent in the agencies set up to control crime as it does within the criminal fraternity itself. All of this has created the most profound difficulties for traditional criminology. Two crises have stretched across the last 20 years: the crisis of aetiology and that of penalty. The metanarrative of progress had as its almost unspoken assumption the decline in crime and incivilities. Yet the highest living standards achieved in the history of our species have been accompanied by a steady rise in the crime rate, while crime itself occurs in all the places it should not as well as being more frequent in all its traditional haunts. The failure of the Great Society programme of the Lyndon B. Johnson administration, the most wide reaching, costly and intensive social democratic attempt to engineer an end to poverty, discrimination and crime, was the prelude to an era where tackling the causes of crime became shorthand not for social engineering but for the necessity of greater discipline in the family or its transmutation into the actuarial calculation of risk minimization. The second crisis, that of penalty, stretches from the prison revolts of Parkhurst to Strangeways today. It is a history of increase, of overcrowding, of a widespread public recognition of futility. It is paralleled by a re-evaluation of the role of policing from the thin blue line to one component in the multi-agency control of crime. All of this repositions the criminal justice system from the agency that is there to control crime to a bit player in the social agenda playing second bill to the family and employment, and dependent itself on public co-operation and support.

And behind these two crises lies an underlying suspicion: for what sort of liberal democratic state is it, that is unable to protect its population from crime yet brings a wider and wider swathe of its population under penal supervision? What sort of freely entered into social contract exists between state and citizen and one citizen and another if inner cities have become areas of curfew at night for women and the elderly and where state coercion is a necessary adjunct to everyday life?

The metanarratives of progress through planning and the rule of law become tarnished and suspect while, more profoundly, the basic categories of crime cease to be fixed entities and become subjects of ambivalence and debate. Categories blur, categories stretch and extend, categories lose their rigidity. Various victim movements are intensely involved in this process of redefinition. Child abuse, for example, is not merely proven to be more extensive than ever thought before, but is also defined in much less tolerant terms. Indeed one can see a long term move from what one might call the 'positive' child abuse of Victorian times ('spare the rod and spoil the child') to the notion that any physical hitting whatsoever is gross and a symptom of parental inadequacy. The Green movement sensitizes us to the frequently invisible crimes of pollution, environmental damage and radiation by lobbying for new statutes and the extension of existing legislation. Most importantly, second wave feminism has had a constant influence on both academic criminology and public debate on crime. Rape, domestic violence, sexual harassment, child sexual abuse, justified homicide all become areas of struggle where categories are reconceptualized, stretched, placed on a continuum which 'blurs' with normality and where there is constant disagreement about demarcations. Just as libertarian socialism informed the radical criminology of the 1970s, radical feminism has been a constant source of inspiration and, sometimes, irritation. The key role it gives to male violence and criminality in the oppression of women and the extraordinary influence it has had on public awareness underscores the leverage which such discourse has had on academic criminology. Meanwhile, a vigorous and heated debate has occurred on all the so-called 'consensual' crimes: pornography, drugs, abortion, illicit sexual relations, and even sado-masochism. Every modern political tendency has entered the arena: socialist feminism and radical feminism, right wing libertarianism and the moral 'majority', neo-liberals and social democrats. What is obvious is that academic criminology, the interior world of scholarship and research, is greatly affected not only by the empirical problem of crime (as well it should) but by the great hubbub of debate in the world outside of it: by politicians, journalists and activists. Whatever, one tendency is clear: the level of debate within criminology has far from subdued (cf. Rock, 1994; Sumner, 1994). Indeed, standing as it does at the crossroads of law and order, at the intersection of morality and immorality, it is a discipline upon which every major intellectual and political current makes its mark.

The crisis of modernity

The crisis in criminology is a crisis of modernity. The twin pillars of the modernist project of reason and progress, the use of law in the control and adjudication of human affairs and the intervention of government to engineer a just social order totter under the weight of their own inconsistencies and ineffectiveness. The legacy of the Enlightenment of the eighteenth century and the scientific revolution of the nineteenth century bequeathed us the two staple paradigms of criminology – classicism and positivism – and it is the challenge to these doctrines which has generated the intense debate characteristic of the late twentieth century. The old certainties of the obvious nature of crime, the central role of the criminal justice system in its control, and the possibility of realizing, by government intervention, a social contract which embraced all citizens have come, one by one, to be cast in doubt. The forces which brought about this transformation are, quite naturally, largely exterior to the discipline itself, although research findings and intellectual currents within the academy have developed and augmented these tendencies. This process has, of course, involved all areas of social policy, although it has been felt most acutely within criminology for it is crime and the anxieties surrounding it which are, as always, the weathervane to change in our society.

The two intellectual currents which signalled the supposed 'end of history' are neo-liberalism – the market philosophy of the New Right – and post-modernism, one reviving a *laissez-faire* past as the key to effective government policy, the other basing its claims on a post-industrial future where all Enlightenment certainties are rendered inapplicable. The collapse of state 'socialism' in the East and the growing doubts with regard to the programmes envisaged by social democracies highlighted the fragility of the metanarratives of progress through sustained government planning. The response politically was the attempted substitution of the market for

metanarrative by the emerging New Right administrations and intellectually by the growth of post-modernism which, similarly, rejected the validity
of metanarratives as a guide to social, political and cultural development.
Both the New Right philosophy of the market place and post-modernism
have had profound effects upon criminology. The former is evident in the
proliferation of texts written from a New Right perspective. In these the
actor is rational and self-seeking, and crime is committed where the balance
sheet of profit and deficit is in the black and where opportunities are
present. No metanarrative of injustice as a motivation for crime nor a sense
of justice and fairness as incorporating us within the bounds of sociability
are deemed necessary. The human calculator exists in a universe of structured temptations and 'opportunities': there is no cause of crime other than
'basic human frailty' (see Felson, 1994; Gottfredson and Hirschi, 1990;
Clarke, 1980). The influence of post-modernism is less obvious and, on the
face of it, might be seen to have only a marginal impact. And it is true that
explicitly post-modern work in criminology only arrived very late in the day
long after the tumult in literature and cultural studies. Yet as Stan Cohen
(1997) has perceptively indicated post-modernist themes were present in
criminology from the early days of labelling theory in the 1960s, through to
abolitionism and social constructionism before coming out as full blown
post-modernism in the late 1980s (e.g. Pfohl, 1985).

Indeed, if one re-examines labelling theory and its critique of traditional
criminology one can find the majority of post-modernist themes. The
concept of the social construction of the label was a precursor to 'decon-
structionism'; the notion of a plurality of voices defining reality was present
in their unruly conception of social order, as was the idea of 'a hierarchy of
credibility', where male, white, older, upper class definers of reality exerted
their dominance. The language of the label and its idealistic power in social
construction was widely explored and is the intellectual progenitor of
'politically correct' terminology today. A conflict theory unwilling to tie
itself to the dynamics of class or a wider overreaching narrative of control
was content to locate power within the everyday micro-politics of human
intervention. Even the transformation of the unitary subject into a locus dis-
sected by competing social texts can be vividly found in the work of Erving
Goffman. But, above all, the perspective drew its orientation from a critique
of the intrusion of the state, both in the form of welfare and of criminal
justice, into the lives of individuals. That is, it accused the state of imposing
a metanarrative, either of determinacy or of evil, which was not only incorrect in its essentialism, but actually self-fulfilling in its effect. The irony,
then, is that post-modernism arrived comparatively early in the post-war
development of criminology and that many of the recent converts to its
cause do not seem to have realized that a rich and developed tradition pre-
dates them (e.g. Smart, 1990).

Yet, while both post-modernism and neo-liberalism were busily writing
off metanarratives, the proliferating new social movements pivoting around
feminism, the environment and ethnicity were creating new narratives with

their own conceptions of progress and social contract. All of these impacted upon criminology, although the role of feminism, particularly centred upon victim movements, has been the most crucial. It is in this mêlée of new ideas, responding to cultural and social change occurring both through the afflu- ent 1960s and 1970s and the recession which followed, that criminology has been set adrift.

Back to basics

It is the core contention of this chapter that to understand the development of criminology, one must situate it in the context of the exterior problems of crime, in particular its extent and perceived distribution, and the wider political and social currents of the time. In the latter instance the major metanarrative concerns the emergence and transformation of liberal democracy and the key idea of the social contract. The changing notion of the social contract has, of course, been the staple of political philosophy within the academy, and the pivot of the social and political discourse in the wider society. This has centred around two problematics: individualism and meritocracy. Namely, how can a society based on self-seeking individuals hang together, and how can a society legitimizing itself in terms of rewards allocated by merit in the market place reconcile gross inequalities of prop- erty and opportunity? These problems of social order have obvious reper- cussions for criminology, the study of legality and disorder, and it is within this discursive flux that criminology has evolved. To point to this seemingly obvious external context does not suggest that the interior history of crim- inology is without its own momentum, nor that it cannot, at times, purpo- sively attempt to cut itself off from outside influences. Indeed, the history of academic positivism within criminology has been precisely to do this: to rewrite the history of the subject as if political philosophy was not its concern (see Matza, 1969) and to consign discussions of the social contract and classicism to the pre-history of the discipline (see Beirne, 1993). It is, of course, clear because such an attempt at blinkered authority has been so successful, that it is necessary to state the obvious.

The challenge to modernism

Let us look first at the major forces which have both disoriented and regal- vanized the discipline. The five factors are the rise in the crime rate; the revelation of hitherto invisible victims; the problematization of crime; the growing awareness of the universality of crime and the selectivity of justice; and the problematization of punishment and culpability. Each of these factors evoked a diverse theoretical response, sometimes exaggerating their relevance, and sometimes evoking an outright denial yet all sensitiz- ing criminology to the breadth of analysis necessary for the explanations

of crime and subverting and undermining the complacency of the modernist paradigm.

The rising crime rate

The majority of industrial countries have seen a considerable rise in the rate
of recorded crime in the post-1960s period. This has had an impact on
theories of causation, has given rise to a crisis within the criminal justice
system because of the experiential rise in demand on it, and has qualitatively upgraded the public's prioritization of crime as a problem. Indeed, of
all the factors, which I shall detail, that have changed our conception of
crime and a reappraisal of the criminal justice system, the rise in crime is
the central motor of change. Let us first look at its effect on theories of causation. The rise in crime in the period 1960–75 occurred at a time of full
employment, when living standards rose to levels greater than have been
known in human history, and in the context of a vast expansion in welfare
provisions. The widely held belief in social positivism – that crime was
caused by bad social conditions – was clearly contradicted, for as the West
became wealthier, the crime rate rose. It is true that in the recession of the
1980s social positivism was to an extent rehabilitated, but the impact on
criminological theory of rising crime in a period of prosperity was profound.
Indeed, most of the major theoretical developments since 1960 have been
a response to this anomaly. Thus on the right, neo-positivism and control
theory, especially in the work of Travis Hirschi, James Q. Wilson, Charles
Murray and Hans Eysenck, picked explicitly on the failings of social positivism and greatly developed theories of individual positivism. In particular, changes in the family were high on their aetiological agenda (see
Mooney, 1998). Causation shifted from a social to an individual level and
the role of informal processes of social control became prioritized over the
formal controls of the criminal justice system. On the left, the immediate
response was to stress the epiphenomenal nature of the 'rise in crime'. This
involved shifting the site of causality from changes in the motivation to
offend to changes in the responses of government and the mass media to
crime. Rises in crime became signs, not so much of any changes in the 'real'
crime rate, but of increased governmental and public responses to crime,
represented sometimes as smokescreens for the vested interests of those in
the criminal justice system, sometimes as metaphors for wider social anxieties unrelated to crime. Starting with labelling theory, left idealism, moral
panic theory, abolitionism and social constructionism all evidenced this
radical change in perspective. Characteristic of this approach is this commentary by Jack Douglas, writing in 1971:

> We are not experiencing a kind of national *crime hysteria*: the rising official rates,
> which the people normally believe are true lead to greater fear of crime, which in
> turn leads to more fear of crime, and so on. On this basis alone, but also because
> it is to the advantage of officials who want more money and more power, *we can*

expect that the official rates will continue to rise steadily for many years to come. But it would be a mistake to believe that this has anything to do with what criminals or other forms of deviants are doing. (1971, pp. 100–1, emphasis in original)

The social positivist pillar of modernism began to look shaky and was disturbed from two sides. Firstly, as crime was increasing despite widespread social amelioration, social positivism was no longer able to explain its incidence in terms of the bottom layer of individuals, the 'difficult to reach', 'problem' families. Secondly, the very nature of crime rates became questioned. They were no longer obvious fixed quantities which governments more or less imperfectly attempted to tackle, but could grow because of the vested interests of those manning the criminal justice system or the 'hysteria' of the public.

Such an increase in crime threatened not only social positivism but the neo-classicist pillar of modernism. For governments all over the Western world committed more and more money to the criminal justice system in order to combat crime, yet the crime rate continues to increase. In the United States such a penal crisis has reached epidemic proportions: the state is unable either to protect its citizens from crime or to maintain a society where imprisonment is a comparative rarity (see Table 2.1).

Now, it could be argued that the crime rate would be even worse if such enormous expenditures were not incurred; indeed, James Q. Wilson (1992) has argued precisely this in 'The War against Drugs'. In any case the inability of the criminal justice system to keep pace with the rise in crime becomes more apparent. Because of this, criminologists of all persuasions shift their attention to the informal systems of the control of crime, whether it is the family, the community, or by public shaming (Braithwaite, 1998). A fundamental shift occurs from viewing the criminal justice system as the thin blue line in the war against crime to viewing the institutions of civil society as being of prime importance.

Lastly, the effect of the growth in crime is to increase public anxiety. The social contract of modernity gives the state the role of monitoring public safety. Yet within a lifetime crime, particularly for urban dwellers, has become no longer a marginal concern, an exceptional incident in their life, but an ever-present possibility. Nor is it simply that government

TABLE 2.1   *US population controlled by penal law, 1995*

	In prison	Controlled by penal law*
Total population	1 in 135	1 in 37
Black males	1 in 24	1 in 13
Black males in 20s	1 in 9	1 in 3

*in prison, on parole or on probation
Source: Mauer, 1997

expenditure on crime control increases and hence public expenditure through taxation, but so does the direct public cost in terms of locks and bolts and home insurance. Crime moves from being a side issue of public concern to a central political issue.

The revelation of invisible victims

The existence of a dark figure of crime unreported to official agencies has been known since the work of Adolphe Quetelet, the Belgian founder of social statistics in the 1830s. Its true extent was a matter of speculation until the first large scale victimization surveys in the United States commencing in the 1960s (the National Crime Survey). The extent of the dark figure revealed varies between surveys, but commonly only about one third of offences are known to the police. Thus the British Crime Survey estimate in 1991 was 15 million compared to some five million crimes officially recorded. The comparison points of the two data sets are fraught with problems, but this does not concern us here. What is of importance is that the crime rate is at least three times the size of the official figures and must be considerably higher given that victimization surveys themselves have a substantial dark figure of crimes unreported to interviewers (see Young, 1988).

So on top of a rising crime rate, we have clear indications that the 'true' extent of crime is extremely widespread. The 15 million crimes in England and Wales would represent one serious crime occurring yearly for every four of the population. Of course, crime is more focused than this, and in urban areas one finds about one half of respondents being victimized at least once in the last 12 months (see Kinsey et al., 1986). Such findings underline the fact that experience of crime is a normal rather than an exceptional event in people's lives. This immediately creates problems for the modernist view of crime. For, far from being the product of exceptional circumstances, such a 'normal' occurrence must have its genesis in widespread conditions within our society. This normalization of crime points to the endemic sources of its origins.

Furthermore, the hidden figure varies considerably with the type of crime committed. Property crime in general has high reporting rates, often because of reasons of insurance, whereas crimes of violence and sexual assault have much lower reporting rates, not only to the police but to conventional victimization surveys. Nor is it merely that certain types of crime have higher hidden figures; crimes against certain victims are revealed much less often in the criminal statistics than others. In general, the more socially vulnerable the victim and the more private or intimate the setting of the crime's commission, the less visible the crime.

Such a distinction between visible and invisible crimes almost turns on its head the modernist paradigm. For it suggests that the image of crime presented in official figures is fundamentally flawed. That is, not only are the figures quantitatively inadequate – and crime is much more common than we have previously believed – but that what we see as the most serious

crimes – violence and sexual assault – are grossly underestimated and frequently occur in intimate and private settings.

Up until now I have talked about the findings from conventional criminological research from the interior of the discipline, but the full force of
this change in orientation has come from movements exterior to criminology. In particular, feminist research and scholarship has profoundly
changed our images of crime. Its task has been to conduct a series of studies
and undertake a systematic analysis revealing the hidden victimization of
women. This has been influenced by the radical feminism of the post-1960s
period. Radical feminism pinpointed violence against women as a central
mode of the control of women in a patriarchal society. It revealed the *extent*
of such violence and it situated it in terms of the *relationship* between men
and women.

The revelation of widespread violence and sexual attacks occurring
throughout the class structure creates problems for the conventional
location of the causes of crime within the lower class and on the margins of
society. It does not preclude class analysis. Certain types of invisible crime
may well be more prevalent amongst the lower classes, but other types of
crime, especially crimes of violence, may be much more widespread and less
class-linked than has traditionally been assumed. The social positivist pillar
of modernism is thus suspect, or at least must be more clearly specified. But
it is not only the positivist pillar which is disturbed by such findings, the intimate, family or private-centred nature of much violence or sexual crime also
creates problems for neo-classicism. The fundamental building block of
classicism based in social contract theory is the coming together of self-
interested individuals who rationally recognize that to avoid a war of all
against all it is necessary to regulate their conduct and to empower the state
to act against activities which violate the general interest. 'Individuals' in
neo-classicism refers not so much to atomistic individuals as individuals
within their families. The family unit is seen as a unitary interest and such
private interests come together publicly in the social contact (Pateman,
1988). Threats and dangers to one's self-interest come from *outside* the
family. Because of this, modernism conceives of the criminal as the stranger.
The exposure of the intimate nature of much violence – whether it is domestic violence, rape, homicide or child abuse – breaches this modernist certainty.

The problematization of crime

Up to this point I have discussed the impact on conventional notions of
crime caused both by its increase in quantity and by the discovery of a wide
range of hitherto unacknowledged offenders and victims. My discussion has
been concerned with the exploration of the dark figure of crime implicitly
assuming, for the moment, that there was indeed a 'real' figure of crime
which could be more and more accurately ascertained. The problematization of crime takes us a stage further. For a whole series of questions have

arisen, both from social movements outside of the discipline and within criminology itself with regard to what actually is criminal and how our conception of crime is constructed. Note that for modernism, crime was obvious: a house broken into, a person assaulted, a car stolen. It was an objective fact out there which could be described more or less accurately and its size ascertained with increasing precision with each advance in measurement. The breach in this orthodoxy occurred from the 1960s onwards with the sustained critique of positivism developed by labelling theorists. In 1967 Edwin Lemert summarized a revolution in thinking about crime and deviance when he wrote: 'This is a large turn away from older sociology which tended to rest heavily upon the idea that deviance leads to social control. I have come to believe the reverse idea, i.e. social control leads to deviance, is equally tenable and the potentially richer premise for studying deviance in modern society' (1967, p. v).

For the labelling theorists the quantity of crime, the type of person and offence selected to be criminalized and the categories used to describe and explain the deviant are social constructions. Crime, or deviance, is not an objective 'thing' out there, but a product of socially created definitions: deviance is not *inherent* in an item of behaviour, it is a quality *bestowed* upon it by human evaluation. To take two examples, to kill someone can be an act of heroism if committed by a police officer confronting armed robbers, or it can be an act of exhibiting extreme immorality if committed by the robbers. To inject morphine can be a legal act of fortunate necessity if engaged in by those who are terminally ill, it can be an act evoking all the prohibitive powers of the state if committed by a street junkie. But these are extreme contrasts; reality, in fact, consists of a series of defined gradations. Thus social definitions of what is criminally violent will consist of a gradient between seriously violent and non-violent and will change, over time, as public sensitivity to violence changes. Therefore, to determine what is the 'real' rate of violence in society will involve two questions: what are the changes in behaviour which might be deemed violent, and what changes are there in public tolerance to violence? It is this recognition of the *dyadic* nature of crime which is the major accomplishment of the labelling tradition. For crime rates no longer are obvious summarizations of items of behaviour 'out there', but are processes in which both human action and definition are subject to change. The dark figure of crime not only expands as more crime is revealed by more sensitive measuring techniques, but will expand if social definitions become less tolerant of crime. Such a position makes the positivist desire for objective and precise measurement, in order to emulate the physical sciences, extremely precarious. Crime becomes problematized; instead of the clear-cut distinction crime/non-crime, it is easier to view behaviour as a continuum between tolerated and criminalized behaviour where the cut-off point varies over time and between different social groups. How hard, for example, does a slap have to be to evoke criminal sanctions? At what point does appropriating other people's property become theft?

Out of the labelling tradition has developed a vigorous social constructionist school of social problems (Kitsuse and Spector, 1973; Pfohl, 1985).
Key to their work is the separation of the study of the genesis of social problems from the study of how social problems are defined. They explicitly
focus on the latter part of the dyad and, with this in mind, trace the moral
career of a problem – how definitions have changed over time – and relate
this to the conflicts of 'claim-makers' over a problem area. They are concerned not merely, quantitatively, with how the size of a criminal or deviant
population changes over time, but, qualitatively, with how the criminal or
deviant is depicted and analysed. From this perspective, crime and deviance
are seen as areas of conflict and debate, experts are seen as having vested
interests which motivate their claims to the problem, and, indeed, positivistic science itself is frequently viewed as an ideology which mobilizes scientific rhetoric in this endeavour. Furthermore, such debates extend out from
the academic world of the experts, to interest groups, the mass media, political law and order campaigns – all of which themselves involve experts in the
process of claims and counter-claims.

This is not the place to critically examine the possibility of fully understanding a social problem area from a position which limits itself to the
genesis and development of definitions and brackets off the problem itself.
There is, of course, the significant danger of merely inverting academic positivism with its 'scientific' claim to objectivity and notion of the 'obvious-
ness' of its subject matter with a perspective which is relativistic and
subjectivist (see Young, 1998). What is of importance at this juncture is that
social constructionism sensitizes the theorist to the constantly problematic,
changing and contested nature of crime and social problems.

It is scarcely surprising that such a perspective should arise within the
academy given the extraordinary level at which the nature, size, limits and,
indeed, existence of social problems are debated within contemporary
society. Over the last 20 years we have seen a burgeoning of pressure groups
seeking both to extend the boundaries of criminalization and to introduce
decriminalization, to redefine the limits of traditional social problems and
to introduce new problems, to recategorize crimes and to redefine problems. Let me cite just a few: the feminist movement, animal rights campaigns, environmentalist groups, anti-racist activists, child protection
agencies, movements both to legalize drugs and to legally restrict other
drugs (particularly tobacco). What exactly is a crime, therefore, becomes
contested and subject to public debate. To take rape as an example, feminist researchers not only argue that levels of rape are much greater than
conventionally recorded, they also trenchantly challenge conventional definitions of rape. Thus rape in marriage becomes in many legislatures a criminal offence and the existence of widespread 'date rape' is claimed. The
argument shifts from what is the 'true' figure of 'obviously' coercive sexual
encounters, stranger rape accompanied by violence, to what exactly is the
nature of rape and what are limits of coercion and consensus in sexual
relationships. The debate begins to centre around what is consenting sexual

intercourse, which is a problem of redrawing the lines between coercive and consensual relationships. Further, it highlights the existence of a continuum: for in an unequal society a large number of heterosexual encounters can be deemed coercive, particularly where the woman is totally dependent on her husband economically, or where her employment prospects are dependent on her male superiors. Some radical feminists would argue that all hetero-sexual relationships are coercive and that rape is simply a matter of degree, whereas others would make much more rigid distinctions. And precisely such a continuum problem occurs with regard to a whole series of other serious crimes, such as child abuse and domestic violence.

There is also a point where the revelation of more and more hidden crime becomes extremely problematic. The exposure of past sexual abuse, for example, becomes at times a seemingly bottomless pit which embraces a greater and greater proportion of the population. What are we to make of claims that over 50% of women have been sexually abused in their child-hood? It is not the aim of this chapter to deliberate on the validity of such assertions, merely to point to the heated public debate which these revela-tions generate. Indeed, organizations are set up to protect the families against what has been called 'false memory syndrome', while therapists specialize in 'unblocking' the memories of supposed child abuse.

The universality of crime and the selectivity of justice

Traditionally criminology has seen crime as being concentrated in the lower part of the class structure and to be greatest amongst adolescent boys. Its focus has been lower class, male and youth. The first serious wave to unbal-ance this orthodoxy was the work of Edwin Sutherland, particularly his article 'White Collar Criminality' written in 1940. He wrote:

> The theory that criminal behaviour in general is either due to poverty or to the psychopathic and sociopathic conditions associated with poverty can now be shown to be invalid . . . the generalization is based on a biased sample which omits almost entirely the behaviour of white-collar criminals. The criminologists have restricted their data, for reasons of convenience and ignorance rather than a prin-ciple, largely to cases dealt with in criminal courts and juvenile courts, and these agencies are used principally for criminals from the lower economic strata. Con-sequently, their data are grossly biased from the point of view of the economic status of criminals and their generalization that criminality is closely associated with poverty is not justified (1940, p. 10)

Here Sutherland, well before his time, captures well the problem of uni-versality and selectivity which was to fixate the criminology of the late 1960s onwards. Crime is much more widespread than the stereotypes of the crim-inal suggest and, furthermore, the criminal justice system selects a particu-lar 'sample' based not on randomness but on the stereotype itself. This time bomb of Sutherland's ticked away until by the 1970s its full implications began to be widely acknowledged. This was due to two types of influence:

a multitude of self-report studies particularly of delinquency which flourished during the period and increased revelations of crimes of the powerful. A whole series of texts pointed to the widespread occurrence of white collar crime: Frank Pearce's *Crimes of the Powerful*, Dennis Chapman's *Society and the Stereotype of the Criminal*, for example, and even in high places, the President's Commission on Law Enforcement and the Administration of Justice (1967).

The revisionism of the early 1970s period pointed to the endemic nature of crime (*universality*), and emphasized the systematic class bias in the focus of the criminal justice system (*selectivity*). And if universality made conventional positivist notions of causation unlikely, selectivity pointed to fundamental problems in neo-classicist ideas of equality before the law. Furthermore, criminology itself became a suspect discipline, for how could the scholar generalize from a sample already chosen by the criminal justice system (see Hulsman, 1986; Sumner, 1990)? Indeed crime, as Hulsman put it, seemed to have 'no ontological reality'.

However, just as the first wave of class-orientated revisionism pointed to the endemic nature of crime the new revisionism with its feminist orientation made a drastic caveat. Feminist criminology not only widened notions of victimization, it also indicated the implications of the extremely low offending rate of women. This in itself was commonplace: criminological texts have always shown that women have a remarkably lower offending rate than men. For example, Sutherland and Cressey in their magisterial *Principles of Criminology* note:

> Sex status is of greater significance in differentiating criminals from non-criminals than any other trait. If an investigator were asked to use a single trait to predict which persons in a town of 10,000 population would become criminals, he [*sic*] would make the fewest mistakes if he simply chose sex status and predicted criminality for the males and non-criminality for the females. He would be wrong in many cases, for most of the males would not become criminals, and a few of the females would be criminals. But he would be wrong in more cases if he used any other single trait, such as age, race, family background or a personality characteristic. (1966, p. 138)

What is of key importance is that feminist criminology brought the matter to centre stage: it hammered home the centrality of the male–female differential. Pivotal work, such as Eileen Leonard's *Women, Crime and Society* (1984), systematically exposed the androcentric bias in criminology. Theory after theory, whether it is differential association, anomie, subcultural theory or social deprivation, breaks down when women are put into the explanatory equation. Furthermore, not only is the importance of informal control rather than the deterrent impact of the criminal justice system highlighted in the low offending rate of women, but the fact that such control is exerted within patriarchy, rather than as a bland social pressure, situates it within the structure of society.

Thus the old certainties of social positivism – that poverty and unemployment lead to crime – become problematic once the criminality of those high in the social structure and women are taken into account. The first should have an extremely low crime rate, which they do not, while women, because of their comparative impoverishment and high rates of unemployment, should have high rates, which they palpably fail to exhibit. Crime thus occurs in places it should not. It does not occur it places it should.

Subsequent events as we approach the end of the century have taken this process further. The endemic nature of crime – at least for males – becomes more evident as crime rates rise; indeed the United States' penal supervision (and that is, of course, of just those who have been caught) becomes commonplace. And for sections of the US population commonplace means normal. In the US as a whole one in three of black males in their twenties are either in prison, on parole or on probation in a 12-month period. The proportions must surely be higher in the great cities of the United States: no shame can presumably accrue from such an occurrence. And as for selectivity a whole series of spectacular acts of discrimination and prejudice have generated widespread public disaffection with the impartiality of the criminal justice system. The Rodney King incident in Los Angeles and the various cases of dramatic injustice in the UK, including the Birmingham Six, the Guildford Four, and much of the activities of the Midlands Serious Crime Squad will serve as examples of the tip of the iceberg of malpractices which growing sections of the public had viewed as commonplace in more mundane policing (see Kinsey et al., 1986).

The problematization of punishment and culpability

The major factor here is the volume of crime. As the amount of crime rises there are immediate problems of how to deal with it bureaucratically with limited resources in terms of detection and disposal. Some measure of selectivity inevitably occurs in terms of where you look for crime, how you decide who is the real criminal, how you prove your case and how you dispose of the criminal. In this process individualized justice is lost; whole categories of people are rendered suspect while justice itself becomes detached from punishment.

The rise in the number of crimes results in an increase in arrests, which represents a dramatic rise of potential input for the criminal justice system. The reaction to this, as in any other bureaucracy, is to attempt to take short cuts and to decrease the possible number of clients. To take short cuts first, an institution like the police faces a growing number of cases per police officer. For example, in England and Wales, despite large increases in personnel, the number of crimes reported by the public per police officer rose from ten in 1960 to 40 in 1990. The temptation here, particularly given government pressure to maintain an economic and efficient service, is legitimately to engage in plea-bargaining, illegitimately to engage in corruption (e.g. by manipulating clear-up figures through 'taking into consideration' ('tic'), by fitting up suspects, by ignoring the gap between 'theoretical' and 'empirical' guilt) (see Kinsey, et al., 1986).

But it is the increased selectivity or 'pickiness' with regard to prospective clients which is perhaps of greatest interest. At the level of suspicion the police shift from suspecting individuals to suspecting social categories. For example, in terms of stop and search: it is more effective to suspect those categories deemed likely to commit offences (e.g. blacks, the Irish, young working class men) rather than to suspect individuals. You trawl in waters with the likeliest, richest harvest rather than take the 'pea in a pod' chance of making an arrest by proceeding on an individual-by-individual basis (see Young, 1995a). The old invocation 'round up the usual suspects' becomes transformed into 'round up the usual categories': individual suspicion becomes categorical suspicion.

The categorical notion of guilt is spectacularly illustrated in the O.J. Simpson case. The extraordinary media attention to this event was a function not only of the celebrity nature of the accused, but of the fact that the case vividly brought together the contradictions between the categories of guilt and innocence presumed in liberal and conservative discourses about crime. Thus from the liberal point of view O.J. Simpson was a black (therefore, innocent), a wifebeater (therefore, guilty), a star (therefore, innocent), and a person rich enough to purchase the 'best' justice available (therefore, guilty). Race, Gender, Status and Class came together with a resounding clash! Furthermore, from a conservative point of view, all of these prescriptions are well nigh reversed. Put this together with astounding police incompetence and corruption, and you have a story of incomparable resonance.

The criminal justice system itself, from police through to judiciary, when faced by too many offenders and too few places to put them, has to engage in a process of selectivity: to distinguish the dangerous, the hardened, the recidivist from the less recalcitrant offender. The proportion of people convicted of crime who are sent to prison declines (in England and Wales in 1938, 38% of those committing indictable offences were sent to prison; by 1993 this had fallen to 15%) and the process of selectivity based on risk management increases. Thus, although the overall numbers of prisoners increases, the chance of an offender going to prison decreases (see Chapter 5). There is little surprise in this: it is the result of expediency rather than leniency. A parallel could be that as the Health Service faces the increasing pressure of patient numbers, hospitals refuse to deal with minor ailments and accidents and attempt to move elderly patients out to nursing homes. Alternative care and alternative medicines, like alternatives to prison, flourish in this predicament.

The impact on the offender of this process of corruption, plea-bargaining and selectivity is to *problematize justice*. The justice one receives becomes a result not of individual guilt and proportional punishment but is more a negotiated process, the result of political or bureaucratic pressure rather than absolute standards. The chaos of reward encountered in the field of distributive justice is echoed in the chaos of punishment within the criminal justice system. Punishment can become divorced from crime; indeed it becomes possible for criminologists to discuss the level and notion of penality as a consequence of various influences in society without the level of crime entering the question. The level of imprisonment, just like fear of crime, comes to be seen as a problem separate from the problem of crime itself.

The new administrative criminology and actuarialism

The rise in crime and the increase in the number of offenders had a profound effect on the working principles of the criminal justice system and on academic theory within criminology. This involves a transition from neo-classicist to new administrative or actuarial criminology (see Table 2.2). The widespread nature of crime, its very *normality*, makes the search for causes less attractive. The new administrative criminology openly criticizes 'dispositional' theories; instead it explains crime as the inevitable result of a situation where the universal state of human imperfection is presented with an opportunity for misbehaviour (Young, 1995a). The task is to create barriers to restrict such opportunities and to construct a crime prevention policy which minimizes risks and limits the damage. An actuarial approach is adopted which is concerned with the calculation of risk rather than either individual guilt or motivation (Feeley and Simon, 1992, 1994; van Swaaningen, 1997). Both the modernist discourse of neo-classicism and positivism are discarded. We are interested in neither liability nor pathology, deterrence nor rehabilitation. The focus is prior to the event rather than after the event, on prevention rather than imprisonment or cure. It is not an inclusionist philosophy which embraces those found guilty of an offence and attempts to reintegrate them into society. Rather it is an exclusionist discourse which seeks to anticipate trouble whether in the shopping mall or in the prison and to exclude and isolate the deviant. It is not interested in crime *per se*, it is interested in the possibility of crime, in anti-social behaviour in

TABLE 2.2   *Neo-classicism and actuarial criminology*

	Neo-classicism	Actuarial criminology
Focus	Crime	All anti-social behaviour
	Actual event	Risk
	Intent	Behaviour
Proof	Proof without doubt	Balance of probability
Goal	Elimination	Damage limitation/harm minimization
Suspicion	Individual	Categorical
Method	Deterrence	Prevention
Agency	State	Private
Locus	Public space	Mass private property
Solution	Reparation	Insurance
Sentencing	Proportionality	Dangerousness

general, whether criminal or not, in likely mental illness or known recalci-
trance: in anything that will disrupt the smooth running of the system. Such
an administrative criminology is concerned with managing rather than
reforming, its 'realism' is that it does not pretend to eliminate crime (which
it knows is impossible) but to minimize risk. It has given up the ghost on the
modernist aims at change through social engineering and judicial intervention, it seeks merely to separate out the criminal from the decent citizen,
the troublemaker from the peaceful shopper and to minimize the harm that
the addict or alcoholic can do to themselves rather than proffer any 'cure'
or transformation.

The shift into late modernity: changing concepts of crime and its control

Before I turn to an explanation of these events let us examine the fundamental changes which have occurred (see Table 2.3).

It is my contention that during the last third of the twentieth century a
dramatic shift has occurred both in our perceptions and in the reality of
crime and its control. This has involved both change and revelation: the
world has changed but in changing has made it more easy for us to perceive
the underlying reality of crime. On the timing of this change, there is
remarkable agreement. 'It all began', James Q. Wilson wrote, 'in about
1963. That was the year that a decade began to fall apart' (1985, p. 15).
And indeed, diverse commentators, whether Wilson, Herrnstein and
Murray in their controversial *The Bell Curve* (1994) or Eric Hobsbawm in

TABLE 2.3 *The shift into late modernity: changing conceptions of crime
and its control*

1 Definition of crime	Obvious	Problematic
2 Prevalence of offenders	Minority	Extensive
3 Incidence of victimization	Exceptional	Normal
4 Causes of crime	Distant, determined, exceptional	Present, rationally chosen, widespread
5 Relationship to 'normality'	Separate	Normal/continuum
6 Relationship to wider society	Leakage	Integral
7 Locus of offence	Public	Public/private
8 Relationship of offender to victim	Stranger, outsider	Stranger/intimate, outsider/in-group
9 Locus of social control	Criminal justice system	Informal/ multi-agency
10 Effectiveness of social intervention	Taken for granted	Problematic: 'nothing works'
11 Public reaction	Obvious and rational	Problematic: irrational 'fear of crime' and moral panics
12 Spatial dimension	Segregated	Contested space

his magisterial *Age of Extremes* (1994), all pinpoint the change that occurred in all areas of life in this decade. The theoretical signal for this change within criminology and the sociology of deviance was undoubtedly the emergence of the new deviancy theory. This early burgeoning of post-modernism vividly grasped the transformation that was under way. It oversaw the shattering of modernity, in particular in its elaboration of the collapse of absolute rules, its insistence on the precarious nature of causality and its stress on the irony of the self-fulfilling and oppressive nature of social intervention as part of a metanarrative of progress.

The changes inevitably caused instabilities in the two spheres of order: that of reward and that of community (what citizens saw as the adequacy of their reward in the market place and how they viewed the balance between their desires as individuals and their responsibilities to the community). The motor behind such a change was rising demands upon citizenship both in terms of formal equality and, substantively, an increase in what was demanded of citizenship. Behind such a surge in aspiration lay the continued incessant development of a market society in the post-war period. The market brings together wide swathes of the population into the labour market, it creates the practical basis of comparison: it renders visible inequalities of race, class, age and gender. It elevates a universal citizenship of consumption yet excludes a significant minority from membership. It encourages an ideal of diversity, a market place of self-discovery yet provides for the vast majority a narrow, unrewarding individualism in practice. It creates 'uninterrupted disturbance of all social conditions, everlasting uncertainty and agitation' yet depends on a relatively uncritical acceptance of the given order. The market flourishes, expands, beckons yet undercuts itself. It does all this but it is not a mere transmission belt: the mores of the market may be the dominant ethos of the age but this ether of aspiration is shaped, developed and given force by the human actors involved. It is in this light that the problems in the two spheres of order, relative deprivation and individuation, must be viewed. For these are the key to the crime wave in the post-war period.

Relative deprivation and individualism

Relative deprivation, it must be remembered, is a creature of comparison. It can occur both when things get better and when they get worse, *providing* comparison is easy or is made easier. It is often absent when the gulf between people is large and has existed for a long time; it is frequently slight when differentials gradually and imperceptibly get worse. To grasp this principle is to move towards an understanding of the last third of the twentieth century. As Eric Hobsbawm charts in *The Age of Extremes* the post-war years saw a massive movement towards full citizenship of each of the subordinate categories of society: the working class, women, blacks and youth. Opportunities increased, greater equality was often realized and much more frequently talked about: expectations rose and by the 1960s the rhetoric of liberty and revolution was in the air. This was not an era of satisfaction, despite full employment and exceptional living standards. The *paradox of equality* is that as differentials narrow differences become all the more noticeable. Relative deprivation did not disappear with rising wealth, it was not ameliorated by widespread gains of citizenship – on the contrary, it was exacerbated. Then after the golden years, the recession of the 1980s and 1990s came – the era of mass unemployment and marginalization. The gains of economic citizenship are dramatically removed and, in a Keynesian era, are seen not as the result of some natural catastrophe but as a failure of government. The mood of the unemployed is not self-blame but system-blaming (see Mooney, 1998). Relative deprivation persists but is transformed. It no longer involves comparison across the serried ranks of the incorporated; it becomes comparison across the division of the labour market and between those in the market and those excluded.

But relative deprivation alone does not explain the rise in crime and disorder from the 1960s onwards. Relative deprivation breeds discontent, which can manifest itself in many ways; crime is only one of them. The lethal combination is relative deprivation and individualism. For Hobsbawm it is the rise of individualism which is pivotal: 'The cultural revolution of the late twentieth century can thus be understood as the triumph of the individual over society, or rather, the breaking of the threads which in the past had woven human beings into social textures' (1994, p. 334). It is individualism which leads discontent to generate the 'Hobbesian jungles' of the urban poor, a 'universe where human beings live side by side but not as social beings' (ibid., p. 341).

Nostalgia and decline

There is a predominant train of thought shared both by those on the left and the right of the political spectrum that the last third of the twentieth century has been a period of decline. The nature of this decline is seen to take many forms: the increase in unemployment, the breakdown of community, the disintegration of the traditional nuclear family, a lack of respect, the lowering of standards, a prevalence of disorder and notably the rise in the crime rate itself. The features stressed in the version of such a decline theory vary with the politics of the commentator although all of them share many of these items as indices of a world turned sour. Crucially, whatever the politics, the role of market society is seen as pivotal in this change. Let me take what at first sight might be almighty strange bedfellows: James Q. Wilson and Eric Hobsbawm. For Wilson, a policy advisor to Nixon and Reagan, a guru of the right, the cause is a culture which emphasizes immediate gratification, self-expression and low impulse control. 'A liberal commercial society committed to personal self-expression' inevitably creates problems of discipline: 'a devotion to self-actualization is at best artistic or inspiring and at worst banal or trivial. In the hands of a person of weak character, with a taste for risk and an impatience for gratification, that ethos is a license to steal and mug' (1985, pp. 247–9). In the end, however, 'we have made our society and we must live with it'. Indeed, Wilson's work is in many ways an attempt to come to terms with how such a liberal 'free' society can work, extending from his initial 'realist' beliefs in the power of law, punishment and policing to his later much greater emphasis on family, the first five years of life, character, and social training (Wilson and Herrnstein, 1985; Wilson, 1991, 1993).

Eric Hobsbawm, the Marxist historian reaches this same conclusion, but this time with considerable irony when he notes how capitalism needs the presence of pre-capitalist values: trust, honour, discipline, commitment to community and to family. Thus he writes:

> As we take for granted the air we breathe, and what makes possible all our activities, so capitalism took for granted the atmosphere in which it operated, and which it had inherited from the past. It only discovered how essential it had been when the air became thin. In other words, capitalism has succeeded because it was not just capitalist. Profit maximization and accumulation were necessary conditions for its success but not sufficient ones. It was the cultural revolution of the last third of the century which began to erode the inherited historical assets of capitalism and to demonstrate the difficulties of operating without them. It was the historic way of the neo-liberalism that became fashionable in the 1970s and 1980s, and looked down on the ruins of the communist regimes, that triumphed at the very moment when it ceased to be as plausible as it once seemed. The market claimed to triumph as its nakedness and inadequacy could no longer be concealed. (1994, p. 343)

So the cause of such a *decline* is a *deficit* and this shortfall is a result of the triumph of market values itself. A market society cannot exist without the oxygen of non-market values and relationships: the market undercuts its own existence. Of course such a deficit is underwritten by the recession of the latter part of the century. Commentators of all political persuasions recognize this, but even social democrats acknowledge that the impact of the recession has been severely worsened by the culture of individualism. The solidarity of the working class community and family which saw the people through the 1930s has given way to fragmentation. In the place of collective values there is every person for themselves, in place of working together there is internecine strife and criminality (Dennis, 1993; Seabrook, 1978).

The diagnosis of decline and deficit is followed, perhaps inevitably, with the prescription of *nostalgia*. Politicians of all persuasions, from social democrats to conservatives, share a preoccupation with the notion of returning to the past, of rekindling the half-warm memories of family, work and community. After all, the essence of the widespread appeal of Etzioni's communitarianism is the attempt to bolt on to a shattered society all the steadfast certainties of the past: a world where everyone pulled together.

A novel bipartisanship of nostalgia is presented before us. It is a world of full employment where the market is extended to embrace the marginalized and absorb individuals – depending on one's political persuasion. It is a society where we must support the family or curb the feckless single mother – depending on one's party preference. It is a time to rebuild community, to return to basics, to encourage the collective values of yesteryear.

There are mistakes both in the prescription and the diagnosis. Much of this centres around the misunderstanding of individualism and of the deficit which is seen as its inevitable result. Let us put the argument in logical order: market society engenders a culture of individualism which under-mines the relationships and values necessary for a stable social order and hence gives rise to crime and disorder. This both Wilson and Hobsbawm would agree on but then Hobsbawm adds an ironic twist: market society is, in fact, dependent on the values and relationships which pre-date it and which the culture of individualism dissolves and disintegrates: I want to examine two key aspects of this argument. Firstly, to what extent is con-temporary capitalism undermined by rising crime and disorder? Secondly, to what degree is the culture of individualism an unmitigated deficit?

In Merton's (1938) famous theory of anomie the cultural ideals of meri-tocracy are subverted by the existing structure of society. In Hobsbawm's critique the reverse is true: the structure of society is undermined by the values. In both, one consequence of such a contradiction between culture and structure is crime and disorder. I am certain that both of these ironies in the constitution of market societies – the first in what I have demarcated as the sphere of justice, the second in the sphere of community, both clearly alluded to by Durkheim – are crucial in the generation of crime in advanced industrial societies. Indeed they are at the core of the claim by radical crim-inologists that crime is an endemic rather than a peripheral feature of social order. Yet it would be as wrong to suggest – as Hobsbawm does – that such endemic disorder is, in fact, a systemic problem *of capitalism* as to suggest – as an earlier generation of radicals maintained – that crime is not much of a problem *for anyone*. Rather we must pinpoint who actually suffers from crime, in this present period, and what are the social consequences of an endemic criminality. Certainly the growth of individualism is the great shaper of the latter part of the twentieth century. Certainly this is a product of market forces; but the impact of the market is at core contradictory, as is individualism itself. For let us clear up, immediately, the notion that capital-ism always needs a high degree of social order. This is true of only specific periods: the universally orderly population of the modernist period was necessary only with Fordist production and full employment. It is in the newly emerging industrial nations that a massive orderly population is necessary, if anywhere. Neo-liberalism triumphed in the First World in the recent period when order amongst the marginalized part of the population – and also the most disorderly – is of declining necessity to capital. The underclass of today are not needed, their labour is unnecessary, the incul-cation of habits of punctuality and discipline irrelevant, their consumption demands useful but easily controllable. The disorder of their communities may be at times an embarrassment to politicians – as in the Los Angeles riots – but their impact is negligible. It is media circus without relevance for capital. The underclass destroy their own areas, they turn in upon each other; they, at times, threaten the police who are specifically employed to be both threatened and threatening. Indeed, leading theorists of the right such as James Q. Wilson speculate as to how far an area has 'to tip' before it is unrescuable and 'realistically' not worth state intervention. New York City, the leading financial centre of world capitalism, can exist with crime rates at a Third World level, yet its economic performance is unabated by the crime that surrounds it. Order must occur, of course, in financial trans-actions and pre-contractual norms exist in order to sustain contracts, as Durkheim pointed out, but this is different matter from that of the crimes of the excluded. It is anyway a matter of speculation exactly what level of honesty and trust is necessary for capital accumulation, a large proportion of which occurs because of precisely opposite pecuniary virtues. The rich and the privileged, by means of gates and bars, by barriers and surveillance, by private guards and public policing, can keep themselves and their prop-erty safe. The suburban shopping mall and the new developments down-town must be swept clean regularly of beggars, small time thieves and drunks, windows must be mended and vandalism erased if customers are to consume effortlessly and without distraction. But none of this poses much of a threat, though it provides a ready rhetoric for politicians and the basis for influential criminological texts (e.g. Wilson and Kelling, 1982).

Neo-liberal policies around the world attempt not only to roll back the state but to redraw the parameters of civil society. They put the social con-tract back on the table and attempt to exclude the lower orders from its orbit. The poor are denied decent education, health care, legal rights and they are, as Galbraith (1992) has pointed out, easily outvoted – their politi-cal rights are not so much denied as rendered inconsequential. And lastly in the field of law and order: the areas which have poor schools and patchy social services also have desultory policing. Here the police force is reactive to gross disturbance, it is not the servant of the local citizenry but its warder. Law and order, like so many aspects of the welfare state, is least provided where it is most needed. Yet law and order, like health care and education, is needed by the mass of citizens. Crime control, in particular, is a political unifier for it is a shared problem for the mass of the population. The capi-talist system itself in the First World requires political order and economic stability but crime with its fitful intransigence and inconsequential rebellion is of no great threat; indeed it is, as Wilson suggests, an inevitable conse-quence of a 'successful' free market system. But what is inconsequential to the system is profoundly deleterious to the citizen and particularly so with the rising demand for a better and safer environment coupled with a general intolerance of violence. We have something of a paradox here: a rising popular demand for law and order at a time when there is a declining systemic need for it. It is for this reason that law and order is of more ideological importance to neo-liberal, politicians of the right whereas it is – or at least *should* be – of more direct material consequence to social democrats.

Crime and deficit

Let us turn now to the problem of individualism and deficit. The language of criminology is rife with the notion of deficit: the causes of crime result from lack of material goods, or falling standards of social training or a general decline in values. Take your pick: the preferred deficit varies with the politics of the commentator yet each involves a loss and an individualistic response to it. I would like to reverse this nostrum: crime is caused not so much because a world has been lost as because a new world has not yet been gained. Let us, briefly, look at each of these deficits in turn, but first of all let me stress that I am not arguing that considerable and often heartless losses have not been experienced during this last part of the twentieth century. The recession has caused widespread misery, whole communities have been destroyed and families torn apart, while the values of the market have profoundly transformed social life. All of this suffering and divisiveness has certainly occurred but its cause has not been simple deficit: it has involved rising demands as well as falling returns, a questioning of conformity rather than a passive deviance, a conflict in standards as well as a lack of values.

To take a lack of material goods first of all. Here surely simple deficit theory works? The recession coupled with the rise of individualism, the material harshness of the market in combination with market values, is frequently seen by social democrats as the obvious cause of crime in the present period. Herein lies a pitfall for radical analyses of crime. The danger is, quite simply, this: that for many social democrats working within criminology the aetiological crisis is over. We are back in the old formula: bad conditions lead to bad behaviour. The rhetoric is simple and seductive: for have not the cuts in the welfare state been swingeing and irresponsible and is not the gap between rich and poor widening? Furthermore, to the conceptual armoury of declining material conditions have been added market values. Conditions have worsened and individualism is rampant in a market society. What else but rising crime could be a result?

It is not as simple as this. Lack of material rewards clearly does not mean absolute poverty; crime rose through the late 1960s with rising living standards: it is relative deprivation which is a potent cause of crime. So perhaps, even here, we should refer to a relative deficit: that is, the relative material standards of individuals compared one to another, a sense of inequality of unjust reward commensurate with merit. So as groups begin progressively to demand greater equality of reward, fuller citizenship, then their relative deprivation increases and, if no collective solution is forthcoming, crime will occur. The prognosis for South Africa, for example, is to be more and more crime ridden unless progress is seen to be substantial, tangible and possible in the future. Half-hearted progress or mere proclamations of equality will not dissolve feelings of relative deprivation; on the contrary they will exacerbate them. Such a situation of fuller citizenship demanded but thwarted is scarcely simple deficit. For it involves not only a static comparison with the more successful, but rising aspirations; it includes people perceiving themselves as being below the line of equality but it also involves people actively stretching the limits. Both Durkheim and Merton realized this: they in no way embraced a fixed, positivistic conception of deprivation (cf. Katz, 1988). Yet social democratic interpretations of crime frequently convey the notion that crime is about simple deficit, that it will disappear as we approach greater equality (it may well not for the paradox of equality is that relative deprivation can increase with greater equality of reward) and that crime itself is somehow something which 'tops up' the income of the poor. This is simply not true: crime, whether street robbery or embezzlement, is rarely committed in order to reach the average median wage. The poor do not steal Beetles but Porsches, looters do not carry home a booty of baked beans but of camcorders, no one – outside of a tiny few – takes illicit drugs to feel normal (see Mugford and O'Malley, 1991). And the rich do not commit crimes in order to ensure a future retirement in comfort. That they already have; they do so in order to excel in their affluence and to exult in their edge over all comers. Further, the rich, as Ruggiero has nicely pointed out, do not pursue crime because of a deficit of opportunities; far from it, they have a surfeit of criminal possibilities just as they do legitimate opportunities (Ruggiero, 1993, 1996). It is a question of being below limits and going beyond limits: it is relative deficit and transgression; a fact recognized by Durkheim and Merton in their invocation of both a sense of unfairness and of infinity of reward.

Let us turn now to the second deficit, that of social cohesion: the decline in the strength of the family and the community. Here a notable political polarization is evident: for if those on the left talk of deficit of reward, on the right the preferred deficit is lack of control. And if social positivism re-emerges in the first deficit, then neo-positivism has even more dramatically re-emerged with the second. The traditional role of biological or psychological positivism has been to explain crime and deviance in terms of the pathology of the individual and to avoid ascribing causes to problems endemic to the structure of society. Thus positivism of the modernist period ascribed deviance to the failure of a few isolated, dysfunctional families. The emergence of mass crime and deviance necessitates a latching on to causes which are *widespread* but which do not imply that there is something drastically amiss with the structure of society. Neo-positivism, particularly the work of Charles Murray (1990, 1994) and Travis Hirschi (Gottfredson and Hirschi, 1990), has focused on the decline of the family and the competence of socialization in the first five years of life. Such a *market positivism* does not question the possibility of human rationality and choice (albeit it remarkably restricted to conformist outcomes) but sees criminal choices as the result of low impulse control and anti-social individualism engendered in childhood. For on the fulcrum of human decision making the long arm of freedom needs the heavy counterweight of early discipline. The widespread nature of such a problem is considered a result of women choosing to have children outside of wedlock or cohabitation. This problem is often seen as localized in an underclass and is a product of welfare dependency. A culture of individualism encourages young women to have children who are inadequately socialized and whose activities are subsidized by the taxpayer. This is not the place to enter into debate with this thoroughly disagreeable and factually incorrect argument but what is of immediate relevance is its notion of how crime is caused by social deficit. Crime is seen to occur because of a failing of the system of socialization, whether it is family or community, single parent or underclass. Crime is the result of a faulty container. The mistake here is twofold. Firstly, to explain crime as the result of a lack of control ignores why people wish to commit crimes. It removes motivation from the equation and thus, ultimately, rules out the generation of criminal motives by the social structure itself. Secondly, it assumes that the container is a physical object which has, so to speak, sprung a leak. The attitude of individuals to the control asserted by their family or community is completely ignored. They are not social actors reflecting on their surroundings but objects more or less controlled by their environment. In fact, habits of obedience, of deference, of willingness to defer to family, neighbours, the local community have all declined partly because of the system's inability to provide acceptable opportunities and partly because of an unwillingness to accept authority just because it is authority. The decline in unthinking obedience is perhaps one of the most significant changes in the twentieth century. This loosening of social ties is not a mechanistic process but a result of greater demand for individual autonomy: its roots lie not in deficit but in aspiration.

Lastly, let us look at the third supposed area of deficit: decline in values. I have already indicated that one of the characteristics of late modernity is an intense debate about values. Crime and deviance are no longer measured by the absolute standards which modernity offered: their definitions are contested and publicly debated. If this is deficit then it is a decline in certainty not a failure of concern. Yet we can go further than this for in the areas of violence and the quality of life one can detect a clear rise in standards. The increased sensitization to child abuse, domestic violence and animal rights are examples which I have already used. But the demand to be freed from the fear of crime and to be able to walk the streets of our great cities at night is part of a general concern for the lived environment and Green issues. This rising demand for law and order is, as I have noted previously (1995b), paradoxical in that it is accompanied frequently by a deterioration of behaviour. Yet the perpetrators and the protesters are not, I suspect, the same people and the frequent finding that the reported rates of serious violence rise much faster than homicide rates suggest that an overall long term change in tolerance is occurring. Such a sensitization does not suggest deficit: indeed, as Norbert Elias has famously shown, we are witnessing a civilizing process rather than an unmitigated tide of barbarism. In particular the entry of women into the labour market and thence more fully into the public arena has led to a growing intolerance of male violence and incivilities.

It is not merely about provision of more opportunities and raising living standards, it is about justice and merit. It is not about more social control, mending the leaks in the system; it is about incorporation: of families and communities whose norms are not simply obeyed but accepted and embraced. It is not a question of creating a monolithic consensus in value but of continuous diversity and change. And in essence, all of this revolves around the notion of citizenship. That is a citizenship which is concerned with equality, a citizenship which is not fixed in limits but subject to rising aspirations, a citizenship whose substance and content is subject to redefinition, disagreement and debate.

Let us return now to individualism. A creature both of Janus and Pandora, the individualism of the latter part of the twentieth century is both contradictory and unpredictable. It is a product of market society, surely, but the way in which individualism develops can have both anti-social and profoundly social consequences. The individualism which begs us to treat others like commodities can also be the individualism which refuses treatment like a commodity. The desire for self-actualization can mean, of course, the cold-blooded pursuit of selfish interests but it can also mean resistance to being put upon. The increasing demand for self-expression can be at the expense of others but it can also be the demand for a world where self-expression is possible. The cult of the individual is at worst a motive for violence to achieve one's aim but it may well involve a growing abhorrence of violence against the individual. In short, if the dark side of the dialectic of individualism is crime and villainy, the bright side is a whole host of new social movements, a new sensibility about the environment, and a lowered tolerance of violence. And there can be little doubt of the central role that second wave feminism and the Green movement have had in the genesis of a new individualism. All of this stands in contrast to many of the institutions and much of the ethos of modernism. The 'benevolent' state which steadfastly destroyed the urban environment with its tower blocks and freeways, which bestowed problems upon a passive public, and created public bureaucracies which were both unresponsive and unreflecting.

3 CANNIBALISM AND BULIMIA

Above all we should realise that certain of our customs might appear, to an observer belonging to a different society, to be similar in nature to cannibalism, although cannibalism strikes us as being foreign to the idea of civilization. I am thinking, for instance, of our legal and prison systems. If we studied societies from the outside, it would be tempting to distinguish two contrasting types: those which practise cannibalism – that is, which regard the absorption of certain individuals possessing dangerous powers as the only means of neutralizing those powers and even of turning them to advantage – and those which, like our own society, adopt what might be called the practice of *anthropemy* (from the Greek *émein*, to vomit); faced with the same problem, the latter type of society has chosen the opposite solution which consists in ejecting dangerous individuals from the social body and keeping them temporarily or permanently in isolation, away from all contact with their fellows, in establishments specially intended for this purpose. Most of the societies which we call primitive would regard this custom with profound horror; it would make us, in their eyes, guilty of that same barbarity of which we are inclined to accuse them because of their symmetrically opposite behaviour. (Lévi-Strauss, 1992 [1955], pp. 287–8)

Anthropophagic and anthropoemic societies

A generation of social commentators have been fascinated by the categories of inclusion and exclusion suggested by Claude Lévi-Strauss in *Tristes Tropiques*. 'Primitive' societies, he argues, deal with strangers and deviants by swallowing them up, by making them their own and by gaining strength from them. They are anthropophagic, whereas modern societies are anthropoemic; they vomit out deviants, keeping them outside of society or enclosing them in special institutions within their perimeters.

Such a viewpoint was quickly embraced by radicals perhaps because it involves a dystopian transition (so attractive left of centre): from a tolerant Arcadian world of the past to the intolerant world of the present (see Cooper, 1967; Young, 1971b). There is little doubt that such a contrast was Lévi-Strauss' intent, although it is debatable whether the swallowing, rather cannibalistic world of anthropophagy is any more tolerant than the anorexic, expelling world of anthropoemia. I doubt it: but the concepts themselves, without the gross conflation of all pre-modern societies into one or the evocation of an inevitable downward decline of tolerance, I think are eminently usable. Particularly if, as embellished by Zygmunt Bauman

(1995), we can acknowledge that all societies have both swallowing and ejecting aspects and we take on board the rather neat observation of David Cooper that such moments can exist in a given society at the same time in different institutions. Thus, the family can spew out the mentally ill, whilst the mental hospital can try to return your relative fully digested and 'normalized' back to the bosom of the family (see Cooper, 1967). Lastly, not only do *societies* have both devices and differing *institutions* specialize, so to speak, in absorption or ejection, but different *sections* of the population can be subject to predominant forces of inclusion or exclusion. Thus Stan Cohen talks of a *bifurcation* with:

> a vision not too far from Orwell's. Middle class thought crime is subject to inclusionary controls; when these fail . . . then 'down the chute'. Working class deviant behaviour is segregated away and contained: if the proles become threatening they can be 'subjected like animals by a few simple rules'. (Cohen, 1985, p. 234)

Visions of social control

Nowhere is such a process of inclusion and exclusion given such a broad sweep as in Stan Cohen's *Visions of Social Control* (1985). Here he sees a long historical movement in the master patterns of social control from inclusive in the pre-eighteenth century, to exclusion from the nineteenth century up until the inclusiveness of the mid-twentieth century onwards (see pp. 16–17). These brush strokes are all too broad to my mind, although to be fair to Cohen he is very aware of the contradictions of each period. My own rendition of this process is more modest: it starts in the inclusive world of the immediate post-war period and it develops into the exclusive world of the last part of the twentieth century. It corresponds to the coda of Cohen's history of social control: a move back to exclusiveness after the destructuring of the 1960s which is, as it turns out, the main subject matter of his book. To a considerable extent, therefore, our concerns run in parallel, yet they differ fundamentally in their mechanisms. Cohen, in my estimation, grants too much autonomy to the control systems. It is as if the apparatus of social control in all its ramifications is bracketed off from the objects to be controlled, whether crime, deviance or disorder and the substantive problems which these create. Once bracketed off, control has its own causality, 'nets' widen and shrink, prison populations rise and fall quite independently of the level of *difficulty* which those who seek to control face. Even more fundamentally the material changes in society which give rise to the different levels and shapes of crime and disorder do not figure at all. The discussion of the transition from an inclusive society to one that is intent on exclusion is thus all on the meta-level of control; the processes of inclusion and exclusion which give rise to problems of crime and disorder (i.e. the transformation of the labour markets and the rise of market individualism) and the problems of exclusion which crime itself creates are ignored. It is almost as if the shadow of the problem has taken precedence over the problem itself. Of course, part of this is a reaction to the conventional wisdom which sees the prisons etc. as simply a function of the level of crime. They are *not*: there is no direct correlation between levels of crime and imprisonment, let alone a one-to-one line of causality (p. 91). Yet this valuable insight of modern criminology has led to a reverse position: that no correlation implies no relationship whatsoever. What, for instance, is one to make of the leading British textbook on imprisonment, Cavadino and Dignan's *The Penal System* (1997), which in the first chapter is able to discuss the crisis of the prisons without discussing the crisis of crime? Complex illustrations are presented to us with every item connected to the others in fascinating flow diagrams without crime being worthy of appearance as a relevant factor.

A widespread problem in the literature is that the totality of the process of control is rarely encompassed. Some theories, as we have seen, focus on 'social control' as if it were autonomous of what was being controlled; some give a social and economic context to the problem but reserve this for explaining the penal or social control system and not for the generation of crime itself. Many conventional theories do precisely the opposite of this, explaining crime in terms of social and economic factors but leaving the criminal justice system hanging in a vacuum. Lastly, nearly all tend to regard social control as, somehow, separate from the public, as if control and social discipline were something unilaterally imposed upon people, for example by the state in orthodox Marxist theory or by the 'carceral archipelago', the wide range of institutions from prison to reform in the community charted by Foucault and his followers.

A fully social theory, one that does not commit such errors of partiality, must deal with the *context* (of both crime and the criminal justice system), with the *currency* (the problem of disorder and diversity which a control system faces) and with *complicity* (the way in which citizens actively participate in social control).

Let me recapitulate the process which I have delineated which brings about the transition from an inclusive to an exclusive society. In the last two chapters I traced the way in which changes in the market place (in the spheres of both production and consumption) gave rise to an increase in levels of crime and disorder and, also, to a problematization of order itself. Rules are more readily broken but also more regularly questioned. Civil society becomes more segmented and differentiated: people become more wary and appraising of each other because of ontological insecurity (living in a plural world where individual biographies are less certain) and material insecurity (a world of risk and uncertainty). The combination of a rise in *difficulty* (crime, disorder and incivilities) and of an increase in *difference* (that is a diversity and debate over rules themselves) results not only in a qualitative change in civil society but in a change in the system of social control, in particular the rise of an actuarial system of justice. Thus exclusion in the market gives rise to exclusions and divisions within civil society, which give rise to quantitative and qualitative changes in the exclusion imposed by the state. And, finally, the responses of the state have repercussions in reinforcing and exacerbating the exclusion of civil society and the market place. The strange anthropoemic machine of late modernity generates a resonance of exclusion throughout its structure with the main motor being the rapidly developing pitch of market relations.

The long term decline in tolerance?

Having sharpened our historical focus and made clear the structures of exclusion, let us now rid ourselves of the notion of a long term decline in tolerance. For exclusion is not based on a simple rise in intolerance as many liberals would have us believe. The contrast that Lévi-Strauss makes is a clear calumny on the contemporary world: for there can be little doubt that the modern urban dweller has a tolerance far in excess of the average pre-industrial society or indeed the present day country dweller. The city spins with a kaleidoscope of subcultures while the electronic media delivers daily a menu of extensive cultural variety, albeit truncated and hybridized to match the locality of listener or viewer. Difference and diversity are the staples of lifestyle, consumerism, of late modernity: we eat our evening meal from a world menu, our supermarkets exhort us to extend our repertoire from the Caribbean to the Mediterranean, the market for popular music makes stars out of the rap dissidents of the Los Angeles ghettos, gay sensibilities imbue our chat shows and enhance our comedians, every diverse nuance of marriage, lifestyle and sexual relations is debated daily.

Late modern societies *consume* diversity; they do not recoil at difference, they recast it as a commodity and sell it in the local supermarket or magazine. What they are less willing to endure is *difficulty*. The transition from modernity to late modernity, I wish to argue, involves a remarkable change: almost a reversal of structures of tolerance. The modern world is intolerant of *diversity*, which it attempts to absorb and assimilate and is relatively tolerant of difficulty, of obdurate people and recalcitrant rebels whom it sees as more of a challenge to rehabilitate and reform. The late modern world celebrates diversity and *difference*, which it readily absorbs and sanitizes; what it cannot abide is difficult people and *dangerous* classes, which it seeks to build the most elaborate defences against, not just in terms of insiders and outsiders, but throughout the population.

The world of modernity

The contrast that I use in this book between the inclusive world of the immediate post-war period ('modernity') and the exclusive world of the last third of the twentieth century ('late modernity') makes this clear. The accent in modernity is anthropophagic: deviants are there to be absorbed. Criminals are rehabilitated, madmen and drug addicts cured, immigrants assimilated, teenagers 'adjusted', dysfunctional families counselled into normality. The difficult, obdurate parts of the population are almost a welcome challenge to the welfare state and its functionaries. And, as Alvin Gouldner pointed out, there is a distinct utilitarian calculus underlying this:

> A central problem confronting a society organized around utilitarian values is the disposal and control of 'useless' men and useless traits. There are various strategies for the disposal and control of useless men. They may, for example, be ecologically separated and isolated in spatially distinct locales where they are not painfully visible to the 'useful'! They may be placed, as American Indians were, on reservations; they may come to live in ethnic ghettos, as American Blacks do; if they have the means to do so, they may elect to live in benign environments such as the communities for the aged in Florida; they may be placed in special training or retraining camps, as are certain unskilled and unemployed American youth, frequently black; or again, they may be placed in prisons or in insane asylums, following routine certification by juridical or medical authorities.
>
> Transition to a Welfare State does not simply mean transition from a standard of individual to collective utility; it also implies a greater involvement of the state in developing and managing the disposal of the 'useless'. In some part, the very growth of the Welfare State means that the problem is becoming so great and complex that it can no longer be left to the informal control of market or other traditional institutions. Increasingly, the Welfare State's strategy is to transform the sick, the deviant, and the unskilled into 'useful citizens', and to return them to 'society' only after periods of hospitalization, treatment, counselling, training, or retraining. It is this emphasis upon the reshaping of persons that differentiates the Welfare State's disposal strategies from those that tended to cope with the useless primarily by custody, exclusion, and insulation from society. The newer strategies differ from the old in that they seek to be self-financing; the aim is to increase the supply of the useful and to diminish that of the useless. (1971, pp. 76–7)

Modernity sought to assimilate; its problem was not the difficulty of the task but the notion of diversity. The stress was on monotone, monoculture, perched, as one might alliteratively put it, on a monorail of progress starting at the 'primitive' world of *National Geographic* and ending in middle class America, the contented Kelloggs' Cornflakes adverts of the early 1960s.

Lévi-Strauss talks of the magical ability of such anthropophagic societies to take individuals 'possessing dangerous powers' to neutralize them, 'even turning them to advantage' (1992 [1955], p. 388). This modernity achieved with virtuosity: it scrutinized groups with alternative values and suggested that they were simply lacking in the values of the establishment: they abhorred pluralism and substituted for a relativity of value an absolutism of standards. Middle class standards were 'normal', 'they' were lacking in normality: 'we' spoke standard English, 'they' were illiterate, 'we' lived in nuclear families, 'their' families lacked structure, 'we' drank malt whisky as a reward for hard work, 'they' took illegal substances because of poor character structure and a pitiful hedonism. Our aggression was normal and desirable: burly, macho-men lined up to receive medals during wars, whilst similar mayhem and violence committed outside of such sanctified cockpits resulted in vaguely similar burly macho-men lined up to engage in prolonged therapy, to control their aggression. We had heroes, they had psychopaths; we had entrepreneurs, they had thieves.

Modernity took the difficult individual and, with a jujitsu-like manoeuvre, transforms their resistance into support for the established order. It was not afraid of the difficult individual; it was not difficulty which threatened modernity but diversity. A whole barrage of experts – psychiatrists, social workers, criminologists – were in the business of explaining away diversity, a positivist social science was evolved which sought to explain the 'remarkable': how differences in values, attitudes and behaviour could possibly occur in a world which was both economically and socially so successful – the end point of historical development. Their task was to convert diversity into deviance.

Inclusivism: its radical wing

The post-war years came to fruition in the permissive 1960s. Just as citizenship in the legal and political sense became extended by class, by age, by race and by gender, so the limits of normality, permissible behaviour within the social contract, were pushed forward. More and more areas of behaviour which were once seen as offences, *by definition* outside of the social contract, became embraced by it. This is manifest in two areas: juvenile delinquency and the so-called 'crimes without victims'. In face of the first rise in juvenile crime in the 1960s the response in many administrations was to make the distinction between the majority of children who misbehave as part of the normal development of childhood and the minority who suffer from more serious maladjustment. In Britain the 1968 White Paper, *Children in Trouble*, summed this up well:

> It is probably a minority of children who grow up without ever misbehaving in ways which may be contrary to the law. Frequently such behaviour is no more than an incident in the pattern of a child's normal development, but sometimes it is a response to unsatisfactory family or social circumstances, a result of boredom in or out of school, an indication of maladjustment or immaturity or a symptom of a deviant, damaged or abnormal personality. (HMSO, 1968, p. 7)

That is, much juvenile offending was normal behaviour, it was no longer criminal in any 'real' sense of the word. Furthermore, neither was the more 'serious' minority truly criminal because it was the result of environmental factors – it was not wilful but determined, a creature not of classicism but of positivism. Thus it was either normal behaviour or a result of something lacking – it was normality or a *deficit* in normality.

In all countries it is youth which is the most frequent source of law-breaking, in its conventional sense. For it is in this age group that burglary, street robbery, theft and public fighting are most frequent. To take juvenile delinquency out of the category 'crime', to capture it in the binary of 'normal youthful behaviour' ('just like we were at that age') and a minority dysfunctional behaviour ('people who were not brought up like us') is inclusion indeed! And to render this latter 'serious' delinquency not wilful but determined by a lack of social training removes that constant spectre of liberal contract theory: the possibility that it might mean class inequality. That is the rational criminal which Beccaria was so aware of – who differed from us not because of a lack of social skills but because of the realization, however primitive, that the given system of property and reward was unfair at core. That is class difference rather than mere deviation from our standards. As John Pitts put it, this was an 'attempt to *decriminalize* and *depoliticize* the youth justice system' (1997, p. 255, emphasis in original). If implemented, at a stroke, a massive part of what is conventional crime would have moved out of the orbit of the criminal justice system. As it was, the political resistance to such reform was immense and the subsequent 1969 Crime and Young Persons Act was very much a fudge even if, looking back from the present, it represents a radical agenda indeed (see Pitts, 1988). The overall intent represented, as Bottoms and Stevenson put it, 'the most developed application of welfare principles to criminal justice ever seen in an English statute' (1992, p. 36). Partial implementation followed, although the welfare impulse was nowhere as substantial as in some European countries (e.g. in Sweden and the Netherlands). Indeed by the 1980s this process of depoliticization in which 'the perpetrators of crime cease to be the objects of political discourse and become instead the objects of a scientific or professional discourse' (Pitts, 1988, p. 150) had proceeded to a remarkable degree. Thus John Pitts notes that Emilia Romagna, the area surrounding Bologna in Italy with a population of 15 million, in 1987 had a 'youth custody' population of two. Ten years previously there had been 400 boys imprisoned.

Other times, of course, had a much more exclusivist vision. The radical nature of these proposals is made clear if we contrast this with a century previously. The Victorians had little difficulty with difference: people actively chose depravity: the street 'Arabs' of Henry Mayhew (1861) were without doubt different to the Victorians who glimpsed them on the edges of Bloomsbury or to the north of Kensington. 'The poor are not like us but different' they might have said, anticipating Scott Fitzgerald (of whom more later). Indeed, as Judith Walkowitz excellently documents, Booth, Mayhew and Greenwood, the urban spectators of the Victorian period, set out on expeditions to chart these differences: 'The literature of urban exploration . . . emulated the privileged gaze of anthropology in constituting the poor as a race apart, outside the national community' (1992, p. 19). And 'to render the "incomprehensible" comprehensible, Booth and his associates applied Lamarckian and Spencerian evolutionary theory to the social world of the slum. They interpreted signs of gender and sexual transgressions as symptoms of biological degeneracy' (ibid., p. 35). The depictions of urban Jewry and the Irish in particular, whether in cartoon or in philanthropic tract, stress racial difference as underlying social difference and, of course, notions of atavism with its roots in the work of Darwin (let alone that of Lamarck and Spencer!). All of this seems like a preview of the world of difference of the latter part of the twentieth century with its stress on the cultural and often racial differences of the underclass. But this takes us too far ahead of the narrative. . . .

What immediately concerns us here is the contrast with the radical inclusivism of the 1960s, the widespread process of defining deviancy down – or lowering of limits of tolerance. And all of this is accompanied by a bifurcation: the normalization of a large part of the 'problem' and the rendering pathological of the minority part. Such a process can be plainly seen in the area of 'crimes without victims'. Let us look briefly at two areas: drugs and homosexuality.

The debate about the legalization of drugs shifted from the notion of drug use being immoral behaviour, an appetite of difference, bohemianism and a rather romanticized heightening of sensibility to that of the drug user being largely inadequate. Our historical images of drugs are transformed. The opium use of Coleridge and De Quincey and the morphine use of the fictional Sherlock Holmes were replaced by the heroin addict with the deficit mantra, 'weak superego, inadequate ego and lack of masculine identification' (see, for example, Chein et al., 1964). So difference once again was transformed into a lack and, as one important consequence, the doubtless positive attractions of heroin were dropped from the literature so that the main motivation for use is depicted as that of tackling withdrawal.

The argument for the legalization of cannabis which occurred in radical circles at this time was naturally ensconced in an inclusivist narrative. Cannabis users were 'just like us', only they smoked cannabis rather than drank lager. They were distinct from heroin users who were deficient in their personalities and behaviour; indeed, one argument for legalization of cannabis was that it kept the two populations apart so that the sociable marijuana user did not pick up bad habits from the anti-social junkie. (Of this I am as guilty as anyone: see Young, 1971a.) The association of cannabis use with the emerging, new Bohemia – a culture of difference if there ever was one – is ignored in this discourse although it is probably this cultural association that explains the moral panic against cannabis use of the period (see Young, 1972).

The myth of the permissive 1960s is so prevalent that it is frequently forgotten how restricted was the narrative of reform (see Greenwood and Young, 1980). The debate on the legalization of homosexual relationships between consenting adults is a case in point. The argument did not centre around the recognition of a gay lifestyle(s) but was about tolerating pathology. Homosexuals were clearly cast as inadequates: they were, as Leo Abse put it in the introduction to the second reading of the Sexual Offences Bill in the House of Commons, 'those who grow up to have men's bodies but feminine souls' (*Hansard*, 19 December 1966, col.1086). Thus the binary normal/deficient was transposed on that of male/female to render gay men as deficient men and, so to speak, honorary females. Furthermore, as 'females' they got together as 'normal' couples in stable relationships and were no more danger to the public than Mum and Dad. Once again a minority of 'inadequates' remained and were separated out in the discourse – the pederasts who molested minors – and these were to remain the focus of legal intervention. At no point was a conception of homosexuality which questioned not only such pathology, but the binary patterns into which it was templated, permitted to see the light of day.

We have seen that the discourse of inclusivity reduced all difference to either similarity or deficit, to either normality or deviance from it. The binary 'like us'/'lacking in us' eliminates all trace of difference. The exclusive world of late modernity begins to change all of this. Difference becomes of paramount value, difference is freely acknowledged, accepted and indeed often exaggerated; what is more problematic is difficulty. The inclusive society is one of high consensus and low difficulty. The consensus is maintained vigilantly whilst difference is systematically denied. For a while this was achieved by the encompassing nature of the labour market, the steady advances of political, legal and economic citizenship and the astonishing material success where each generation was better off than the one before it and each generation realized the highest living standards in human history (see Chapter 1).

The transformation in late modernity

Earlier I detailed the exterior events which undermined and then transformed modernity. The social world became simultaneously more diverse and much more difficult. A pluralism of value, the result of immigration and subcultural diversity, made it impossible to maintain absolutist standards. And difficulty abounded: the total recorded crime rate for England and Wales in 1995 was 11.5 times that in 1955, the rate of violence was almost 20 times. A diverse and more difficult population confronts the moralist of late modern times: patterns of virtue have gone for ever, rigidity of standards is part of a bygone age, while crime itself has become normal, part of the everyday experience of the citizen.

It was because of such dramatic changes that the structure of tolerance and intolerance of late modernity began to reverse the strictures of the modern world. Diversity became tolerated, indeed differences in lifestyle were celebrated while difficulty became less and less tolerable. This involved a transition in Lévi-Strauss' terms from the anthropophagic to the anthropoemic which is perhaps why so many writers at the cusp of the early 1970s felt so attracted at that time to his metaphor.

The exclusive world necessitates the development of new modes of social control. The swallowing, incorporating world of the post-war period becomes transformed into one which is more ejecting, separating and excluding. The transition is reminiscent of Lévi-Strauss' dichotomy but it is not as simple as this. The late modern world is both ingesting and ejecting, it absorbs diversity and it provides a gradient of tolerance which is both including and excluding. The change in the various institutions of social control are a response to the transformation in the problems which the system faces. They are a response to tackling a more diverse world and one where crime and disorder are much more widespread. That is an increase in *difference* and in *difficulty*. It is important to stress this seemingly obvious fact that the problems facing a society largely determine the methods evolved to tackle them because there is a frequent tendency to separate them. To believe, for example, that the police, the prisons, the multi-agency systems of crime prevention, etc. develop quite autonomously from the problems they are set up to tackle; furthermore, that the modalities of control which are set up to circumscribe the world of crime and deviance have great similarities to those in the 'normal' world. Thus we can perceive a similar ethos permeating society: social control is not confined to the police patrol and the penitentiary.

The mode of exclusion is, therefore, different from the past and corresponds to the realities of the present. It does not present itself as an on/off switch of inclusion or exclusion: either you're inside society or you're not. Rather it is a sifting process which occurs throughout society, for exclusion is a gradient running from the credit rating of the well-off right down to the degree of dangerousness of the incarcerated. Its currency is risk, its stance is *actuarial* – calculative and appraising. The image of society is not that of a core of insiders and a periphery of outsiders but more that of a beach where people are assigned to a gradient of positions in a littoral fashion. At the top of the beach there are the privileged sipping their cocktails, their place in the sun secured, while at the bottom there are creatures trapped in the sea who can only get out with great effort and even then are unlikely to survive. The beach has its gradient in between but this does not preclude at its extremes sharply segregated worlds, whether of the super-rich or the underclass.

The rise of actuarialism

In Frankfurt, the financial heart of continental Europe, many roads lead to oblivion.

You can shoot up behind a dustbin, you can curl up on a stairwell. Or you can walk past the shining glass headquarters of Germany's leading banks and enter a pleasant room with potted plants and at state expense, pump yourself full of heroin.

Europe is on the cusp of a revolution. In Zurich, addicts are given heroin on prescription and injected on city-subsidised premises. A council employee stands by as the addict injects; doctors are on hand; the exact dose is monitored on a computer. In The Netherlands, from next May, city authorities in Amsterdam and Rotterdam will start giving heroin to addicts in a trial run. And in German cities such as Hamburg and Stuttgart, drug experts are pressing for similar schemes to that in Frankfurt: no heroin handouts – not yet – but a controlled environment for hard-drug abusers. If there is a debate about marijuana in Germany, it centres on whether one should be allowed to smoke and drive. Hard-drug addiction is the problem, and so that is where solutions are being sought. . . .

It's easy to deduce why city elders have been willing to experiment with hard-drug policy. Boutique owners do not like comatose addicts sprawled in their doorways; inner-city residents are tired of paying for private security companies to drag overdosing teenagers out of pedestrian precincts. Thus, out of a sense of decorum, a concern for property prices and turnover, solid burghers are supporting state subsidised heroin rooms. (Roger Boyes, *The Times*, 1 December 1997)

A major motif of social control in late modern society is actuarialism. This involves, as we have seen (Table 2.2, p. 45) a transition where there is a concern less with justice than with harm minimization and where causes of crime and deviance are not seen as the vital clue to the solution to the problem of crime. The actuarial stance is calculative of risk, it is wary and probabilistic, it is not concerned with causes but with probabilities, not with justice but with harm minimization, it does not seek a world free of crime but one where the best practices of damage limitation have been put in place; not a utopia but a series of gated havens in a hostile world. The actuarial stance reflects the fact that risk both to individuals and collectivities has increased, crime has become a normalized part of everyday life, the offender is seemingly everywhere in the street and in high office, within the poor parts of town but also in those institutions which were set up to rehabilitate and protect, within the public world of encounters with strangers but within the family itself in relationships between husband and wife and parent and child. We are wary of scoutmasters, policemen, hitch-hikers, babysitters, husbands, dates, stepfathers and stepmothers, people who care for the elderly – the 'other' is everywhere and not restricted to criminals and outsiders. Its causes are increasingly unsure and this uncertainty is compounded by its seeming ubiquitousness. Both individuals *and* institutions face the problems of sorting out the safe from the risky and doing so in ways which are no longer cast iron and certain but merely probabilistic.

Rules themselves have become problematic in a pluralistic society where rules overlap to be sure but are never identical between one group and the other; they change over time and have changed, *without doubt*, within the lifetime of everyone. So it is no longer a question of right and wrong, more what is the likelihood of your rules being broken, and when the unit of risk becomes your chance of victimage, assessment of individual responsibility becomes less and less relevant. If you are the manager of a shopping mall or a mother seeking to protect her family, whether the likely transgressor is mad or bad, following rules or being unable to engage in rule-following behaviour, is of little consequence. Thus the line between free will and determinism becomes not only blurred but in a sense irrelevant. *You want above all to avoid trouble rather than to understand it.* You want to minimize risk rather than morally condemn behaviour.

Actuarialism and 'The New Penology'

The use of such actuarial discourse was convincingly pinpointed by Malcolm Feeley and Jonathan Simon in their seminal article on 'The New Penology' (1992). Their description of the phenomenon is excellent but their explanation of its origin commits the familiar error of attempting to divorce or fudge the concept from the problem of rising crime. Thus they explicitly note how the discourse arose in the United States when there had been a 'massive increase in the level of incarceration over the past decade and a half during which rates of reported crimes have risen only modestly' (ibid., p. 450). They bring in a series of explanations laterally: the impact of current systems theories of management from other fields such as public policy and commerce and the present intellectual fashions in law and economics (see Feeley and Simon, 1994). Thus they comment: 'the factors accounting for the rise of actuarial justice in the criminal process have origins in technologies developed elsewhere' (1994, p. 185). Indeed they seem to write off crime as a relevant factor. The link between the pressure on the criminal justice system and changes in its discourse and practice becomes fudged. Feeley and Simon admit to external pressures but they see the new penology as both the 'cause and effect' of the growth in the penal population.

Furthermore, not only do they separate out actuarial changes in the criminal justice system from crime, but they seem to see actuarialism as a propensity of control agencies rather than an attitude prevalent both in institutions *and* in the population at large. In part both these absences are a product of bracketing off 'risk' and indeed being uncertain whether there have been any actual changes in risk rather than the perceptual or the phenomenal.

In an important sense actuarialism is morally neutral, it is part of a postmodern sensibility which Zygmunt Bauman terms *adiaphorization* – 'the stripping of human relationships of their moral significance, exempting them from moral evaluation, rendering them "morally irrelevant".' (1995, p. 133). Thus Jonathan Simon writes of a future actuarial scenario where:

> the background security system could become intrusive and coercive. In the name of improving safety and lowering social costs, numerous social controls could be put in place to govern the way people work and live. These controls would differ markedly from traditional juridical social controls. One example is drug use. . . . If drugs are out in the eighties, it is because they are perceived as driving accident risks up, and productivity down.
>
> The control system is changing as well. In the near future the security system could effectively limit drug use by imposing urinalysis screening as a condition of

employment. To use drugs would no longer be to challenge the moral sanction of the state and expose oneself to punishment, but instead to risk being denied access to the system. Rather than being defined as a deviant malefactor, the drug user becomes the self-selected occupant of a high-risk category that is channelled away from employment and the greater access it brings.

And he adds in a footnote:

> As this essay is being written drug use has suddenly become the hot political issue of the moment. But it is a strangely unpolitical debate in which no one can articulate the moral dilemma. The policy thrust is toward systematic drug testing. And the rationale is pure risk. People who use drugs are harming themselves and hurting the economy. (1987, p. 85)

Actuarialism and the risk society

It is extraordinary that the academic discourse on actuarial justice develops separately from the rich vein of sociological scholarship concerning the nature of a 'risk society' (see Beck, 1992; Giddens, 1991). This is particularly so in that Jonathan Simon wrote an extremely prescient piece entitled 'The Emergence of the Risk Society' in 1987 which has a much wider compass than the now famous series of articles on the new penology and actuarial justice (Feeley and Simon, 1992, 1994; Simon, 1993; Simon and Feeley, 1995). But even the original article (quoted above) is concerned with the response to risk rather than risk itself, as its subtitle indicates: 'Insurance, Law and the State'.

For Anthony Giddens the concept of a risk society is concerned with the nature of risks in late modern society and with what he calls 'the calculative attitude' which individuals and collectivities develop in *response* to such risk:

> To live in the 'world' produced by high modernity has the feeling of riding a juggernaut. It is not just that more or less continuous and profound processes of change occur; rather, change does not consistently conform either to human expectation or to human control. The anticipation that the social and natural environments would increasingly be subject to rational ordering has not proved to be valid. . . .
>
> Providential reason – the idea that increased secular understanding of the nature of things intrinsically leads to a safer and more rewarding existence for human beings – carries residues of conceptions of fate deriving from pre-modern eras. Notions of fate may of course have a sombre cast, but they always imply that a course of events is in some way preordained. In circumstances of modernity, traditional notions of fate may still exist, but for the most part these are inconsistent with an outlook in which risk becomes a fundamental element. To accept risk as risk . . . is to acknowledge that no aspects of our activities follow a predestined course, and all are open to contingent happenings. In this sense it is quite accurate to characterise modernity, as Ulrich Beck does, as a 'risk society', a phrase which refers to more than just the fact that modern social life introduces new

forms of danger which humanity has to face. Living in the 'risk society' means living with a calculative attitude to the open possibilities of action, positive and negative, with which, as individuals and globally, we are confronted in a continuous way in our contemporary social existence. (1991, p. 28)

What I want to do is discuss the basis of such a notion of risk in the area of crime and deviance and how this results in a 'calculative' or 'actuarial' attitude in individuals, in institutions and in the criminal justice system itself.

Living with strangers: the six components of risk

A 'real' rise in risk

As I have documented throughout this book, the vast majority of countries in the developed world have experienced a rise in crime in the last 30 years. Such a crime rate has been accompanied by a penumbra of incivilities and crime has become increasingly internecine in its nature so that predatory behaviour and disorder is more and more implosive within each neighbourhood and social group.

Revelation

The mass media, the pressure group activities – and even the criminological researcher – have presented to the public a wider range of crime and on a greater scale than ever before. National crime surveys inform us that we can at least double (if not quadruple) the official crime rate, pressure groups indicate abuse occurring within the family often as much (if not more) than in the world outside, institutions which serve to protect and safeguard the vulnerable are seen to be sites of crime (from homes for the elderly to the orphanages of the Christian Brothers or the Sisters of Mercy), police and prisons are exposed as prime sites of corruption, violence and drug dealing. And on top of this, the illicit activities of white collar and corporate criminals are every day presented on our televisions and in our newspapers. No doubt some of this is inaccurate and a proportion misleading and mischievous, but the world which we *experience* as risky is *revealed* as risky on a wider and wider scale in all areas and parts of the social fabric.

Rising expectations

Risk is not a fixed objective thing: it rises or falls as our tolerance of a particular behaviour or practice changes. The change in public attitudes over the last 30 years has shown every indication of the 'civilizing influence' of a greater demand for a refinement in our behaviour towards each other and for an enhanced quality of life. Indeed the rising demand for law and order, which is often seen negatively as a sign of growing public authoritarianism may, more positively, be viewed as increasing demands for security, safety and civility in everyday life. One look at the area of violence confirms this, where a whole array of crimes have become a major focus of public concern: for example domestic violence, rape, child abuse and violence against animals. The entry of women into public life, consequent on their incorporation into the labour force, is no doubt a major influence on this, with rising demands being made on the level of civility both in public spaces and within the home. The area of public space is of interest in this respect in that it represents an area where women, because of increased economic and social equality, place themselves more at risk from male abuse but also demand more propriety. The greater use of pubs by women is a humdrum example of this two-way process, and is encouraged by the brewers for precisely these reasons.

Reserve

The greater mobility of people in modern society results in a decline of communities where people live most of their life and which centre around their workplace. This results in a significant drop in information, about neighbours, acquaintances, or chance encounters in the street. One has less direct knowledge of fellow citizens and this, together with living in a much more heterogeneous society, leads to much less *predictability* of behaviour. Unpredictability combined with risk generates a greater wariness in an actuarial stance towards others.

Reflexivity: the uncertainty of uncertainty

A key aspect of the late modern world, over and above the sensitization to risk, is the problematization of risk itself. Not only is the metropolis an uncertain world of dangers, but the level of risk itself is uncertain. In contrast to the modern world of predictable anxieties and dangers it is a world of uncertainty in that each level of risk will be questioned by experts and public alike. The fears come and go: carjacking, BSE, AIDS, road rage. They flicker on the screen of consciousness, something is going on but we are not sure who or what to believe. Whereas experts once concurred, they now seem to make a point of disagreement. From global warming to the ozone layer, from BSE to satanic child abuse, disagreement is the norm to an extent that the experts themselves begin to look shaky and to purvey just another opinion. But this is not a phantasmagoria, as some writers would have it (e.g. Furedi, 1997); city life is scarcely an Arcadian dream: if there was not a rational core of unease the images would not be able to find any purchase in the public consciousness.

Refraction

The mass media carry a plethora of images of crime and deviance gleaned from across the world. These media commodities are characterized like all news by their atypical nature – they are 'news' because they surprise and shock. Without doubt such imagery in its sheer quantity and in its garishness must cause 'fear' of crime disproportional to actual risk. Yet it is only one factor out of six, but it is often presented as *the* factor which determines public assessment of risk – as if fear were merely a metaphenomenon of television viewing.

Umwelt and the management of risk

The awareness of risk generates an actuarial attitude in the citizen of late modernity. This is an attitude of wariness, of calculation and of reflectiveness. Some of these calculations will involve seeking for opportunities: urban life is full of excitement and pleasure as well as risk. The citizens of all the great First World megalopolises – London, New York, Paris, for example – share the same habits of reserve, of abrasiveness with strangers, of 'ducking and diving': of avoiding trouble and seeking gain.

Anthony Giddens discusses the way in which human beings generate around themselves a feeling of bodily and psychic ease. 'If we mostly seem less fragile,' he notes, 'than we really are . . . it is because of long-term learning processes whereby potential threats are avoided or immobilized' (1991, p. 127). He builds on Goffman's notion of an *Umwelt*: a core of accomplished normality with which individuals and groups surround themselves. Taking inspiration from studies of animal behaviour, Goffman begins the section of *Relations in Public* designated 'normal appearances' with this remarkable imagery of the *Umwelt*:

> Individuals, whether in human or animal form, exhibit two basic modes of activity. They go about their business grazing, gazing, mothering, digesting, building, resting, playing, placidly attending to easily managed matters at hand. Or, fully mobilized, a fury of intent, alarmed, they get ready to attack or to stalk or to flee. Physiology itself is patterned to coincide with this duality.
>
> The individual mediates between these two tendencies with a very pretty capacity for dissociated vigilance. Smells, sounds, sights, touches, pressures – in various combinations, depending on the species – provide a running reading of the situation, a constant monitoring of what surrounds. But by a wonder of adaptation these readings can be done out of the furthest corner of whatever is serving for an eye, leaving the individual himself free to focus his main attention on the non-emergencies around him. Matters that the actor has become accustomed to will receive a flick or a shadow of concern, one that decays as soon as he obtains a microsecond of confirmation that everything is in order; should something really prove to be 'up', prior activity can be dropped and full orientation mobilized, followed by coping behaviour. . . . (1971, p. 238)

The *Umwelt* has two dimensions: the area which one feels secure in and the area in which one is aware; the area of apprehension. The lioness sleeps tranquilly on the veldt, her eye every now and then taking in the activities in the distance. In human society it is a moving bubble which shrinks and expands wherever one is: whether, for example, one is at home or in the urban street. The nature of the *Umwelt* varies by social category. It is strongly gendered: Goffman noted that the *Umwelt* of women differed from men. Clearly, recognizing predatory sexual signs as well as signals of possible violence from men both in public and in the home is an important part of the social repertoire of women. Anyone who has conducted a criminal victimization survey knows that it is possible to identify and differentiate, 'blind', between women and men merely by looking at their avoidance behaviour patterns. Researchers talk of the 'curfew' at night of urban women (see Painter et al., 1989). The *Umwelt* is strongly racialized: ethnic groups are aware of areas of safety and danger and in racist discourse, minorities are represented as signals of fear and danger to the majority population. It has strong dimensions of age: schoolchildren have a vivid sense of space and safety (see Anderson et al., 1994); whilst street gangs and home boys actively police their turf, providing both security for themselves and alarm for others. Lastly, *Umwelt* is, of course, crucially constituted by class: the middle class by virtue of the cost of area, by the use of motor car, by private club and fancy restaurant seek to separate themselves from the undesirables, the 'dangerous classes', even when in transit through the busy city centres of Manhattan and London.

The signs of danger need not be crime itself or the threat of it, but more subtle perceptions of possible risk and the escalation of danger. Goffman was perhaps the first academic to note the problem of incivilities, way ahead of Wilson and Kelling's famous 'Broken Windows' (see Chapter 5, p. 127). Thus:

> When an individual finds persons in his presence acting improperly or appearing out of place, he can read this as evidence that although the peculiarity itself may not be a threat to him, still, those who are peculiar in one regard may well be peculiar in other ways, too, some of which may be threatening. For the individual, then, impropriety on the part of others may function as an alarming sign. Thus, the minor civilities of everyday life can function as an early warning system; conventional courtesies are seen as mere convention, but non-performance can cause alarm. (1971, p. 241)

He cites an example of sexual harassment which graphically indicates the continuum nature of crime. This is from Meredith Tax's article in *Women's Liberation: Notes from the Second Year*:[1]

> A young woman is walking down a city street. She is excruciatingly aware of her appearance and of the reaction to it (imagined or real) of every person she meets. She walks through a group of construction workers who are eating lunch in a line along the pavement. Her stomach tightens with terror and revulsion; her face becomes contorted into a grimace of self-control and fake unawareness; her walk and carriage become stiff and dehumanized. No matter what they say to her, it will

be unbearable. She knows that they will not physically assault her or hurt her. They will only do so metaphorically. What they will do is impinge on her. They will use her body with their eyes. They will evaluate her market price. They will comment on her defects or compare them to those of other passers-by. They will make her a participant in their fantasies without asking if she is willing. They will make her feel ridiculous, or grotesquely sexual, or hideously ugly. Above all, they will make her feel like a thing. (Tax, 1970, p. 12)

Goffman is convinced that the condition of 'uneventfulness' is a moral right of a citizen (see 1971, p. 240); such a level of trust is part of the nature of civilized life. And he detects an overall deterioration in this quality of life:

The vulnerability of public life is what we are coming more and more to see, if only because we are becoming more aware of the areas of intricacies of mutual trust presupposed in public order. Certainly circumstances can arise which undermine the case that individuals have within their *Umwelt*. Some of these circumstances are currently found in the semi-public places within slum housing developments. . . . Certainly the great public forums of our society, the downtown areas of our cities, can come to be uneasy places. Militantly sustained antagonisms between diffusely intermingled major population segments – young and old, male and female, white and black, impoverished and well-off – can cause those in public gatherings to distrust (and to fear they are distrusted by) the persons standing next to them. The forms of civil inattention, of persons circumspectly treating one another with polite and glancing concern while each goes about his own separate business, may be maintained, but behind these normal appearances individuals can come to be at the ready, poised to flee or to fight back if necessary. And in place of unconcern there can be alarm – until, that is, the streets are redefined as naturally precarious places, and a high level of risk becomes routine. (1971, pp. 331–2)

The area of security, of the *Umwelt*, shrinks apace as we enter the latter third of the twentieth century (see Chapter 2): it shrinks because of actual risk but also, as we saw in the last section, because sensitivity to risk rises whilst knowledge of others diminishes. But what can one say of the area of apprehension? Here the paradox of a drop in knowledge of immediates is associated with a globalization of knowledge of the wider outside world. *The area of security, of the* Umwelt, *thus decreases whilst at the same time the area of apprehension vastly increases.*

Lastly, there is another side of *Umwelt*, not touched upon by Goffman, but with obvious relevance and with parallels in animal behaviour. The lioness gazing fleetingly across the veldt is mapping out not only an area of security and one of apprehension but also looking for indications of prey and the possibilities of predation. In human terms the city is not only an area of security and insecurity but of opportunities for excitement, interest, gain and action. The *Soft City* of Jonathan Raban is an emporium of possibility as well as a labyrinth of danger.

Recalcitrant modernity and the critics of risk

There is a body of thought which sees fear of crime and perceptions of likely risk as a phenomenon quite separate from the actual risk of crime itself. Indeed 'fear' of crime is regarded sometimes as a problem autonomous from crime. Fear and concern about crime then become metaphors for other types of urban unease (e.g. urban development), or a displacement of other fears (e.g. racism, psychological difficulties). The 'real' or 'true' fears are separated from crime itself and this exercise is achieved by contrasting the 'gap' between the 'real' risk of crime and the evidence of 'disproportionate' fears. Women and old people are the most frequently cited examples of evidence that such a disproportionality exists. This is not the place to enter into a discussion of the concealment of risks of crime against these groups either by under-reporting or by avoidance behaviour which, so to speak, 'artificially' lowers the rates. I have analysed this extensively elsewhere (see Young, 1988, 1992). What is vital to reiterate, however, is that groups vary in their evaluation of the grossness of crime and that each item of risk is weighted differently by them. Women tend to view violence with greater abhorrence than men, but it is grotesque masculinism to suggest that because they worry more about violence, they are suffering from a form of irrationality which necessitates an expert unravelling their 'real' causes of discontent.

Crime, then, is refracted through the subculture of a group; it can never be perceived 'objectively' as naive 'realists' and their critics seem to believe. But there is more to it than this: within the notion of crime as a metaphor for other forms of urban unease is implicit the belief that crime is somehow *separate* from the other problems of society. Yet in fact, as numerous theorists have pointed out, crime is part of a continuum with other forms of anti-social behaviour and, indeed, as radical criminologists have never ceased to argue, the values which underlie much criminal behaviour are not distinct from conventional values but are closely related to them (see, e.g., Currie, 1997a). To talk, then, of crime as a metaphor for urban unease is a bit like saying that fire is a metaphor for heat; that it is somehow unrelated, but excessive heat is the real problem and that the fascination with these flames that flicker around us is merely a distraction brought upon us, no doubt, by the mass media and the crime control industry (e.g. Baer and Chambliss, 1997).

My argument is that because human behaviour is always a subject of evaluation and assessment there can be no one-to-one relationship between 'risk' and 'fear': arguments which are based simply on the level of correlation, for or against, are positivist blind alleys which lead nowhere. What is necessary is to enter into the subculture in order to discover the significance of crime within it. To conduct qualitative research on the group is the only way to work out lines of causality (Sayer, 1984). In some cases almost metaphorical relationships will be found (but even here they are metaphors grounded in reality), in others the relationship will be stark and close (see Young, 1992).

Human evaluation takes time, it does not happen in an instant, as if we were talking of particles colliding with each other in the physical sciences. This mistake befuddles the debate about public attitudes to crime in the present period, particularly in the United States. Even such sophisticated commentators as Simon and Feeley can construct a false puzzle about public attitudes to crime:

> What accounts for such intense fear? And what accounts for the dramatic increase in fear in recent years? Shifts in levels of fear of crime are not well-understood, and the answers to such questions are both complex and incomplete. But one important piece of the puzzle is well-charted if not well-understood: the intensity of public concern with crime is not directly or strongly related to the magnitude of crime. Indeed in recent years, concern about crime has increased despite a decline in overall rates of victimization. To be sure, some groups have experienced significant increases; young people from twelve to fifteen years of age, for example, experienced a 34 percent increase in violent crime victimizations during the 1980s. And citizens of our poorest inner-city neighborhoods, in particular young African-American males, have experienced significant increases in violence over the past decade. Still, the groundswell of support for more and more punitive crime measures in recent years has come after a decade of steady or declining crime rates for suburban middle-class whites, that segment of the population from which the strongest support for new get-tough measures comes. Why is this group which in other respects seems relatively insensitive to the well-being of people in communities distanced from themselves by poverty and race, and which is otherwise so sceptical of increases in government expenditures, so responsive to threats that in an objective sense affect them less now than at any time in recent memory? And why, when they generally resist increased government spending, are they willing to support vast new expenditures for crime control measures of dubious efficacy?
>
> Fear by itself is an inherently unsatisfying explanation for the formation of recent crime policy. Indeed, it is difficult to explain the fear itself, in its own right. And the very lack of any clear correspondence between objective risk and fear suggests that discourse, including the discourse of crime and penality, must be fundamental input to fear itself, along with factors such as neighborhood disorder, economic anxiety, and changes in racial demographics. (1995, p. 154)

I have quoted this at length, although such views are echoed regularly elsewhere (e.g. Chambliss, 1994a, 1994b; Platt, 1996) because it most thoroughly describes this perplexity. Briefly in response to this it should be noted that a central plank of the conundrum is that in the recent years the crime rate for the United States has levelled: for example the homicide rate (one of the more reliable statistics) was 10.2 per 100,000 in 1974 and 9.5 in 1993. In between this it has fluctuated, sometimes being as low as 8.0 (1985) (see Figure 3.1). William Chambliss quite correctly posited that the FBI has often capitalized on these fluctuations by claiming increases in violence when over the longer period there was, if anything, a slight decline (see Chambliss, 1994b). This rosy positivistic vision is dependent on public memory being extremely short, yet it is undoubtedly longer than these authors allow for. Any middle-aged person in the United States will be only too aware that over the last third of the century (the period that concerns us here) there has been a dramatic increase in violence. In 1966, for example, the homicide rate was only 5.9 per 100,000 and the simple fact is that those who are careless enough to be mystified by public attitudes confine themselves to the plateau of the post-1973 period. For example, Chambliss' graph to illustrate this (1994a, Figure 2; 1994b, Figure 3) commences at this point but if he had started it just a few years earlier it would have shown a period of rapid growth up to this exceptionally high plateau (the present homicide rate is seven times that of England and Wales, and that of young men is a staggering 52 times). Could it not be that the American public is sick to its back teeth with this inordinate slaughter of its young people? Could it not be that they are willing to back intemperate policy and imprisonment in order, they hope, to achieve some abatement of the problem?

The progressive moment of late modernity

The critics of risk portray the risk of crime as greatly exaggerated, and the public as cultural dupes manipulated by the mass media and the risk control industries. They have a rather irritating habit of talking learnedly of the transition to late modernity whilst still feeling it necessary, in a good old-fashioned modernist tone, to inform their readers what are the 'real' risk rates and the 'real' causes of public fears. They fail to take on board two of the key elements of late modernity: public reflexivity about risk and a deep-rooted scepticism about experts.

The critics of risk take their arguments too far. The emergence of a risk society, as the development of late modernity itself, is a contradictory phenomenon. For the greater public awareness of risk is part and parcel of what are essentially progressive and democratic processes occurring throughout the world in the late twentieth century. The first is that of environmentalism, the Green movement. The awareness of the dangers of pollution in the atmosphere, in food, in our drinking water, in the city and on the beach, is undoubtedly a great step forward. Secondly, there is a greater repugnance of violence, an awareness of the hidden violence against children and women, in particular, and of violence against the other species that inhabit our planet, both domesticated animals and wildlife. Here both feminism and Green politics have made their mark. The above two demands are subsumed by a more general desire that citizenship should encompass a degree of control of the world that surrounds us, from the quality of life in the streets of our cities to the accountability of public bodies. Lastly, we have become increasingly sceptical of experts both in their right to define *our* problems and their ability to provide solutions. Three major political strands lie behind this greater awareness of risk: the Green movement, feminism and libertarianism. Thus, talk of 'risk' rates,

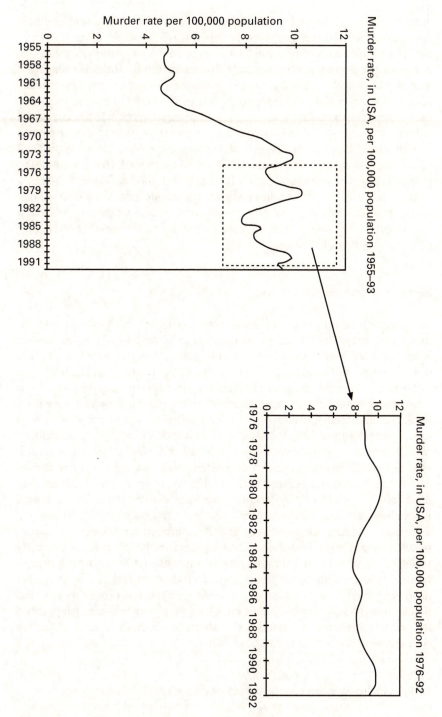

FIGURE 3.1   *The murder rate in the US, 1955–93 (Archer and Gartner, 1984; Maguire and Pastore, 1995)*

debate about safety and security, scepticism about figures and political turmoil about solutions can scarcely be regarded as an abnegation of politics, as authors such as Frank Furedi would have it. 'Risk rates' have become a democratic currency, part of a reflexive audit of our affairs. To hinge the question on whether they have actually risen and whether they are phrased in an alarmist fashion fundamentally misses the point. In some instances they have risen, in many cases they are exaggerated, but what is important is that the base line of evaluation has increased as has the demand for a higher quality of life. The point is that we are increasing our level of social scrutiny and demand. Furthermore, the very existence of a debate about the levels of risk, of which the writers on risk are part, is *in itself* one of the great gains of late modernity. It is not so much that modernity has failed to keep its promise to provide a risk-free society as that late modernity has *taken seriously* this promise, has demanded more and realized the greater difficulty of its accomplishment.

Social exclusion and the citizen

I have indicated how social exclusion has its roots in the general problems of society and of its citizens. It is not simply a top-down phenomenon as some commentators would like to think; that is, it is not merely a product of the criminal justice system, of the ordinances of the local and central state – although, of course, these are very much part of the process. Rather it has roots in the material and moral reality in which individuals seek to live their lives: the actuarial attitude which is wary of risk and circumspect about moral uncertainties. The tendencies to essentialism and to demonization have their resonances everywhere. The forces of social exclusion are ubiquitous in society, yet they are not generated by illusion: there are real risks and moral uncertainties out there albeit played upon by politicians and members of social control bureaucracies, particularly within the criminal justice system and private security sector ('the crime control industry'). Thus when Claude Lévi-Strauss talks of anthropoemic societies, societies which exclude and expel their members, he is right to emphasize society rather than the state or elite interests. But it is always necessary when analysts use phrases like 'society' and 'social control' to ensure that these are not being used as shorthand for the desires of the powerful. Power exists throughout society for the phenomena of inclusion and exclusion could never be fully understood if they do not embrace the demons and desires of the powerless as well as the powerful.

Inclusion and exclusion as the causes of deviance

I have up till now in this chapter focused upon the forces of expulsion which propel the individual or group out of society. This follows Lévi-Strauss and, of course, the labelling tradition. In the latter we should note how the stress is on how deviancy becomes difficulty because of overreaction of society and the state. Edwin Lemert's (1967) classic distinction between primary and secondary deviation, the first the 'natural' variation that occurs within society, the second the deviation which is a product of reaction itself, is a case in point. And, in this tradition, the *secondary harm* generated by intervention is often seen as more of a problem than the *primary harm* which occurs if no intervention had been attempted. The debate over the legalization of drugs is still, quite rightly, dominated by this type of argument. Similarly, the concept of *deviance amplification* formulated so imaginatively by Leslie Wilkins (1964) and developed and popularized by Stan Cohen (1972) and myself (1971b) follows this line of thought, adding to it a conception of process accelerating in severity through time. Thus forceful social exclusion exacerbates the problems of the excluded and makes more of a problem than there was in the first place, and so on. Thirty years of juvenile justice legislation have held this in mind both in statute and in practice.

But theories of exclusion and inclusion are not only concerned with social reactions to crime and deviance, they are obviously also linked to their causes. Broadly speaking there are two conventional types of explanation of the causes of crime: a cultural and a structural, loosely associated with conservative and liberal political discourses respectively (for an example witness the debate over the nature of the underclass between 'culturalists' such as Charles Murray, 1990 and 'structuralists' such as William Julius Wilson, 1987). Cultural theories suggest that crime occurs because of a lack of culture, of socialization, of symbolic embeddedness in society, community and the family. Hans Eysenck's classic formulation (1970), involving three discrete levels, is a useful illustration. Criminality occurs because:

- the individual is genetically less capable of being socialized;
- his or her family was inadequate at the business of social training;
- the values socialized were incoherent, inconsistent and contradictory.

These three interacting levels of inadequacy come together to produce a lack of cultural incorporation of the individual. More recent theories on the right of the political spectrum replicate such a formula: Gottfredson and Hirschi's *A General Theory of Crime* (1990) fits this well, as does Wilson and Herrnstein's (1985) *Crime and Human Nature*. This approach suggests that crime and deviance occur because of lack of inclusion in the culture of a given society. Crime occurs because of a *deficit of culture*. Such a model has been associated with individual positivism and its ideological attractions are clear: deviance occurs not because of material inequalities or differences in culture but because of the lack of an unquestioned and moralistic *absolutist* culture (see Taylor et al., 1973).

The second approach is also a deficit model: but, in this case, crime and deviance are seen to occur because of a lack of material goods – because of inequality, poverty, unemployment, etc. It is concerned with absolute deprivation: people commit crime because they are not included in the economy. The policy correlate is that crime and disorder will disappear if work and income is provided. Such a view of social exclusion is commonplace; it informs, for example, the policies of both the Clinton and the Blair administrations. This social positivism was severely shaken by the experience of the 1960s when full employment and rising living standards across the Western world were accompanied by rising crime rates (see Chapter 2). For it was not absolute deprivation but *relative* deprivation that was the source of social disquiet and such a subjective experience of inequality and unfairness is related to meritocracy, not opportunity, that is, the allocation of reward by merit rather than merely the opportunity to earn a living.

Thus both the deficit model favoured by the political right (individual positivism) and that by the left (social positivism) are flawed. The first sees a lack of inclusion in the culture of society, the other a lack of inclusion in the economy, as the wellspring of disorder. But, as I have discussed in Chapter 1, both ignore the subjectivity of the citizen, the ability of human actors to stand back and assess fairness and their ability to create cultural difference rather than just reproduce a monolithic, given culture. So the two competing strands are about different types of exclusion (or more accurately lack of inclusion, because it is not an active process); that is, lack of cultural or economic inclusion. The present debate over exclusion in Europe revolves around discussion centred on such flawed conventional wisdoms.

The critique of the two positivisms

The critique of the two positivisms is part of the legacy of sociological thought. It is embedded in the work of Durkheim but the most influential single article is Robert K. Merton's 'Social Structure and Anomie'. Written in 1938, this is probably the most cited article in the history of sociology and explicitly targets both individual and social positivism. The rejection of individual positivism points to the way in which crime and deviance, rather than being a pathology of individuals, is the 'normal' response generated by the culture and structure of society. Further, Merton is aware of the paradoxical findings that many poorer countries have lower crime rates than richer countries and that crime does not necessarily decrease with a rise in living standards. His criticism of social positivism is exceptional in its clarity:

> This theoretical analysis may go far toward explaining the varying correlations between crime and poverty. Poverty is not an isolated variable. It is one in a complex of interdependent social and cultural variables. When viewed in such a context, it represents quite different states of affairs. Poverty as such, and consequent limitation of opportunity, are not sufficient to induce a conspicuously high rate of criminal behavior. Even the often mentioned 'poverty in the midst of plenty' will not necessarily lead to this result. Only insofar as poverty and associated disadvantages in competition for the cultural values approved for *all*

members of the society is linked with the assimilation of a cultural emphasis on monetary accumulation as a symbol of success is anti-social conduct a 'normal' outcome. Thus, poverty is less highly correlated with crime in southeastern Europe than in the United States. The possibilities of vertical mobility in these European areas would seem to be fewer than in this country, so that neither poverty *per se* nor its association with limited opportunity is sufficient to account for the varying correlations. It is only when the full configuration is considered, poverty, limited opportunity and a commonly shared system of success symbols, that we can explain the higher association between poverty and crime in our society than in others where rigidified class structure is coupled with *differential class symbols of achievement.*

  In societies such as our own, then, the pressure of prestige-bearing success tends to eliminate the effective social constraint over means employed to this end. 'The-end-justifies-the-means' doctrine becomes a guiding tenet for action when the cultural structure unduly exalts the end and the social organization unduly limits possible recourse to approved means. (1938, p. 677, emphasis in original)

Crime is, therefore, not a result of personal pathology but of cultural and social pressures stemming from the heart of society:

For our purposes, this situation involves two important features. First, such anti-social behaviour is in a sense 'called forth' by certain conventional values of the culture *and* by the class structure involving differential access to the approved opportunities for legitimate, prestige-bearing pursuit of the culture goals. (ibid., p. 676)

It is a result of the famous contradiction between culturally induced ends and available means and it is augmented by an individualistic stress on success, on ends over means, which is part of American cultural values.

  Let us rephrase Merton's formulation in terms of our present discussion. *Crime occurs where there is cultural inclusion and structural exclusion.* He reverses the dictum of individual positivism: crime is not the result of a lack of culture but of embracing a culture of success and individualism. He, therefore, recontextualizes social positivism: it is not material deprivation *per se*, nor lack of opportunity which gives rise to crime, but deprivation in the context of the 'American Dream' culture where meritocracy is exhorted as open to all.

Inclusion/exclusion: a late modern bulimia

All of this takes us by a long route back to Lévi-Strauss and his metaphors of the anthropophagic and the anthropoemic, those societies which are social cannibals and those which vomit deviants out. What Merton suggests as the paradigm case for a discontented society is one which does both: it voraciously devours people and then steadfastly ejects them. A bulimic society: '**bulimia**: a condition of continuous, uncontrolled hunger. When compensated for by forced vomiting or overdoses of laxatives the condition is called *bulimia nervosa*' (*Collins Encyclopaedia*, 1995, p. 145). The social order of the advanced industrial world is one which engulfs its members. It consumes and culturally assimilates masses of people through education, the media and participation in the market place. A ubiquitous mass media, proliferous in its channels, takes up a greater and greater proportion of leisure time and carries with it global images of success, of expectations and desires. Most crucial of all is that there is the image of what is a normal lifestyle, what goods and level of comfort can be expected if we play the game. There are images of the lifestyle of the stars, to be sure, but there are also images in soap operas and in the incessant succession of fictional dramas and factual news stories of the rewards of everyday life. Much of this imagery is taken in out of the corner of one's eye: it is the backcloth to the drama and is absorbed daily without being the centre of attention. The comfort of apartments, the model of car, the style of leisure and the freedom of lifestyle – all are absorbed by the viewer. The media carries, therefore, images of what level of comfort is to be expected and what consumer items are associated with success. It carries notions of reward but also measures of merit: success is open to all, *your* success depends on how hard you try. Both the American Dream and the dreams of Europe and Australasia permeate the world. And they are carried not only in the 'factual' stories of the newsroom and the documentary but in the fictional stories of television drama. We know from studies of non-Westerners watching television that these backgrounds make a great impression on the viewer (see Lull, 1991). As Thompson puts it:

> When people watch international news, for instance, they pay as much attention to street scenes, housing and clothing as to the commentary which accompanies the pictures from foreign lands. (1995, p. 176)

It was the constant images of everyday life in the West that did much to engineer the final collapse of Stalinism in the East. But if such imagery has leverage abroad, how much more will it have within a society?

The mass media is, of course, not the only instrument of inclusion in our society. Mass education prepares children for work and inevitably carries notions of career, of meritocracy and success, while the market itself, particularly as a place of consumption, encourages participation and involvement. Only the most steadfast minority can resist its encroachments: only by banning access to newspapers, radio, television, by running one's own schools and frowning on extra-group friendships can cultural isolation be achieved.

The test case in the heart of Philadelphia

By the measure of this argument discontent in late modern societies is not a product of simple exclusion but a bulimic process of inclusion and exclusion. What more ready test of this hypothesis could be made than with regard to the phenomenon of the 'underclass'? Surely, here is an excluded population, cut off from the outside society, where disorder and incivility have become part of the torn fabric of everyday life and where cultural alienation has generated remarkable differences in lifestyle and aspiration? William Julius Wilson in his pathbreaking book *The Truly Disadvantaged* (1987) outlines precisely such a process of *social dislocation*. Blacks became concentrated in the urban centres of the United States by the attraction of work in the factories of Los Angeles, New York, Chicago and Detroit. The deindustrialization of the 1970s brought about by the flight of capital to the cheaper labour markets of South East Asia left these people stranded. The growing black middle class, encouraged by equal opportunities legislation, obtained jobs, often in the government bureaucracies, and quit the ghetto for the suburbs. Left behind were a dislocated people, cut off from economic opportunity, spatially segregated both by class and race. The number of 'marriageable' men declined with the lack of work and the inability to support families, which resulted in the growth of single parent, female centred families. Children grew up without either role models of everyday work or the practices of the nuclear family. A culture emerged which was low achieving, ill suited for the disciplines of work, unstable in its family structure, with excessive emphasis on masculinity and where crime and violence abounded. The urban underclass, according to William Julius Wilson, was born.

Here we have a classic social democratic account of the formation of an underclass: economic and social exclusion (exacerbated by spatial segregation) leads to social disorganization, a lack of culture – a social group excluded from the cultural mainstream of American society. Recall and compare the account of underclass formation given by Charles Murray (1990, 1994): the welfare state creates a culture of dependency whose menfolk are unwilling and unable to take up the possibilities of work and where womenfolk are encouraged by benefits to become single mothers. A culture antithetical to the work ethic of the wider society is created which is racked by crime and disorder because of the inability of single mothers to adequately socialize their sons and because work has little attraction compared to theft and the illegal economy. Here, the culture created by the welfare state excludes its members from the social and economic institutions of the mainstream. Murray's account is the very reverse of Wilson's, although the resulting culture itself is seen to be rather similar in its difference, disorganization and alienation from the core values of American society.

These two authors clearly represent the two types of exclusion that I have talked of: where the group is excluded because of exclusion from the economy, and where 'self-chosen' exclusion is seen to result in a lack of ability to socialize children into the wider culture. In both these instances, the 'underclass' is seen to lack culture. But, finally, let us note that there are authors both on the left and the right who start from the position that black culture is different from the mainstream to begin with: those on the left, of whom Wilson is particularly critical, who see black culture as an alternative culture of struggle, fight-back and survival and those on the right who see it as alien in the sense of naturally intransigent, ill-disciplined and unassimilable. Thus we have four positions in all: two that portray the underclass as lacking in culture and two who see it as an alternative culture. None of them would characterize it as the very embodiment of dominant culture.

Against these positions, Carl Nightingale in *On the Edge* (1993), his remarkable study of the black ghetto of Philadelphia, counterposes an analysis which is incisive and convincing. For he argues that what it is vital to understand is not only the alienation but, paradoxically, the degree of inclusion of black youth in American culture. This process of cultural inclusion has increased over time; furthermore, it is augmented rather than diminished by economic and social exclusion and it is this assimilation which is the key to understanding the violence of their lives. He begins his book:

> This is a . . . book about some American children. But *American* is not the word most Americans commonly use to describe them. Overall, the nation's preferences run instead to phrases like 'alienated youth', 'ghetto kids', 'them', or 'you people', and in more hateful moments, 'punks', 'wolf packs', 'welfare queens', or 'niggers'. . . . But the favorite term nowadays is 'underclass', a term one liberal scholar defined, in part, as 'a vile and debased subhuman population'. Americans do have access to more respectful names for the kids in this book: '*African*-American' is one of them. But '*all*-American' (as in apple pie or the kid next door) is almost never a first choice.' (1993, p. 1, emphasis in original)

And he notes how it became clear to him, just like Merton before him, that crime and incivility relate to the American Dream:

> Poor, on welfare, left behind by emigrating employers and community leaders, racially excluded, feared and despised by many Americans, then thrown into prisons: how could the children described in this book be more alienated from the American mainstream than that?
>   In fact, it was only by getting to know some poor urban African-American children much closer up that I could grasp just how thoroughly American their lives have been. (ibid., pp. 5–6)

Thus he details how it is their immersion in the American Dream which fuels their anger. First of all he charts their exposure to American mainstream culture. The market readily embraces them in an enthusiasm for sneakers, cars, clothes, jewellery:

> Already at five and six, many kids in the neighborhood can recite the whole canon of adult luxury – from Gucci, Evan Piccone, and Pierre Cardin, to Mercedes and BMW . . . from the age of ten, kids became thoroughly engrossed in Nike's and Reebok's cult of the sneaker. . . . (ibid., pp. 153–4)

Television is watched avidly. African-Americans watch half again as much television as whites: in the average black household the television is on for

11 hours per day. The culture is in fact permeated by the mainstream. Nightingale points to what he calls 'the didactic use of violence' – the notion that problems can be readily solved by violence – which constitutes such a major motif in American cartoons, feature films, law and order strategies and, indeed, foreign policy. He notes that 'forceful parenting' rather than *laissez-faire*, is a key component of African-American child rearing, reflecting traditional rather than liberal values. He points to the extent to which the neighbourhood backed Bush during the Gulf War – which occurred at the same time as the interviews. But his explanation of their enthusiastic embracing of conventional values does not involves simple transmission through television and the market place, but has a dynamic rooted in compensation.

Like Merton, he stresses that tension is created by the combination of economic and social exclusion with cultural inclusion, but to *compensate* for this discrepancy, cultural identification is given an even greater emphasis:

> Inner-city kids' *inclusion* in mainstream America's mass market has been important in determining those kids' responses to the economic and racial *exclusion* they face in other parts of their lives. And, indeed, kids' experience of exclusion and of the associated painful memories has made their participating in mass culture particularly urgent and enthusiastic, for the culture of consumption has given them a seductive means to compensate for their feelings of failure. (ibid., p. 135, emphasis in original)

Here he goes further than Merton and, in the tradition of subcultural theory, travels quite closely to Albert Cohen in *Delinquent Boys* (1955). Cohen, it will be remembered, was interested in the intensity of the delinquency of lower class boys, in its expressivity and in its negativism. Crime was not simply an alternative instrumental route to achieve the material goods denied them, as would be the expected outcome of the Mertonian paradigm. Often, in fact, it palpably failed to achieve such instrumental aims; instead it was, Cohen suggested, an act of a revolt, an *inversion* of the middle class standards encountered in school. Delinquency was neither a result of a lack of conventional values nor some alternative set of norms, but it bounced off conventional values, sprung with a psychodynamic of its own. There are differences, of course: Cohen is talking about the school whilst Nightingale talks about the mass media and the consumer market, and whereas Cohen's 'reaction formation' is an inversion of conventional values, Nightingale's compensation is an overidentification with those values. But these differences are easily resolved if we acknowledge that the school is the chief carrier of undiluted meritocratic values of work, discipline and reward, whilst the wider commercial culture is not: it is a celebration of luck, hedonism, leisure, fun and good fortune. Identification with the wider culture as a compensation is simply not the same as identification with school. Furthermore, we are speaking of a world 40 years on from *Delinquent Boys* – where the wider culture places a much greater emphasis on hedonism and expressivity than the more balanced motifs of the past. It would not be going too far to suggest that much of present day mass culture is itself a compensation for the failures to deliver of the system, for the disappointments of the citizen. In the 1930s, black and white Hollywood movies portrayed an elite world of wealth and leisure which allowed the mass of the population for a few hours to lay aside the problems of work and money, in short, to *escape*. In the present day Technicolor world of expressivity, violence is a theme which can actually be replicated out on the streets. It provides ready rhetoric and role models for the play-acting of the gang. It can script reality rather than provide an escape from the real world. But more of this later.

Carl Nightingale's theory is, thus, a critique of those who believe that the problems of the underclass are a result of simple exclusion, the social isolation theories of William Julius Wilson and his associates (e.g. Sampson and Wilson, 1995). Such theories of alienation explain much but they do not go far enough.

> These forces of economic and racial alienation explain increases in fatal violence and the erosion of community only when viewed along with forces which have helped the inner city become more included in the mainstream. (ibid., pp. 74–5)

But it is also a critique of those theories which portray the ghetto as a repository of alternative values. Rather they have a *surfeit* of American values. Let's recast this in terms of identity and difference: Nightingale sees the Philadelphia underclass as lacking identity, of being the same as 'us' only less so, not as inhabiting a different world as part of a series of separate multicultures. If anything he tends towards the argument of a loss of difference, from the African-American culture of the past, to an absorption in the American mainstream.

Here we have a bulimic world of cultural inclusion and social exclusion, followed by overidentification in order to compensate, an inclusive moment, and then, presumably, an even greater awareness of the exclusive nature of social structure. But we can go further than this by adding parts of this process which Nightingale only touches upon. How does the underclass react to this overidentification coupled with rejection? The most obvious answer is through crime and, in the case of youth, through the creation of gangs and criminal subcultures. These could be construed as somehow alien to the wider culture, a position long debated in criminological theory, but modern ethnography graphically demonstrates that this is not true. For example, let us look at Philippe Bourgois' ethnographic study of El Barrio, East Harlem, New York City. Here there is a distinct parallel with Carl Nightingale's work, for just as he sees African-American culture being assimilated into the mainstream, Bourgois even more dramatically notes how the culture of Puerto Rican immigrants comes to be part and parcel of American culture:

> I . . . want to place drug dealers and street level criminals into their rightful position within the mainstream of U.S. society. They are not 'exotic others' operating

in an irrational netherworld. On the contrary, they are 'made in America'. Highly motivated, ambitious inner-city youths have been attracted to the rapidly expanding, multibillion-dollar drug economy during the 1980s and 1990s precisely because they believe in Horatio Alger's version of the American Dream.

Like most other people in the United States, drug dealers and street criminals are scrambling to obtain their piece of the pie as fast as possible. In fact, in their pursuit of success they are even following the minute details of the classical yankee model for upward mobility. They are aggressively pursuing careers as private entrepreneurs; they take risks, work hard, and pray for good luck. They are the ultimate rugged individualists braving an unpredictable frontier where fortune, fame, and destruction are all just around the corner, and where the enemy is ruthlessly hunted down and shot. (1995, p. 326)

But such a measure of success – the crack dealer with money to burn one day yet down on his heels the next – is only for a few. The vast majority of people in the ghetto have to deal with failure, and this failure results from the internalization of the values of the wider society so is articulated in terms of self-blame rather than seen as a fault of the system. The excluded because of their cultural inclusion blame themselves for their own exclusion. Bourgois concludes:

At the same time, there is nothing exotically Puerto Rican about the triumphs and failures of the protagonists of this book. On the contrary, 'mainstream America' should be able to see itself in the characters presented on these pages and recognize the linkages. The inner city represents the United States' greatest domestic failing, hanging like a Damocles sword over the larger society. Ironically, the only force preventing this suspended sword from falling is that drug dealers, addicts, and street criminals internalize their rage and desperation. They direct their brutality against themselves and their immediate community rather than against their structural oppressors. . . . There is no technocratic solution. Any long-term paths out of the quagmire will have to address the structural and political economic roots, as well as the ideological and cultural roots of social marginalization. (ibid., pp. 326–7)

But no such long-ranging policy of social and political inclusion is forthcoming for this bulimia of exclusion. In fact the very reverse is true: the United States criminal justice system has expanded at an unprecedented level and its focus is the underclass of the ghettos.

Lastly, we must chart the final moment of exclusion. The inclusive moment of creating a criminal subculture based on all-American notions of work as an area of rugged individualism and competition and sanctioned by a film industry which carries the message of didactic violence, blurs the notion of criminal and non-criminal, of good guy and bad guy, of hero and crook, is followed by exclusion in the most draconian fashion imaginable. For, as we have seen, the US criminal justice system focuses upon ghetto youth with unparalleled intensity. One in nine of those aged between 20 and 29 is in prison in any 12-month period, one in three is on probation, parole or in prison. The criminal justice system constitutes their lives, constructs their identity, impinges upon them daily. The last expulsion of a long bulimic process is in place. What a strange world this is of inclusion and exclusion: a *bulimia nervosa* of the social system where at one point the outside world touches and shapes the underclass, whilst at another point it rejects and expels it.

The myth of difference

An immediate question arising from this discussion of the way in which the wider culture impacts on and shapes every aspect of all but the most cocooned of subcultures, is whether our society although prone to exclusion is, like the inclusive society before it, fairly culturally homogeneous. The vaunted diversity of late modernity is a myth. Thus Russell Jacoby writing in *New Left Review* is scathing about what he terms the 'myth of multi-culturalism':

> Let me put my cards on the table: multiculturalism and kindred terms of cultural diversity and cultural pluralism are a new cant. Incessantly invoked, they signify anything and everything. This is not simply an example of sloppy terms; these phrases have become a new ideology. To put it provocatively, multiculturalism flourishes as a programme when it weakens as a reality. The drumbeat of cultural diversity covers an unwelcome truth: cultural differences are diminishing, not increasing. For better or worse only one culture thrives in the United States, the culture of business, work and consuming. (1994, pp. 121–2)

In contrast, cultural differences described by anthropologists diverge 'dramatically'. He cites Ruth Bendict in her classic 1943 *Patterns of Culture*:

> At least no one would confuse Dobuan growing practices with those of present-day farmers or suburban gardeners. 'Yams are conceived as persons', Bendict wrote of Dobu farming, 'and are believed to wander nightly from garden to garden. . . . Incantations lure the roaming yams to remain in one's own garden at the expense of the garden in which they were planted. (ibid., p. 122–3)

And he continues:

> In a premodern world, separate groups might develop singular cultures, but in highly organized American society the maintenance of unique cultures is improbable; neither the means nor the requisite isolation exist. To talk of distinct American 'cultures' denotes something very different from the culture of the Dobus. The American cultures partake of a larger American industrial society; they carry its signature in their souls and their wallets.
> To put this sharply: America's multiple 'cultures' exist within a single consumer society. Professional sports, Hollywood movies, automobiles, designer clothes, name-brand sneakers, television and videos, commercial music and CDs pervade America's multiculturalism. These 'cultures' live, work and dream in the same society. Chicanos, like Chinese-Americans, want to hold good jobs, live in the suburbs, and drive well-engineered cars. This is fine – so does almost everyone – but how do these activities or aspirations compose unique cultures? (ibid., p. 123)

Russell Jacoby, further, points out that even those who are economically excluded from society only too readily share its culture. And here, with immediate relevance to our discussion, he cites Nightingale's study of Philadelphia.

Thus Jacoby's case is that multiculturalism is absent in modern societies where the market connects and brings together citizens. The consumer culture of late modernity engulfs all apart from a few expressedly separatist groups and recently arrived immigrants. There is much to be said for this perspective: the notion of separate cultural essences, parallel to the diversity of biological species, is a fallacy. Human cultures are constructed by crossover, by hybridization and by innovation. They have no distinct existence in a loosely interrelated society and even between countries and continents there are, in Edward Said's phrase, overlapping territories and 'intertwined histories' (1993).

But is this to deny the sense of diversity which late modernity brings us? I think not; the problem is not so much with Jacoby's observations as with the lens that he uses. For, armed with the binoculars of multiculturalism, he surveys the United States and is only willing to concede diversity where difference is great, separate and 'essentially' distinct. But we should not expect the criterion of wandering yams to substantiate our detection of difference! Difference in late modern societies is a question of accentuation, stress, reinterpretation, and recontextualization of general values. It encompasses a stress both on the global and the local levels. Perhaps this will be clearer if we move our gaze from low in the class structure, up towards the rich and famous. But first of all let us identify what we mean by subculture because this is the key concept of diversity in a plural society.

The concept of subculture

David Downes, in his study of working class delinquency in the East End of London, invoked the definition of culture formulated by C.S. Ford, namely: 'learned problem solutions'. That is, subcultural responses are jointly elaborated solutions to collectively experienced problems. It is necessary, therefore, to explore and understand the subjective experience of the actor. Downes writes:

> Whatever factors and circumstances combine to produce a problem derive from the individual's frame of reference – the way he looks at the world – or the situation he confronts – the world he lives in and where he is located in the world. (1966, p. 6)

In short: subcultures emerge from the moral springboard of already existing cultures and are the solutions to problems perceived within the framework of these initial cultures.

Culture is seen as the ways people have evolved to tackle the problems which face them in everyday life. It includes language, ways of dress, moral standards, political institutions, art forms, work, norms, modes of sexuality – in sum, all human behaviour. People find themselves in particular structural positions in the world and, in order to solve the problems which such positions engender, they evolve subcultural solutions to attempt to tackle them. That is, people in every structural position evolve their own *subculture*. And, of course, the major structural axes are those of age, class, ethnicity and gender. These shape people's lives in the context of the space they occupy (e.g. whether they live in the inner city or rural areas) and the particular time and country we are talking about. So the structural predicaments which give rise to problems for different groups are varied and stratified throughout society. Subcultures overlap, they are not distinct normative ghettos: the subculture of young black working class men will overlap a great deal with that of their female counterparts. But there will also be distinct differences stemming from the predicaments of gender. People in the same structural position can also evolve different subcultures and these will change over time. Mods, rockers, teds, punks may all be varieties of attempts by working class youth to deal with similar problems. For subcultures are human creations and can vary as widely as the imagination of the participants involved.

All human beings create their own subcultural forms and although we often tend to use the term for the young and the deviant, this is just a matter of focus. Policemen and social workers, for example, form their own subcultures which are, in their way, as developed and exotic as those that exist in the underworld.

Subcultures, therefore, relate to the wider values and structure of society, and to the local problems and predicament of particular groups. In a highly interrelated society, they cannot be hermetically separate – even if their members try – and far from consisting of 'essences' – cultural dispositions which merely unfold – they change constantly, as the problems of each group change over time.

Subculture and diversity

The concept of subculture allows us to gain insight into the nature of diversity in late modernity. Subcultures occur throughout society, they are the differently accentuated interpretations of the wider values which vary by age, class, gender and ethnicity. They are constructed in relation to each other by bricollage, reinterpretation and invention. It is a frequent mistake to identify ethnicity with diversity, thus a multicultural society is seen as one in which there is a series of cultures independent of each other: separate essences each involving a replay of the culture of origin of the group concerned. This is a mistake because ethnicity is only one strand of subculture and the subcultures constantly change. To understand the subculture of the playground in my local secondary school in Stoke Newington, North

London, for example, it would be useless to think merely of a series of ethnic cultures: African-Caribbean, African, Turkish, Kurdish, Irish, English, Jewish, etc. more or less co-existing and jostling together. These strands occur, of course, although they are never static and always developing, but there is no end of crossover between young people as part of their evolving youth culture, there are differences and similarities between the subcultures of the boys and the girls and there is an extraordinary cross cutting of class beneath it also (see Back, 1996).

This focus on subculture as a unit of diversity rather than the atomistic, separate cultures beloved of multiculturalism, each with a separate ethnic core, allows us to appreciate the notion of late modern diversity. It is not that the old immigrant cultures based on ethnicity do not occur, but they are rather like cultural dinosaurs which either adapt or disappear. Of course, as in some culturalist Jurassic Park nationalists and separatists attempt to revive such cultures – sometimes with success for a short time, but the current of history runs against them. Lastly, the emphasis on subcultures allows us to note the fashion in which, through relationships of ageism, sexism, racism and classism, some subcultures exert power over others, indeed create problems for others in which the evolving subculture is an attempted solution. Subculture thus emphasizes conflict and power, unlike cultures, which are functional and unitary in their interests.

Difference then is related to subculture and subcultures connect the global and the local. That is, they are part of a global culture which is in late modernity very much a product of a market society (see E. Currie, 1977a): it stresses individualism, consumerism, it attempts to legitimize itself through meritocracy and has a strong emphasis on self-expression and actualization. That such values permeate society allows critical theorists such as Jacoby to presume that there is no such thing as diversity. He is correct, of course, to emphasize that the ethnic ticket has been grotesquely exaggerated ('does the fact that salsa sales surpassed ketchup sales signify that the United States has become culturally diverse or just that more people eat Mexican-American food?', 1994, p. 125) but the local variation between people by age, class, gender and ethnicity relates to a range of problems from the changed complexity of the labour market to the diverse pursuit of identity in a world where normative contours are blurred and shaded. In a society where market forces penetrate every corner, particularly in terms of consumerism, one would expect the broad brush of market values to tar every crevice of the social structure. Indeed, we have seen precisely this in our examination of Nightingale's study of the Philadelphia ghetto. Yet the social fabric is scarcely so closely interwoven as it was in the inclusionist period up to the early 1970s when employment was full and monolithic, when careers tended to span a lifetime and domestic and leisure roles were tightly cast and designated. The rise of an exclusive society involves, we should recall, the unravelling of the labour markets and the rise of a widespread individualism concerned with identity and self-actualization. Role making rather than role taking becomes top of the agenda.

Subcultures do not disappear but they lose their rigidity, they are more diverse in a late modern world and involve crossover and transposition of values from one to another (cf. Taylor, 1999, where subcultures are seen to vanish) and they involve much change in character and membership over time (Ruggiero and South, 1995). Such an argument has clear parallels with the debate in cultural studies about globalization: that a process of cultural imperialism is occurring, a so-called McDonaldization of world cultures into an increasingly uniform US mould (see Schiller, 1992 [1969]; Ritzer, 1993). The arguments against this are diverse (see Thompson, 1995) but, for our purposes, one of the major criticisms is the way in which local cultures *hybridize* the global tendencies: reinterpreting, transposing and rearranging them to fit local contexts. A whole series of manoeuvres can occur between what would seem a uniform message and its effect upon people's culture and beliefs; hybridization is one, but it is quite possible for the cultures to be aped *ironically* (see Nightingale, 1993, on 'gangsta' culture), or queer theorists on gay irony (see Plummer, 1995, pp. 138–43) or converted *intransigently* or simply ignored and *neutralized*. If this is true of local cultures, it is all the more true of subcultures, with their bringing together of the concerns of age, class, gender and ethnicity. Further – and much more radically – as Paul Willis has argued, the market forces by their emphasis on human choice and self-actualization set off a process which goes far beyond the confines of simple passive consumerism. The market, rather than prescribing conformity, presages diversity:

> The market is the source of a permanent and contradictory revolution in everyday culture which sweeps away old limits and dependencies. The markets' restless search to find and make new appetites raises, wholesale, the popular currency of symbolic aspiration. The currency may be debased and inflationary, but aspirations now circulate, just as do commodities. That circulation irrevocably makes or finds its own worlds. . . .
>
> Commerce and consumerism have helped to release a profane explosion of everyday symbolic life and activity. The genie of common culture is out of the bottle – let out by commercial carelessness. Not stuffing it back in, but seeing what wishes may be granted, should be the stuff of our imagination. (1990, pp. 26–7)

Part of the problem of diversity is, as I have suggested, the lens used. Russell Jacoby's is of such low definition that the world easily seems one-dimensional to him; only the cultural dinosaurs – he mentions the Hasidic Jews and the Amish – seem to represent real cultural differences. And, of course, if one was looking at, say, Britain or the United States the other cultures which would appear dramatically different would be the recent immigrant cultures of, for instance, South Asia or the Middle East. It is probably only for a short time that such dramatic differences will remain but, more importantly, it is not such isolated cultures which subjectively experience high levels of deprivation and discontent. This is associated with a significant degree of assimilation because it is only where expectations become in line with those of the wider population that injustices can become apparent. It is *relative* not *absolute* deprivation which generates discontent. Crime, for example, occurs where relative deprivation is highest and for relative deprivation to occur there has to be a degree of assimilation. Thus the crime rate of the first generation of African-Caribbeans in Britain was low, whereas that of their second generation offspring was high. In contrast the crime rate of the less assimilated South Asian population is only recently beginning to rise as assimilation occurs (see Lea and Young, 1993).

The rich are different

Let us turn once again, as promised in the last chapter, to F. Scott Fitzgerald and his famous cogitation on difference. It is encapsulated in a remark which Fitzgerald made to Ernest Hemingway:

'You've got to admit it Ernest the rich are different from us.' To which Hemingway replied 'Yes, they have got money.'

This terse interchange captures elegantly the problem of similarity and difference. The rich are, of course, part of the wider society and in many ways they variously share the values of the wider culture. But they also inhabit social territories with pressures and advantages compared to those below them and develop a style of life, a sense of identity, a mode of coping (or lack of it) quite different from other people. The vast majority of the population do not live beyond the bounds of material necessity, they would not know how to spend more than half a million pounds on the day's shopping as did Sir Elton John, they do not understand the plethora of serial temptations and pitfalls that confront presidents, they cannot understand the impossibility of going to a shop, pub or restaurant unharassed which is part of the daily life of successful popular musicians or film stars. Such a difference is underscored by the fact that many politicians, entertainers and even royal families feel it necessary to present themselves as being 'normal' just like everyone else. Such a situation was epitomized by Elvis Presley. In his later years Elvis was rumoured to have by his bedside two books: a bible and a pharmacopoeia. On one side his presentation of himself and his own sense of identity was rooted in being a decent, God-fearing Southern boy, a 'normal' man by those standards; on the other his life was so transfigured by his fame, from that fateful day in Memphis when 'That's Alright Mama' was played on the local radio station, that he could no longer be 'normal' in public, or in his relationships in private. Indeed, a most abnormal diet of uppers and downers was necessary to help him manoeuvre his way through the maze of unlimited money and gross adulation, while trying to find that muse which forever eluded him.

Returning to Philadelphia

The culture of the ghetto is closely linked with that of the outside world, is dynamic, is propelled by the contradictions of opportunities and ideals, of economic citizenship denied and of social acceptance blocked. It is neither a lack of culture nor an essentially different culture. But it *is* different: it is a subculture bricollaged out of wider culture which stresses certain values and transforms others. In the very act of compensation it overidentifies and it underidentifies. Here both Nightingale and Jacoby are wrong, for at some point selection and exaggeration becomes difference. It is irretrievably linked but it is different: this is, in fact, the meaning of diversity in late modern societies. It is overlap and choice, accentuation and transformation. It is also a subculture which in this process creates possibilities as well as blocking others. Its members see themselves through the situation but then, at the same time, as they are existentially creative they tend to essentialize themselves. The subculture creates essential notions of masculinity, it accepts rigid distinctions and even plays upon racial stereotypes.

Let us consider for a moment the mechanisms involved in bulimia. The actors, themselves, in the process of cultural inclusion experience relative deprivation which is rendered even more chronic by their compensatory overidentification with the American values of consumerism and competition. Their criminality is shaped by this individualism as it is informed by the notion of justified violence. The legitimacy of orderly behaviour is thus easily undermined, 'techniques of neutralization' abound. But the paradox of inclusion/exclusion is not only expressed in terms of access to material goods – cars, clothes, apartments – it is also evidenced in a loss of identity. You will remember from Chapter 1 Jimmy Feys' admonition that social exclusion creates problems of identity. Denied access to the full status of citizenship – a sense of indignity for many rubbed into them daily by their treatment on the streets by the police, or of being unable to take up the role of husband and breadwinner portrayed daily against the backdrop of comfortable homes that make up the sets of so many television dramas, feared because of stereotype and prejudice – lower class youth have the most extraordinary crisis of identity and self-worth. It is not just relative deprivation, then, that they confront but ontological crisis. One solution to crisis of identity is to emphasize features, to draw clear delineating lines, to suggest that your being is fixed and resolute. In short, to exaggerate and to essentialize oneself and one's difference from others: the 'hard' man of macho-culture whose toughness of physical features is contrasted to the derogatory 'softness' of women or of men acting like women. Thus both heterosexual masculinity and the 'otherness' of women, 'soft' men and homosexuals are essentialized. Hollywood, following on from the likes of Marvel comics, contributes well here. Richard Sparks notes:

> One of the most striking features ... is the evident, indeed exaggerated muscularity. Many stars of earlier periods (John Wayne perhaps most obviously) have

presented emphatically and heftily masculine figures but with few exceptions (Kirk Douglas in *Spartacus*) the detail and definition of their physique has not been dwelt upon so lingeringly. Stallone and Schwarzenegger are not just male heroes: their pumped up bodies signify (nay, yell) 'Masculinity' as if these days one *showed* masculinity by presenting it in excess – a prototypical, warrior essence. . . .

We see masculinity 'hyperbolized' in the ultra-physiques of Schwarzenegger or Stallone; or else we have the hyper-masculine' close-to-the-edge dangerousness of the Mel Gibson character in the *Lethal Weapon* films. (1996, pp. 355–6, emphasis in original)

Paul Willis, in his celebrated *Learning to Labour* (1977) describes how the lads create an identity which is macho, anti-female, racist and anti-intellectual, in order to survive. Similarly, such a toughening of identity, the process of essentialization, occurs across the world, wherever lower class male adolescents are marginalized. It is like some general law of the lower reaches of society where the division between the sexes and hostility to the middle class is a common feature although the target of the racism varies: sometimes white on black, sometimes black on white (see Messerschmidt, 1993).

Of course such a process of creating an essence, a stout and solid identity, is only one half of the equation. The other is the images projected upon the underclass by the wider public. Here, as we saw in Chapter 1, a more pervasive ontological insecurity spurred on by the exigencies of late modernity also has a tendency to essentialize – perhaps not spurred on as acutely as by the predicament of the youth themselves but certainly the repository of massive forces tending towards exclusion within society as a whole. In the next chapter I will trace how this process of essentialism can turn to demonization – to placing the blame for society's ills on certain parts of the social structure.

Note

1. The original notion of incivilities and crime as a continuum clearly comes from radical feminist activists in the early 1970s. See, for instance, the account of 'little rapes' in Medea and Thompson's *Against Rape* (1974). See the discussion in Chapter 5.

4 ESSENTIALIZING THE OTHER: DEMONIZATION AND THE CREATION OF MONSTROSITY

We have concerned ourselves up till now with the discussion of the actuarial response to the risk of crime, that is to the problem of *difficulty*. We must turn now to the second problem, that of *difference*: that is, how do both individuals and society as a whole tackle the problems generated by a more diverse social order? In Chapter 1 I delineated the way the exclusions arising from the changes in the labour force and the individualism of a market society gave rise to relative deprivation and a breakdown in social control which together create a rise in crime. It is this material discontent and conflict which is the currency of difficulty. But I also noted that there were grave ontological problems in a late modern society. The disembedding of the self from the secure tracks of family and work, the circumstances of uncertainty and multiple choice, the reflexivity of scepticism and anxiety meld together both material and ontological insecurities. And such a combination is one where the displacement and projection of focus is very likely (see Luttwak, 1995; Holloway and Jefferson, 1997). But note also that such fears are grounded in the difficulties arising from crime and other social problems. They are not free-floating illusions. Both distortion and refraction of fears are ever likely, and in a world of plurality and difference it is on to the deviant other, either the actual criminal or cultures which although perfectly law abiding are perceived somehow as alien, that such projections are likely to be made.

In the inclusivist discourse of the modernist period the deviant other was portrayed as a faded, imperfect image of the normal. It was a lacking: a lack of socialization, of social graces, of civilization, of self-control ... whatever. In the late modern period, difference becomes recognized, indeed elaborated; on this level the creation of deviant others as scapegoats is considerably obviated, but as we shall see, the anxieties arising out of the late modern world constantly undermine any stability. Multiculturalism is precarious: the ecumenical world is always liable to fundamentalism and split; it is because of the ever-present possibility of demonization that it is worth our while to look at the culture dynamics of difference in the late modern period.

The multicultural epoché

> Phenomenology has taught us the concept of phenomenological *epoché*, the suspension of our belief in the reality of the world as a device to overcome the natural attitude by radicalizing the Cartesian method of philosophical doubt. The suggestion may be ventured that man within the natural attitude also uses a specific *epoché*, of course quite another one than the phenomenologist. He does not suspend belief in the outer world and its objects, but on the contrary, he suspends doubt in its existence. What he puts in brackets is the doubt that the world and its objects might be otherwise than it appears to him. We propose to call this *epoché the epoché of the natural attitude*. (Schutz, 1967, p. xliii, emphasis in original)

Alfred Schutz famously documented the taken for granted world of everyday life; a world secure in that doubt was suspended and replaced by the epoché of the natural attitude, the suspension of knowledge that the social world around us is a human and contingent creation. Peter Berger and Thomas Luckmann in *The Social Construction of Reality* point to the way in which the institutions of society, the meanings given to behaviour become accepted as an objective reality, a thing of solidity rather than an arbitrary product of human artifice. Thus the terrors of anomie, of an awareness of existential aloneness and isolation, are protected by this suspension of doubt. For 'the institutional order represents a shield against terror. To be anomic, therefore, means to be deprived of this shield and to be exposed, alone, to the onslaught of nightmare' (1967, p. 119). The precariousness of human existence, the need for a viable *Umwelt* necessitates a whole series of defensive mechanisms. Berger and Luckmann call them, somewhat grandly, the 'conceptual machineries of universe-maintenance', amongst which are two processes: 'therapy' which is the measures by which potential deviants are kept within the fold by convincing them that their deviant thoughts, desires, etc. are not alternative causes of action but lapses of insight and decision, and 'nihilation' where alternative norms and values are rendered without meaning – and seem a 'lack' of the taken for granted 'normal' world rather than other worlds. These are rather like the way in which the inclusivist rhetoric of the modernist period portrayed deviance as a lack and split the social world into 'us' and those who 'lack' our values. Indeed Berger and Luckmann were writing at precisely such a time. The two sources which might unsettle the natural attitude are dreams, fantasies – the dark side of consciousness and, most importantly from our perspective, the multiple realities of different subcultures and societies. For these alternative worlds hold out the possibility that one's own life is relative and without any absolute meaning. What matters here is that the transition into late modernity manifestly exacerbates such ontological insecurity. For the disjointed world of work and family no longer provides the embeddedness in society which makes for an easy acceptance of the taken for granted, whilst the diversity of lifestyle and culture experienced within urban society, and presented through the mass media, constantly undermines any notion that one's world is obvious and certain. Helmut Schelsky (1957) depicts such a situation in the evocative phrase 'the market of worlds' and talks of the 'permanent reflectiveness' which such a situation provokes.

Late modernity is a world of increased difficulty and diversity: if the heightened awareness of risk leads to an actuarial attitude so does the plethora of alternative worlds presented to the individuals whose own *Umwelt* has been severely weakened by loosening of the bonds of work and family. Surely in such a situation traditional 'conceptual machineries' will be severely strained and new defensive strategies developed and elaborated?

Thus the phenomenological epoché by which the natural world is rendered suspect, by which the everyday world around us ceases to be taken for granted and comes to be regarded as a phenomenon, is aided by relativism. To know that there are indeed other ways of doing things which in their own world are considered just as everyday as one's own takes away security. The plethora of worlds presented to the citizen of late modernity seeks to make every citizen into his or her own phenomenologist! The natural epoché, so secure in the post-war First World of consensus, material certainty and embeddedness, becomes threatened on every side by the diversity of urban life and by the cultural multitude presented every day in a globalized mass media. An attempted solution to this is what I will call the multicultural epoché. That is, the bracketing off, the suspension of doubt characteristic of the natural epoché is so to speak multiplied. Each culture is bracketed off from the others in its own exclusive zone just as actuarially each group builds material and economic barriers in order to minimize risk. And in both the moral act of attempting to create normative ghettos and the physical act of attempting to create a zigzag of material barriers within the city (from one-way systems which re-route traffic away from your area to actual gating), adiaphorization occurs. For no hint of moral evaluation is permitted, rather the distinctions are justified as 'natural' and any interchange of their boundaries is characterized by wariness rather than by judgement of merit.

Ontological insecurity in the cultural revolution

The cultural revolution that swept the developed world in the 1960s was the pivotal event in the last third of the twentieth century. Social commentators from Eric Hobsbawm (1994) to Amitai Etzioni (1997) stress this movement – however different their interpretations – and this revolution, together with the economic changes in the labour market, is, of course, the main shaker and mover in the transition from an inclusive to an exclusive society. The cultural revolution arose on the back of the market place. As Paul Willis puts it:

> The market is the source of a permanent and contradictory revolution in everyday culture which sweeps away old limits and dependencies. The market's restless

search to find and make new appetites raises, wholesale, the popular currency of symbolic aspiration. The currency may be debased and inflationary, but aspirations now circulate, just as do commodities. That circulation irrevocably makes or finds its own new worlds. (1990, pp. 26–7)

The demand is for a world in which individuals can develop and give their lives meaning; for one where human diversity can flourish. It engendered a world where a thoroughgoing process of detraditionalization occurred, where the old accepted structures of family, work and community became looser and where authority itself was questioned. Let us note that the accent on self-fulfilment, and consequently diversity, contradicts with that of security. Ontological fulfilment and ontological security are at loggerheads and not merely because of the values of others (although this is a great part) but because the individual's own choices and search for meaning challenges a secure taken for granted world. There is not, therefore, merely social contradiction but also a psychological split where ontological certainty is stretched between the comfort of stability and the need for change.

But the cultural revolution promised much. What a brave new world this is where the emphasis is on the social construction of reality, of making one's own lifestyle rather than acting out a predetermined essence. A brave new world where difference could be respected and where authority was treated with suspicion, where no longer would one culture proclaim its unchallenged dominance, where white, middle class, middle aged males (some dead, some almost so) no longer set the rules, and where, in England, a post-war world of upright backs, strange moustaches and clipped accents – fuel for a whole generation of satirists – could be jettisoned for ever!

A widespread way of dealing with the problem of diversity and ontological insecurity is multiculturalism. This doctrine spread across the developed world: more pronounced in the Anglophone countries than others, most dramatically developed in the United States and a central platform of liberalism – although, at least, lip service is paid by many to the right of the political spectrum. Here, against the supremely inclusivist notion of a melting pot where diversity was lost in the ethos of the dominant culture, multiculturalism allowed people to be themselves, to develop their differences and to tolerate deviation. The irony of this project is that the contradictions inherent within it, together with the pressures and anxieties present in the wider social context, constantly come together to subvert it. Thus, as we shall see, the attractions of essentialism, of absolutely the opposite impulse to 'the market in worlds' re-emerge sometimes in a social form and even in the form of a return to biology as an explanation of human behaviour.

But first of all let us look at the shape of multiculturalist ideas. Let us contrast inclusivist analysis with that of multiculturalism. Take homosexuality, for an example (see Table 4.1). Here multiculturalism is, on the face of it, progressive.

Male homosexuality is cast in multiculturalism as gay culture, analogous to ethnic subcultures; its negative side is not seen as a cultural form but in the value-neutral, actuarial formulation of 'risk'. Gay cultures themselves

TABLE 4.1   *Inclusive and exclusive images of homosexuality*

Status	Liberal inclusivism	Multicultural exclusivism
'Normal'	Stable homosexual couple JUST LIKE US	Gay culture/s DIFFERENT FROM US
'Deviant'	Pederast LACKING US	Unsafe sex, Danger AIDS RISK

are not a subject for criticism, and certainly not moral censure; what is to be criticized is the risk inherent in unsafe sex – and this, it is stressed, can occur in all sexual relationships (heterosexual included). Similar to intra-venous drug use, these risks are detached from their subculture and are viewed neutrally as risks where harm must be minimized.

The multicultural solution to the ontological crisis

Paradoxically one solution, albeit precarious in the long run, to the onto-logical vicissitudes of late modernity is multiculturalism. In many ways this is an easier adaption than to tremulously hold on to the old single society of inclusivist values. Nostalgia for the old days of consensus and stability needs a lot of effort in a diverse society with an ever more critical citizenry. Multiculturalism actively embraces the threat to the natural attitude, it brings diversity into the benign sector of its *Umwelt*. Let us look at its com-ponents:

- *pluralism*: the social world consists of a plurality of cultures reflecting the diversity of countries of origin but also gay cultures, religious communi-ties and regional and national differences;
- *celebration*: such a diversity is celebrated, nurtured and elaborated by the institutions of education, politics and the mass media;
- *equality*: all cultures are seen as equal; the inclusivist motion of the superi-ority of one culture (the 'dominant' culture) over all others is seen as a disgraceful ethnocentricity. What was once seen as disorganization is seen as differential organization. For example, we identify various family structures and talk little of inadequate family structures (for a commen-tary on this see W.J. Wilson, 1987);
- *adiaphorization*: the phenomenon of adiaphorization noted with regards to the actuarial approach to risk is replicated here in terms of culture. Other cultures are not morally evaluated; items of their agenda may be frowned upon (e.g. clitoridectomy and judicial amputation), but these are seen as separate from the cultures themselves, which are there to be cel-ebrated rather than judged;
- *essence*: the various cultures are seen as having essential natures,

historically formed. The inclusivist world was, of course, essentialist: our world was the essence and theirs lacked it. But here we have a multi-culturalism, a world of different and separate essences. Each culture has its own 'natural' norms like different species in nature – just as in the childhood cartoons where each species of animal is given a different propensity together with a different regional accent;

- *ascription*: people belong to particular cultures; they are sometimes unaware of their 'roots' and have to discover their own heritage, but it is as if they were making contact with their personal essence. Self-identity is achieved by self-recognition and cultural identification;
- *distance*: the urban dweller visits different cultures as a shopper, as a diner, or as a tourist to a designated area (Chinatown, Catholic West Belfast, gay Manchester, Little Italy, etc.) but he or she cannot change culture nor would cultures actively proselytize.

The function of such a multicultural package is quite clear. It gives solidity to each individual (they have their own essence and bulwark against onto-logical insecurity) and avoids the unsettling of the natural attitude by ascrib-ing different behaviour to others with differing essences. It accepts the relativity of norms without granting relativity of choice. And, just as the actuarial attitude created a wariness of risk, the distancing in multicultural-ism allows for a cultural wariness, cloaked in notions of respect and toler-ance. It creates a world of exclusive enclaves to replace the inclusive world of the post-war period. It is important to realize the remarkable nature of the multicultural project. For the momentum of modernity is to produce a world which is open, disembedded, ambivalent and fragmented: a world of choice and creation of self and lifestyle. Multiculturalism forecloses on this, it grants diversity yet divests the actor of choice.

This is why gay culture is such a fulcrum of debate and fascination, for it is above all a *created* subculture; friendships are not inherited with job, family or community; areas are palpably manufactured – Christopher Street in New York City is not Chinatown, the gay subculture is not discovered through the examination of tradition or history, but manifestly improvised out of a bricolage of straight and innovated styles from skinhead haircuts to an adulation of Sandie Shaw and Judy Garland. Yet essentialism constantly reasserts itself. Let me quote at length Ken Plummer's remarkable ex-egesis of this in *Telling Sexual Stories*:

> To understand just what has happened to same-sex experience during the past century it may help to start with an exercise in imagination. Picture, if you can, a microscopic experience of homosexuality: an erotic eye for the same sex, two people – or more – responding with their genitals to each other's bodies, two people of the same sex feeling emotionally content when close to each other. Such experiences are probably ubiquitous and universal. Imagine you were born in the nineteenth century and have wandered into the late twentieth century. A wholly different world appears before you: what has happened to such microscopic experiences? In many big cities, you will find that a massive network of talk and

activity has flourished around these seemingly small and personal experiences. There are bookstores and video shops, . . . bath-houses and porno-houses, bars and clubs, hi-energy discos and low-energy poetry readings, theatre companies for lesbian and gay theatre, health clinics and restaurants, gay men's choruses and lesbian communes; there are groups of every conceivable interest. . . . Hundreds of thousands of men and women have come over the past two decades to live their whole life from within this world, . . . A small experience has become a major cultural form. . . .

But more than this: the experience has also been transformed into a major way of *being* in the world. For in every major western city throughout the world, people have become 'gay' or 'lesbian' or even, since the late 1980s, 'queer' all over again! Identities are built around sexuality; an experience becomes an essence; . . . Of course this is just what the medical practitioners were doing in the nineteenth century when they created their rogues' gallery of perverts. But now the identity is no longer imposed, stigmatisingly, from without. It is instead embraced, willing, from within. This, the story goes, is what that microscopic experience 'really' meant all along: it was a sign of a deep-seated, truly different nature. (1995, p. 86, emphasis in original)

As Plummer documents, the drive to essentialism is embraced by gays. This stance creates its own contradictions, for as Frank Mort puts it:

The gay community has circulated its own quasi-essentialist identity around the idea of an ethnically-based interest group. As a form of everyday commonsense it has sat somewhat awkwardly with the knowledge produced from a generation of academics and researchers. Here, despite the different frames of reference, a dominant strand of argument has been to assert the relativism of homosexuality, both historically and in relation to different societal milieux. The 'social constructionist' paradigm, as it has come to be termed, has worked to deconstruct more unified and stable projections of the homosexual self. (1994, p. 208)

The basis of the appeal of essentialism

In the inclusivist years of the 1960s and early 1970s, the progressive call was for an equality which ignored difference, which was coupled with a mind-set which minimized difference. This was true in terms of culture: similarities of belief were celebrated and a melting pot advocated, and it was true of sexual orientation: the gay couple were seen as identical to the heterosexual couple and equality of treatment and respect was *therefore* demanded and this was true of men and women. As Lynne Segal puts it:

What is troubling to some older feminists such as myself is the turnaround in feminist writing from an original denial of fundamental difference between women and men in the early Seventies to a celebration of difference by the close of that decade. (1987, p. x)

Thus the progressive rhetoric which stressed that blacks and whites, gays and straights, men and women, even 'normal' people and so-called 'deviants', were the same, and hence the obvious injustice of unequal treatment, became transformed into the notion that people were different, that difference must be recognized and respected in the form of equality of treatment. This was combined with a form of essentialism: that these differences were based on essences which were seemingly fixed and timeless. There are many reasons why such essentialist notions of difference appeal in the present period, but let us first of all examine the appeal of essentialism itself.

Essentialism can be claimed for oneself or one's group or it can be applied to others. The attractions of self-essentialism are various:

1 *It provides ontological security*: by obviating choice it gives solidity to a social world which is, as Berger and Luckmann have stressed, a human creation and therefore always liable to doubt, unsettling feelings and, at the extremes, panic and terror. It provides the dictum that we do it this way because this is the way we have always done it and because it is the correct way of doing things.

2 *Absolution of responsibility*: it takes human choice out of one's actions, thus absolves one of moral responsibility and, therefore, any criticism from others or need to change one's behaviour, e.g. 'the junkie role' is constructed around the essence of the biologically (i.e. chemically) determined addict (see Young, 1971b). Thus all sorts of devious and malicious behaviour can be explained away by the addictive molecule rather than the actor. Such a relief from adult responsibilities can be particularly attractive in this present period of high unemployment where there is a 'crisis of masculinity' (see Auld et al., 1986). Similarly, the members of a street gang can attribute much of their machismo and chauvinism to their essence of masculinity and perhaps ethnicity: They have 'manly flaws' (Liebow, 1967) which explain the 'need' for sexual variety, gambling and drunkenness (see also Bourgois, 1995).

3 *Justifying the unacceptable*: similarly, other more institutionalized and threatening behaviour can be justified by essentialism. Thus marching in a triumphalist fashion, with drums and strange outfits, through republican areas in Northern Ireland can be justified as part of a cultural heritage and a key component of self-identity. Various highly dubious practices from genital mutilation (both female and male) to the political domination of particular areas can be justified as fundamentalist religious practices ('written in stone') or as the nationalist invocation of the accumulated weight of historical tradition.

4 *To assert superiority*: the most common usage of essentialism is to justify superiority, whether racial, gender or class. For example, patriarchal dominance can be asserted by referring to biological superiority or to superiority through socialization or training. Conversely, some recent 'cultural' or 'radical feminists' can assert the inherent superiority of women as an uncontestable argument for social change (e.g. Dworkin, 1980).

5 *To claim unity of interest*: the claim of an essential unity of interest between all women, all blacks, etc. allows differences in status and privilege within such groups to be ignored – sometimes conveniently. For example, in terms of equal opportunities policies it is an advantage to relatively privileged individuals to be able to claim identity with groups who have a very low average chance of jobs, housing, etc.

6 *To defend oneself*: essentialism may not simply be used as an excuse but may be invoked by members of a relatively powerless group to claim that their behaviour is as 'natural' (thus permissible) as anyone else's. Gay essentialism, as we shall see, claims that as homosexuality is one's biological nature, it cannot be a subject of blame and has a natural parity with heterosexuality.

Essentialism is a paramount strategy of exclusionism: it separates out human groups on the basis of their culture or their nature. The advantages have always been there throughout human history but there are obvious reasons why the above strategies should appeal as we enter the late modern period. Ontological insecurity rises; vast numbers of individuals and groups suffer crises of identity. In such a moral climate fundamentalism has great appeal, as has the reassertion of basic or family values. The entry of women into the public sphere poses greater challenges to masculinity and engenders conflict whilst the marginalization of lower working class men generates macho-cultures which wear their gender essentialism like a badge. Let us turn now to the process of essentializing the other.

Essentializing the other[1]

Just as one's own group is frequently seen as having an essence which has its advantages, so are the stereotypes we apply to other groups. The advantages parallel those of self-essentialization:

1 *It provides ontological security*: in an intensely pluralistic world where we are increasingly aware of alternative lifestyles and normative choices, the ontological threat of relativism is ever present. If homosexuality is a choice of lifestyle this obviously threatens the identity of the red-blooded heterosexual male! If the boundaries between men's work and women's work are beginning to blur and erode then an intransigent masculinity can seize an essential difference to justify resisting any incursions on the male role. The essentializing of others takes away alternatives as choice; rather they are simply the attributes of other social groups *different* from ourselves. Gay people are homosexual, that is their nature, other people are intensely religious – that is part of their culture, women are intuitive, emotional, close to their feelings and love looking after children, etc.

2 *It legitimizes both privilege and deference*: it allows us to maintain and accept positions of superiority or inferiority. In a world where the

distribution of reward and privilege is supposed to be meritocratic, yet is palpably unfair and chaotic, the belief in the essential and radical differences of ability of people allows the rich to sleep easy and the poor to accept their lot. We have already seen Scott Fitzgerald's reflections on difference but elsewhere he reflected more elaborately on the rich:

> They are different from you and me. They possess and enjoy early, and it does something to them, makes them soft when we are hard, and cynical where we are trustful, in a way that, unless you were born rich, it is difficult to understand. They think, deep in their hearts, that they are better than we are because we had to discover the compensation and refuge of life for ourselves. Even when they enter deep into our world or sink below us, they still think that they are better than we are. They are different.

3 *It allows us to blame the other*: essentialism, as we shall see, is a prerequisite of demonization: of blaming a group either within or without society for the systemic problems which society faces.
4 *It is the basis for projection*: it allows us to securely project on the other, the baser and uncomfortable parts of oneself. As Dave Morley and Kevin Robins put it:

> Yet the stranger, the foreigner, is not only among us, but also inside us. He is, says Julia Kristeva, 'the hidden face of our identity' (1991: 20). What is hidden or repressed, creates in us a sense of existential unease and foreboding. What has been alienated in the construction of our identities comes back to haunt our imagination and disturb our peace of mind. (1995, p. 25)

To project what we perceive as unsavoury helps us allay these nightmares and makes more coherent and delineated our chosen identity.

Biological and cultural essentialism

Essentialism can either involve the belief that the tradition of a group generates an essence (cultural essentialism) or that such a culture and patterns of behaviour are underwritten by biological differences (biological essentialism). There has been a tendency in recent years for arguments with regard to the biological basis of essentialism to be revitalized. Some of this has been the result of traditional preoccupations of those on the right, for example biological justifications for supposed racial and working class inferiority. Thus, Herrnstein and Murray's bestselling book *The Bell Curve* (1994) argues that there is a racial and class basis to IQ and hence the present inequitable social structures of the West are based on actual biological differences; even more sinisterly, Philippe Rushton's (1995) excursion into the fashionable world of evolutionary psychology suggests that supposed black–white differentials in crime, aggressiveness and sexuality relate to essential differences between the 'races' generated by their attempts to thrive in different physical environments.

What is more surprising is that such claims as to the biological basis of social difference are echoed in more progressive parts of the political spectrum. Thus Lynne Segal writes:

> Feminists have fought fiercely to demolish the significance given to the biological in determining the social inequalities between women and men, and the contrasts we draw between 'femininity' and 'masculinity'. But today some feminists, with equal passion, appear to have gone over to the opposite camp. (1987, p. 7)

And Ken Plummer notes how the supposed discovery of a biological basis of homosexuality was greeted with enthusiasm by some parts of the gay community:

> For many, it is a biological story of natural difference. It is a culture creating its own essentialist story of identity – 'Homosexuals are born, just as heterosexuals are born. This is what I think, feel, know and there has been no evidence to prove otherwise', says Larry Kramer – a leading gay activist. And when in 1991, Simon LeVay (re)discovered the biological basis of homosexuality through his study of the shrinking hypothalamus, he became a celebrated character in gay culture. (1995, pp. 86–7)

Indeed T-shirts in the gay community soon proclaimed 'Thanks for the genes, Mom', or just 'Xq28', the supposed region of the genome where the 'gay gene' was situated (Fernbach, 1998).

Even more bizarre is the continued use of racial categories by progressives working in community relations and by left of centre councils. Here we have the category 'race' which the majority of biologists assure us has no scientific meaning (see Rose et al., 1990). The paradox is that those most opposed to racism find themselves utilizing racially based or, indeed, racist categories. Certainly, they are more willing to use them than anyone else outside of the far right. In vetting parents for adoption, for example, many social services pursue policies which make the South African Nationalist Party in its heyday seem half-hearted in its racial policies. Paul Gilroy (1986) has termed this process ethnic absolutism and is a trenchant critic of such policies. As John Pitts and his colleagues in their critique of Anglo-American race relations policies note:

> It is the idea of identity as ever capable of being 'finished' against which Gilroy wishes to argue, and it is one of the characteristics of 'identity politics' that it has to implicitly or explicitly posit social and individual identity as an *essence*. The seemingly inescapable polarities of essentialist and pluralist ways of thinking dog the politics of race as they have dogged much social scientific and critical work. Integration and anti-racism must surely be understood as processes rather than events, in which a dialectic of *change* must be assumed if they are to mean what they claim to mean. . . .
>
> From this conceptual ground, Gilroy has lent his weight to work which

re-evaluates an unquestioning commitment to 'same race placement' policies. Buried in current discourses about racial identity which inform child protection and child care practices there is, arguably, a 'myth of origins' in which the restoration of the abandoned child can only be achieved by the construction of a positive identity conceived in terms of cultural 'roots'. (Cooper et al., 1995, p. 139, emphasis in original)

They contrast this with French policies where:

Within French political discourse, the subsumption, but not the annihilation, of notions of identity within those of 'sociality', the recognition that all personal identities are social, multifarious and changing, may offer something worthwhile in the effort to reconstruct a social work politics which reconciles attention to 'differences' within a universalised struggle to create 'the good society'. (ibid.)

The fallacy of essentialism

John Lea and I, writing in 1984, note the fallacy of such essentialism:

the behaviour of a particular group relates to its specific history and the opportunities and constraints which that brings. [such] theory is opposed to any notion of 'natural' . . . tendencies of a particular group whether this be established in a genetic, racist fashion or by means of a cultural essence transmitted relatively unaltered over time. Nowadays the belief in a pre-written genetic script determining the behavioural characteristics of a group has little audience. Culturalist theories have a more pervasive influence, however. From the latter standpoint the essential characteristics of a group are seen to be determined by cultural traditions whose 'essence' can be discovered by the discerning analyst. Thus a Jewish propensity for finance is discovered, or an African propensity for rhythm identifiable in contemporary black America. Such theories abound in the discussion of ethnic groups and their history, and stretch from music (jazz as the direct expression of African culture in America) to politics (Jews are innately quiescent in the face of adversity), and embrace all those writers, of the right or left in politics, who see the behaviour of second-generation immigrants as a cultural replay of their ancestry.
   The point is not to deny cultural legacies and traditions but to emphasize that they are constantly changed, reinterpreted and reworked in the face of changing circumstances. The immense variations of human behaviour cannot be accounted for in terms of the genetic script or the cultural essence. Those who a generation ago were talking of Jewish quiescence in response to persecution presumably now speak of the innate aggressiveness of Jewish culture. The relationship between one generation and the next is a process of *reworking* rather than a process of *transmission*. (1984, p. 131, emphasis in original)

This, then, is the critique of essentialism: Firstly cultures do not involve timeless essences; in contrast, they can change rapidly over time if circumstances change just as they can remain static if conditions are unchanging. Cultures and subcultures are the ways of adapting to the problems facing people: different cultures represent different circumstances. Secondly, they are never pure in form but contain contradiction, conflict and disagreement. Lastly, and most definitively, they are not separate from each other but involve interchange of ideas and symbols, and this exchange involves transposition and transformation. It is not a question of a multicultural batch of threads intertwining but of a bleeding of colour and texture. Or, to change to the more usual metaphor, cultures are *hybrids*, they are rarely isolated species. Such a hybridization has become increasingly evident in the present period of globalization.

If we reject such essentialism, it follows that we must discard the notion of multiculturalism which proposes a mosaic of fixed essences glued to their historical past, part of an epoché which assumes that these essences never change and never encroach on or challenge each other. To do this is not to deny pluralism and diversity. This course is that of those conservatives who wish to return to a nostalgic world of consensus and conformity. Rather it is precisely such a medley of cultures which gives vitality to the late modern world. For not only is such a world attractive and desirable, there is no going back to 'the good old days' of monoculture and blandness. But it is a pluralism which interweaves and where the dyes of each strand interpenetrate and change. It is a world of crossover and hybridization, not of separatism and assimilation; one where cultures constantly transform, disappear, yet where difference constantly re-emerges in new and synergic ways.

Floya Anthias gives clarity to this in a review of recent texts on ethnic relations, where she makes the following extremely useful contrast:

> A distinction can be drawn between multiculturality (which involves diversity, cultural penetration and hybridity) and multiculturalism (difference, cultural reproduction and enclavization). . . . Multiculturalism is the interventionism that seeks to reproduce and preserve. Multiculturality is the removal of barriers to the legitimacy of different ways of being and is not dedicated to reproduction. Multiculturality goes along with both hybridity and assimilation. Neither is to be feared as a loss or a demise of a group although assimilation is an ideology and practice of forced acculturation and therefore deeply delegitimizing. Multiculturalism focuses on the reproductive process of culture rather than the transformative ones. (1995, p. 298)

The belief in fundamental and considerable cultural differences between people living in the same society – however illusory in their basis, however *invented,* the traditions (see Hobsbawm and Ranger, 1983) – can be devastating in its consequences. Listen to Robert Hughes bitterly denounce the 'culture wars' of contemporary America:

> It is too simple to say that America is, or ever was, a melting pot. But it is also too simple to say none of its contents actually melted. No single metaphor can do justice to the complexity of cultural crossing and perfusion in America. American mutuality has no choice but to live in recognition of difference. But it is destroyed when those differences get raised into cultural ramparts. People once used a dead

metaphor – 'balkanization' – to evoke the splitting of a field into sects, groups, little nodes of power. Now, on the dismembered corpse of Yugoslavia, whose 'cultural differences' (or, to put it plainly, archaic religious and racial lunacies) have been set free by the death of communism, we see what that stale figure of speech once meant and now means again. A Hobbesian world: the war of all on all, locked in blood-feud and theoretic hatred, the *reductio ad insanitatem* of America's mild and milky multiculturalism. What imperial rule, what Hapsburg tyranny or slothful dominion of Muscovite apparatchiks, would not be preferable to this? Against this ghastly background, so remote from American experience since the Civil War, we now have our own conservatives promising a 'culture war', while ignorant radicals orate about 'separatism'. They cannot know what demons they are frivolously invoking. If they did, they would fall silent in shame. (1993, pp. 15–16)

Cultural essentialism allows people to believe in their inherent superiority while being able to demonize the other, as essentially wicked, stupid or criminal. There is a terrible irony here which Zygmunt Bauman points out, which is the transformation of liberal rhetoric into the language of exclusion. Inclusivist rhetoric had as its progressive moment the stress on the way in which biological differences (whether of 'race', 'gender' or age) were not rooted in any essential differences but were social products. Human nature was plastic, malleable – social diversity was a product of differences in socialization not essence. Black/white, male/female, even adolescent/grown-up were social constructs. Men were not naturally aggressive; the right upbringing would create social harmony. Criminals were not born but made. Biology could not be used to justify behaviour or to infer superiority or inferiority. Furthermore – and here is the hope of progress – by the patient devising of institutions we can change our children, our fellow citizens and ourselves: we can thus socially engineer a better society. Education can instruct, democracy dispel authoritarian attitudes, prisons rehabilitate and clinics cure and modify behaviour. For people are not prescribed other than to be first of all malleable and, second of all benign and peaceful towards each other, if only the social circumstances were there to mould and permit. This viewpoint was the central motif of both US and Soviet attitudes to human progress in the post-war period. The old tyrannies of blood and soil are supplanted; human beings are, in fact, very similar under the skin of culture, and culture and behaviour can easily be changed.

The transformation which Bauman points to is one which supplants biological essentialism with cultural essentialism:

paradoxically, the ideologies that currently accompany the strategy of communal identity-building and the associated policies of *exclusion* deploy the kind of language that was traditionally appropriated by *inclusivist* cultural discourse. It is culture itself, rather than a hereditary collection of genes, that is represented by these ideologies as immutable. . . . Much like the castes or estates of the past . . . they can never mix; and they should not mix lest the precious identity of each should be compromised and eroded. In a grotesque reversal of culture's history, it is not cultural *pluralism* and separatism, but cultural *proselytism* and the drive towards cultural unification that are now conceived as 'unnatural' – as an abnormality to be actively resisted and defied. (1995, p. 188)

People are born with cultures; they are seen to be constituted, given identity by their cultures. Without their specific cultures, they are not part of the human race as the earlier assimilationist ideas suggest, but nothing, people without culture, the 'other' who are those left in the margins of the cultural map outside of the habitable enclaves of each tribe and culture.

Social diversity begins to be seen like bio-diversity: a series of species that cannot (and should not) interbreed, that should be preserved in their pristine distinctiveness and, of course, which 'naturally', if regrettably, conflict with each other. Thus Bauman points out how multiculturalism is unable to combat the new racism because the latter is more and more frequently (from Bosnia to Northern Ireland and from White Supremacy to the Nation of Islam) expressed in precisely the same cultural terms:

The root of the present weakness of the so-called 'anti-racist' cause so poignantly felt throughout Europe lies in the profound transformation of the cultural discourse itself. Within the framework of that discourse, it has become exceedingly difficult to advance without contradiction (and without the risk of criminal charges) an argument against the permanence of human differentiation and the practice of categorial separation. This difficulty has prompted many authors, worried by the apparent inability of the 'multiculturalist' argument to challenge, let alone to arrest, the advance of pugnacious tribalism, to double their efforts in the refurbishing of the 'unfinished modern project' as the only rampart still capable, perhaps, of stemming the tide. Some, like Paul Yonnet [1993], go so far as to suggest that the anti-racist forces, preaching as they are mutual tolerance and peaceful cohabitation of diverse cultures and tribes, are to blame for the growing militancy of the exclusivist tendency. (ibid., pp. 188–9)

Conditions for a successful demonization exercise

When faced with my demons
I clothe them and feed them
And I smile
Yes, I smile, as they're taking me over.
('Strange Glue' *International Velvet*, Catatonia, 1998)

Essentialism provides a cultural basis for conflict and is the necessary *prerequisite* for demonization of parts of society. Demonization is important in that it allows the problems of society to be blamed upon 'others' usually perceived as being on the 'edge' of society. Here the customary inversion of causal reality occurs: instead of acknowledging that we have problems in society because of basic core contradictions in the social order, it is claimed that all the problems of society are because of the problems themselves. Get rid of the problems and society would be, *ipso facto*, problem free! Thus, instead of suggesting, for example, that much high risk, deleterious drug use is caused by problems of inequality and exclusion, it is suggested that if we get rid of such drug use ('just say no', lock up the dealers) we will no longer have any problems. The solution then becomes the appointment of such potentates as drug czars in order to eliminate the problem from society as if it were a cosmetic problem rather than one of the interior structure and values of society itself. Crime, then, is a major currency of such demonization. That is, the imputation of criminality to the deviant other is a necessary part of exclusion. Racial demonization, for instance, is inevitably associated with accusations of criminality. Contemporary examples are the characterizations of Albanians in northern Greece and in Italy as the source of the majority of crime (see Karydis, 1992).

In Great Britain such a process was evident in the controversial issuing, in July 1995, by Sir Paul Condon, Commissioner of the Metropolitan Police, of a letter to 40 community leaders which suggested that the majority, perhaps as high as 80%, of London muggers were black. This was seized upon by the media as a major breakthrough in plain talking. At last someone had the guts to admit what every Londoner knew: that most crime in the city was caused by black people (see J.Q. Wilson, 1987). I was greatly agitated by the naivety of such pronouncements and spent a considerable time in the subsequent fortnight appearing on television features and giving newspaper interviews to attempt to counter this misinformation. The problem was not so much numbers – although 80% was far too high a figure – but context. (For a London survey see Harper et al., 1995.) The point was that street robbery is carried out largely by poor, young, adolescent boys who live in the inner city. It is an amateurish crime, however serious its consequences. In London, because of the balance of population, a large proportion of muggers will be black, in Newcastle, in the north of England, they will inevitably be white, as they will in Glasgow. Indeed, in Glasgow they will most probably be Catholic rather than Protestant as the Catholic population is much poorer. There would be understandable public outrage, however, if a Scottish Commissioner of Police were to produce street robbery statistics by religious affiliation. And it would be a bizarre criminology which was based on religious preference and rates of crime. Perhaps one could imagine theories correlating belief in Original Sin and rates of burglary, or access to the confessional and assault rates in Sauchiehall Street, Glasgow! Such demonization involves taking crime out of its structural context and apportioning blame to the group themselves. Of course, this is *not* to deny differential crime rates between groups as some liberals do, for to deny these would be to ignore different structural positions (see Lea and Young, 1993). Rather it is to locate such crime within the actual core problems of the society.

Let it be said that such a process of demonization was probably unsuccessful in this case. There was a wide variance in the media reporting of these figures as well as considerable caution both within the media and by outside public bodies and, finally, given the indigenous nature of British blacks, it is unlikely that the widespread public could be galvanized into a 'successful' moral panic. As we have seen (Chapter 1) such moral panics are less likely to be achievable in the late modern period.[2] Where such a racial demonization is more easily possible is when it involves recently arrived immigrants, perhaps illegal, across the borders of the First World (see Karydis, 1996). Here every instance of criminality is often highlighted in the mass media (see Spinellis et al., 1996) and the very fact of their illegal nature is seen as a criminal 'master status' which quite falsely indicates their guilt of all other types of crime as obvious and tautologous. The demonization process taken to its extreme *allows* the perpetuation of atrocities. As Stan Cohen graphically depicts in his study of human rights violations, it permits behaviour against others quite outside what is considered normal civilized behaviour. He lists a whole series of 'techniques of neutralization' of responsibility one of which is victim blaming:

> The most common forms of victim blaming are variations on the themes of 'they started it', 'they had it coming' and 'they got what they deserved.' As with the doctrine of necessity, these justifications appear either in the current context (reacting to immediate resistance, provocation and violence) or the historical narrative in which the current victim is alleged to have been the original perpetrator. As we know from the atrocities of the last few decades – whether in Northern Ireland, Rwanda, the former Yugoslavia or the Middle East – there is virtually no end to the historical spiral of conflicting claims about which group is the original, 'real' or ultimate victim.
>
> Other forms of 'denial of the victim' are less explicit (though decodable) in the official response to the outside world but clearer in the internal ideology through which governments ensure that their own citizens are cooperative perpetrators or complicit bystanders.
>
> These include: First, *dehumanization*: disparagement of the victim groups by repudiating their humanity. They become a lower form of being with less right to comparison with other humans, less ability to feel and less entitlement to compassion or empathy. They are savages, gooks, slits, vermin, animals, two-legged monsters. Violence is 'the only language they understand'. Second, *condescension*: the other is regarded not so much as evil or sub-human but to be patronized as inferior, primitive, childlike, uncivilized, irrational and simple. Third, *distancing*: the dominant group ceases to feel the presence of others; they virtually do not exist. Because their very presence is not acknowledged, they cannot be seen as victims. (1995, p. 79)

This passage clearly illustrates how the language of essentialism (often combined with nationalism) can be used to demonize and dehumanize others and, as a consequence, to generate a vocabulary of motives which allows inhumanity.

Yet the demons are not only the strangers that have come amongst us, but the people who have become strangers. Immigration alone scarcely provides sufficient stock of folk devils to placate the troubled identity of late modern society. The two most important indigenous scapegoats are the underclass and drug addicts. These two modern folk devils have key explanatory roles in conventional discourses about crime. Interestingly their prototypes have a very similar narrative form:

1 *Temptation:* 'Normal' single mother is tempted into living off the state; 'normal' person is tempted into trying drugs.
2 *Petrification:* The single mother begins a family who become part of a 'dependency culture'; the drug taker becomes dependent, becomes a drug addict and is caught or trapped in the situation.
3 *Disturbance:* Their dependency culture produces sons who suffer crises of masculinity resulting in the formation of gangs and incessant criminality; the drug addicts rob to keep up with the costs of their ever-increasing habit. They are both major contributors to the total crime figures of the nation.
4 *Nemesis:* Pitiful lives, pain, misfortune are seen to be the inevitable outcomes, and from the hell of the sink estate to the overdose on the stairwell it is portrayed as self-inflicted.

Here, then, the deviants are tempted: they chose voluntaristically their deviance rather than being impelled by any social circumstances (it is their fault, not society's), they become taken over by the determining essence of dependency, they're seen to be the cause of society's problems rather than their problems being caused by society; moreover they repeatedly cause a remarkably large proportion of society's problems and, finally, they do harm to themselves. Who could quarrel with their demonization?

Such demonization has the following three components: distancing, the ascription of an essentialist other, and the reaffirmation of normality. *Distancing* basically involves explaining crime or deviancy in a way which denies that it has any relationship with the core values and structure of society. Much of establishment criminology has this as its project (see Young, 1997). Ascribing an *essentialist other* is to suggest that the deviance is a product of some deviant essence inherent in the individual or group (and, by definition, *not* a characteristic of 'us'). The *reaffirmation of normality* allows, in a Durkheimian fashion (see Erikson, 1966) the boundaries of normality to be drawn more definitely and distinctly. Every folk devil sharpens the image of the normal person in the street: in these instances, the normal family and the 'normal' non-drug user (ignoring whiskey, strong lager, gin and tonic, cigarettes, barbiturates, Valium, Prozac, beta-blockers, etc, etc!). The single mother, particularly, calls forth strong images of what one might call *the essential family*, that is the family as it is and always used to be: Mum, Dad, two kids, house, garden, the cat, 'Dad the breadwinner', Mum the nurturer and provider of a little extra income, breakfast together in the morning, dinner on the table in the evening and lasting more or less for ever.

Demonization and the manufacture of monsters

Up until now I have talked about the demonization of groups; let us turn now to focus on individuals: to the manufacture of monsters. This is, of course, not an either–or: very often the monsters are set in the context of the demonization of a group. Thus the boy murderers of James Bulger were seen to spring from the context of single mothers and the underclass and, indeed, represented a clear indication of the pathology of the group (see Mooney, 1998). Just as moral panics seem to have increased in frequency (see Chapter 1) so the phenomenon of intense media and public focus on individuals seems to have increased in pace. As I write, in Britain, two examples are the paedophile Sidney Cooke, and the child murderer, Mary Bell. The first set off a panic by his release from prison and the second because she received money for the publication of her biography. The mass media is full of their pictures, the press relentlessly hunt them down, the public expresses wide concern; in the case of Cooke, crowds riot for law and order (i.e. for action against paedophiles) outside a police station in Bristol, the commentators speculate endlessly in their columns and afternoon shows. This is not the place to enter into a full analysis of such phenomena, but it is important to relate them to our general argument.

1 Their 'wickedness' is clear cut: Cooke, Bell, Hindley, the Wests have committed gross and exceptional crimes; there is, unlike in nearly every other crime case widely reported in the media, little if no debate as to their false accusation and innocence (cf. Louise Woodward, O.J. Simpson). There is also a noticeable difference from many moral panics where the wickedness of the group stigmatized is much more ambiguous (e.g. mods and rockers, drug users, new age travellers).
2 They are seen as monsters, creatures who are *essentially* different from us. Their acts are 'unbelievable', impossible to imagine oneself doing, on the 'edge of human comprehension and empathy'.
3 The discourse does not omit the notion of causation. That is, their wickedness is, indeed, manufactured by society – it is not a free-floating spirit of evil. Rather, and this is particularly true of Mary Bell, it is seen as a product of a monstrous family background (sado-masochistic, prostitute mother who conspired to sexually abuse her). Their background is essentially different from 'our own'.
4 They are beyond redemption. Being essentially cast as monsters, they cannot change. No time in prison can redeem their wickedness. They should preferably stay in prison, or other coercive institution, for ever or, in the case of the paedophiles, be chemically castrated.
5 The risk is extraordinarily exaggerated. Cooke was feared even though he was in voluntary custody in a police station and had been under constant observation by police and probation officers in his short period outside prison. The discourse is as far away from the actuarial as can be imagined.

6 The mass media play a key role in the demonization: they hunt for the deviant way ahead of the police, and often hold the police responsible for inadequately dealing with the case. The criminal justice system is thus on the defensive rather than being in a morally entrepreneurial role.

7   At the end of the twentieth century, the bookstores are full of books on crime, though this title will certainly not find a place on the same shelves. In the massive Waterstones bookstore in the city of Manchester, England, where I live, the ground floor display area has recently been rearranged so as to accommodate, right at the front of the store, several hundred new titles, on topics like Serial Murderers and Sexual Crimes of the Twentieth Century. Several of these new books are companion volumes to movies on release in the city's cinemas, or, in some instances, are simply the original text on which the movies are based. The movies in question – *Shallow Grave*, *Silence of the Lambs*, *Reservoir Dogs*, *Natural Born Killers* and others – focus heavily on interpersonal violence and murder and also place great emphasis – in the manner of many earlier cinematic genres – on the idea of the 'criminal mind' (not least, as a way of dramatising the detection of the originating criminal act) but also – to a significant extent, movies which emphasise the idea and contemporary social presence of Evil. Similar moral and psychologistic pre-occupations are now also widely apparent on prime time television. (Taylor, 1999, p. 1)

The public have always been interested in crime and in monstrous behaviour from the Jack the Ripper hysteria of the last century to the present day. But as Ian Taylor graphically indicates, the quantity of coverage has exponentially increased, in every variety of the mass media, and there is a global quality to the interest. We share serial killers: the coterie of journalists from around the world outside West's trial at Winchester Crown Court is a case in point. Serial killers, particularly serial sexual killers, come into a category of their own. The combination of sex and violence is no doubt the most widespread pornography available, an example of what might be called legitimized pornography which has great appeal, as the tabloids and Andrea Dworkin have discovered to their good fortune, which you can both simultaneously condemn and cite widely (see Young, 1981).

8 Finally, it should be clear that such a sequence in all its detail but with the reverse valence occurs when individuals are beatified by the public and the media. Thus the process can produce both monsters and saints, wicked women and fairy princesses. This occurred with the response to the death of Princess Diana: all flaws were forgotten and an image of perfection was projected on to her.

The monstrous is, therefore, outside of us. It is an alien quality possessed by these monstrous others. Such a presumption is a calumny in the era of the Holocaust when seemingly perfectly normal people have acted in diabolical ways, or of total war where 'heroes' on every side burnt, bombed and exterminated innocent civilians, where human desire and sexuality has frequently taken malign and bizarre forms, and where ethnic cleansing has supported rape and massacre in Rwanda and Bosnia. To accept the binary – the normal and the monstrous – is to deny the monstrous in all of us: the dark side of our aggression and our sexuality.

But to explain such monsters merely as a projection of every man's inner psyche, the epitome of our darker selves rather like Michael Crichton's *Sphere*, is insufficient. The questions are: why do we need such projections more at certain times than others? Why are certain groups more liable to such projections? How do we facilitate such projections? What trick of mind allows us to essentialize, to dehumanize others? I am not, of course, denying or forgetting the question: how could they have done these acts? Rather, I am saying that this is not the only question; both how does society manufacture 'monsters' and how do we manufacture our representations of monsters, must be answered. Furthermore, a too declamatory focus on 'how could they do such things?!' serves to suggest that the causality was outside of the orbit of the 'normal' world, that it has no relationship to our own reality.

Essentialism and the criminology of war

Ruth Jamieson (1998), presents a strong case for a 'criminology of war'. She points out that the disinclination of contemporary criminology to foreground war is 'astonishing', particularly given the massive victimization involved. Amongst the arguments she musters is the clear parallel between violence in war time and that which occurs on the home front. Both frequently involve the same group of people (i.e. young men) and the state rhetoric for war is very similar to that of the 'war on crime' (for law and order comparisons, see Steinert, 1998). Furthermore, such conflicts in late modernity are more and more frequently intra-state and internal than between states. Ethnic conflicts often conflate and obfuscate criminal and political interests. The relationship between the political and the criminal blurs: the same individuals, whether it is in Northern Ireland or Bosnia, drift from one group to another, and the soldier unsupervised and off duty can easily be the criminal whether it is the corruption of the UN forces in Somalia or the constant thuggish behaviour of the British UN forces in Cyprus. The official role of soldiers often becomes that of policeman; the militarization of policing by the formation of para-military units, the increased co-operation with military personnel, and the 'upgrading' of the weapons used and extent of violence further blur the lines between engagement in war and the pursuit of crime control (see Kraska and Kappeler, 1997; also Lea and Young, 1993).

But it is in the mobilization of aggression that there is an extraordinary parallel between war and crime. In order to create 'a good enemy' we must be able to convince ourselves: (1) that they are a cause of a large part – maybe all – of our problems; (2) that they are intrinsically different from us: that they epitomize wickedness, evil, degradation, etc. That is to pinpoint and essentialize. The first principle allows one to direct one's animosity towards them, the second gives one 'permission' to use violence, often of an extreme nature. In war the government orchestrates such a comparison, the soldiers carry out the acts of violence. In crime, the government or law enforcement agencies are active in the comparison: thus we have 'a war against drugs' directed by a 'drug czar'. The essentializing of the 'drug barons' as the epitome of evil and the 'addicts' as the embodiment of degeneracy allows the campaign to focus aggressively and justifiably on its target. Who, as Nils Christie nicely put it, could fail to mobilize against such a 'good enemy' (Christie and Bruun, 1985). But the process of essentialization also facilitates the aggression of the criminal against his victim. This is most clear in the so-called 'hate crimes': crimes based on racism or homophobia (see Berk, 1990; Herek and Berrill, 1992). However, one should be aware that the notion of hate crimes based on group animosity and prejudice is certainly much wider than this. Much of male violence against women is based on a misogyny which has clear notions of essential deviance: witness the litany of 'slag', 'whore', 'bitch' which often accompanies such attacks and which contrasts with patriarchal binary of the 'good' woman (Lees, 1997; Mooney, 1999).

Iris Young in her influential *Justice and the Politics of Difference* (1990a) extends this argument, arguing that violence is a major form of oppression (together with exploitation, marginalization, powerlessness and cultural imperialism). She sees it as particularly linked to cultural imperialism and focused upon gays, lesbians, Jews, African-Americans, Latinos and women. Thus she would extend the notion of hate crimes, with their essentialist underpinnings, to the majority of violence. This rather turns the conventional notion of violence on its head. That is, instead of being instrumental and random, it is seen as cultural and oppressive: a product of cultural othering. Nancy Fraser (1997, p. 200) cautions us about taking this too far, pointing to instances of violence (e.g. against striking workers) which are not a form of cultural imperialism and one could extend this to include a range of 'normal' criminal events (e.g. fights in pubs, robbery). However, even in cases of street robbery there can be little doubt that cultural othering greatly facilitates the ability of the offender to excuse his acting outside the realms of normal civilized behaviour.

Essentialism and social exclusion

It should be obvious from the above discussion that essentialism greatly facilitates the process of social exclusion. It furnishes the targets, it provides the stereotypes, it allows the marshalling of aggression, it reaffirms the identity of the in-group – those with power and handy rhetoric – but we can go a little further than this, because social exclusion confirms and realizes essentialism. David Matza, at the end of *Becoming Deviant* (1969), discusses the relationship between essentialism and social exclusion. He draws several lines:

1 Social exclusion threatens the sense of identity of an individual or group, it makes them ontologically insecure and thus open to the embracing of essences. (See the discussion in the last chapter.)
2 The actors can embrace these essences in order to compensate for the lack of identity. The famous example he gives is Jean Genet who on being accused of being a thief becomes indeed that, for he embraces the master status, the essence, 'thief' as an organized core of his being. (Or at least this is how his biographer, Sartre, depicts it: see *Saint Genet*, 1964.) We have seen how such a process of embracing the essence bestowed upon the deviant can be taken up ironically, mockingly and transformatively. But even so, it still shapes individuals' notions of themselves.
3 Finally, and crucially, social exclusion by blocking off opportunities, both materially and in terms of the possibility of embracing alternative identities, can self-fulfil itself. For example, a man forced into a situation where he has little means of earning a living other than thieving, can come to believe that he *truly* is a thief, while the onlookers can find their prognosis confirmed for – lo and behold, the man they designated 'thief' continues thieving.

Matza calls this the 'intricate bogus' of essentialism. The answer to how we know that a person is essentially a thief is the recurrence of his thieving behaviour. Take away the material and ontological reasons for recurrence and it seems to be the product of an essence which is centred in the individual and by definition repeats itself.

Returning to Philadelphia, Carl Nightingale notes the level at which the ghetto culture makes heroes of the rap and hip hop singers who turn 'the language of racial hatred on its head, transforming the label "nigga" and the violence and sexual conquest of their songs into a badge of authentic blackness' (1993, p. 132). He adds:

> By choosing to use the word *nigga* – with its deliberately unshed and definitive evocation of racial exclusion and stereotype – in a wry and ironic attempt to save face, kids end up accepting the word's evocation of self-contempt. The identity also helps impose a rigid uniformity on the ideal image of black masculinity, which enforces inner-city boys' all-too-prevalent tendency to repress or aggressively express their overwhelming memories of pain. Nor, unfortunately, does it do much to allay suspicious white Americans' proclivities toward linking race and violence. Indeed, if the history of inner-city social life is partly based on some sort of 'cyclical' dynamic, the most important one is not a 'self-perpetuating' cycle of poverty passed from generation to generation. Instead the crucial dynamic involves white racism feeding off the self-portraits of those young black men it has trapped in the seduction of its caricatures. (ibid., p. 133)

I quote this excellent passage because it captures the recurrent bogus nature of essentialism in a nutshell, but here it is not just a single individual who is cast in a mould, but a whole race and a whole generation.

Herein is the deceptive nature of essentialism. For, on the one hand, conservatives insist that these essences are reality (a thief is a thief, the feck-less are without drive, young blacks are violent) whilst on the other more liberal commentators will insist that these presumptions are mere illusions. They are prejudice invoked against poorer parts of the community and more vulnerable individuals whilst in reality people are more or less similar. In reality, the social system produces people who appear as if constructed as an essence. *It is neither essence nor illusion* but a world of appearances which appears as if it's constructed of essences, whose very reality has a stolid, stereotypical quality.

Notes

1. Actuarialism and essentialism can and do occur at the same time. For example, a concern for the management of risk and the control of risky populations can occur at the same time as the demand for their heavy stigmatization, the hot pursuit of justice ('three strikes and you're out'), the possibilist belief in the elimi-nation of crime, drug use, etc. On one side then we can have a careful actuarial grading of intervention (the littoral metaphor of control) which involves the minimum level of intervention, and most importantly expenditure, necessary to achieve a level of insurance from risk for selected populations. That is, it seeks not to eliminate crime but to achieve graded harm minimization for various bands of the class structure. On the other hand we can have an almost reckless public expen-diture which, like a real life version of the Hollywood *Terminator 1, 2* and *3*, seeks to eliminate crime at all costs, whether financial or judicial. And, of course, we can have one discourse riding on another. That is we can have a moralistic pursuit of penality combined with an actuarial management of the huge warehouses of offenders which such a justice policy throws up. Indeed, the combination of a public judicial system pursuing retributive justice and a privatized penal system carefully counting each actuarial penny is familiar: one with its eye on the actors, the other with its eye on the shareholders.

The simultaneous existence of both discourses has palpably confused Jonathan Simon and Malcolm Feeley's valuable analysis of actuarialism, in which they seek a dominant actuarial tendency to such an extent that the US penal explosion, in par-ticular, can only appear as an anomaly (see Simon and Feeley, 1995). Their con-fusion is most evident in terms of the underclass. From an actuarial point of view the management of the underclass is clearly a problem of hiving them off, creating gates and barriers which keep them in their own reserves, causing problems for themselves and minimizing problems for others. From the point of view of essen-tialism and the demonization of the underclass, however, it is necessary that the forces of law and order enter their territory and hand out justice often in a draconian and indiscriminate fashion. Both of these tendencies occur in late modern societies (see Lea and Young, 1993).

These twin discourses of actuarialism and moralism correspond to the twin ten-dencies in late modern society: one to lose metanarrative, and any idea of, progress (rather than progress as the technical goal of the control of risk), and the other to actively engage the 'enemy' and to essentialize and demonize in the bargain. Two images of the criminal thus co-exist, *homo actuaris*, where all are capable of crime but to varying, discernible degrees, and *homo criminalis*, where the criminal and the non-criminal are clearly demarcated.

Finally, it should not be assumed that we can put an easy political label on actu-arialism. For actuarialism can exist in a positive, progressive light as well as in the negative fashion to which we are perhaps more accustomed. Actuarialism, for example, could well be part of an ideology of reducing the intervention of the criminal justice system. It could be linked with abolitionist and minimalist tendencies (see van Swaaningen, 1997). Indeed, this is the form in which it appears in the debate on drugs policy where advocates of *harm minimization* are pursuing what amounts to an actuarial policy over and against those who would advocate a war on drugs and an intemperate use of criminal justice sanctions.

2. Even the most celebrated moral panic about blacks and crime, that described by Stuart Hall and his colleagues in *Policing the Crisis* (1978), was certainly unproven on both these counts of ascertaining that there was a media consensus and that public opinion was actually mobilized (see Sumner, 1981; Waddington, 1986; Downes and Rock, 1982).

5 THE CRIMINOLOGY OF INTOLERANCE: ZERO-TOLERANCE POLICING AND THE AMERICAN PRISON EXPERIMENT

In this chapter I wish to point to two of the most publicly manifest examples of social exclusion by the criminal justice system. Here the exclusionary tendencies in civil society are easily matched, and augmented, by state-initiated attempts to maintain order. Such interventions have reached their most pronounced form in the United States, as have the exclusionary tendencies of civil society – but the advocacy of zero-tolerance policing and of increasing imprisonment have ready resonances around the developed world.

> In the book I wrote some time ago with George Erdos, *Families Without Father-hood*, we tell a story about zero-tolerance, confident, policing in Sunderland in 1941. Three boys were sharing a Woodbine one Sunday morning in the loading bay of a town-centre store. A policeman appeared at one end of the short back lane, another at the other. The boys were marched home to their parents. (The boys and the policemen both walked a mile.) Their fathers smoked. The policemen smoked. But boys of twelve were not allowed to smoke. They certainly could not thumb their noses at generalized adult authority by smoking in public. The boys whose fathers were not away fighting in the war were in trouble with their fathers. All of them were in trouble with their mothers.
>
> If any journalist had seen fit to write an article condemning the waste of police resources on a trivial – and victimless – offence when their fathers and brothers were being killed at the front or at sea, his editor would have wondered what on earth his point could be. If the editor had published it, the public would have had difficulty in understanding what was being proposed – that because their fathers were absent, their sons should be allowed to flout rules that they would have upheld if they had been at home?
>
> When policing was detailed and consensual, we conclude, it was low-key, good humoured and effective. Of these three boys from working-class homes in terrace houses without gardens and opening straight onto the street, the products of depression and war, one became one of the town's best ship-yard welders, one a bank manager, and one the head of a polytechnic. (Dennis, *Zero-Tolerance: Policing in a Free Society*, 1997, p. 2)

The diversity of late modernity evokes a nostalgia for the inclusive, secure world of the past; the rise in crime and disorder characteristic of the period creates the demand for a quick fix, a panacea, in order to conjure back the secure streets and backyards of childhood memories. Father is at work (or at war), Mother at home, the bobby is on the beat, mischief is caught in the bud, and ill-doing firmly dealt with. Put the film on fast rewind: back to the future. . . .

The last third of the twentieth century witnessed a rise in crime in all advanced industrial countries with the possible exception of Japan. The increase occurred early in some countries, such as the United States, later in others, such as the Netherlands, but it seemed for a long time remorseless and inevitable. It occurred through periods of full employment and in the recession of the 1980s. Sometimes its force was dramatic: in one year alone in England and Wales (1991) the rise in the recorded crime rate was one and a quarter times that of the total crime rate in 1950. Often its impact was gradual but far-reaching in its eventual consequence. It occurred despite massive rises in living standards, expenditure in the criminal justice system and on crime prevention and measures of personal security. Experience of crime moved from the exceptional to become part of normal everyday life (Lea and Young, 1993; Garland, 1997) and the precautions against it seemed at times like some ghastly Maginot Line of colossal cost and minimal effectiveness. For a time the slogan became 'Nothing works' and the crime statistics were awaited with apprehension: as one Metropolitan Police Commissioner put it, they became like 'the sins of the community . . . annually visited upon the police'; and he noted that 'the "figures" beast has the strength of years in its veins and is an unconscionable time dying' (Newman, 1985, pp. 14–15).

Indeed by 1986 the London police, always traditionally eager to claim crime as 'their' problem, were only too ready to issue disclaimers; witness the bitterness of this Metropolitan Police document:

> It also seems wrong in principle that some of our more vociferous critics are allowed to enjoy multiple bites at the same cherry. On the one hand the Left argues that government policy has spread and intensified relative deprivation which they argue is criminogenic. At the same time they vilify the Force for failing to stem rising recorded crime rates and protect vulnerable Londoners. The government, on the other hand, pursues an economic policy, which includes a Treasury driven social policy, that has one goal – the reduction of inflation. Any adverse social by-products are accepted as necessary casualties in the pursuit of the overall objective.
>
> It might be more constructive to judge Force performance against a forecast that had taken account of extrinsic social and economic factors. (Metropolitan Police, 1986, pp. 115–16)

Yet at long last the tide seems to have turned (or at least halted). Between 1993 and 1995 the crime rate in 12 of 17 advanced industrial countries declined (Home Office, 1996) and various agencies of crime control began, once more, to claim the crime rate for themselves. None more so than in New York City, where the crime rate plummeted by 36% in three years (1993–96) and where some are claiming a 'miracle'. Indeed 'police leaders and consultants travel around the country preaching the new science of crime reduction and seeking miracles of their own' (Lardner, 1997, p. 54), whilst Commissioner Bratton who presided over the big change cheerfully announced 'Crime is Down in New York City: Blame it on the Police', George Kelling has embarked on a world tour expounding on the 'Broken Windows' philosophy which supposedly informs the miraculous event (Kelling and Coles, 1997) and, over a short period of time, the NYPD has become the most visited and researched police department in the world.

It comes as no surprise, therefore, that our own Home Secretary, Jack Straw, should announce in the first speech to a party conference since the Labour Party came to power, that he wanted 'zero tolerance of crime and disorder in our neighbourhoods' (September 1997), while the incoming Prime Minister of Ireland, Bertie Ahern, in May 1997 pledged himself to zero-tolerance with Bratton's Irish-born deputy John Timoney at his side (Shapiro, 1997).

A seminar in Westminster: the miracle revealed

On an afternoon in July 1997 I was invited to a seminar of the right wing think tank, the Institute for Economic Affairs. It was the day after the launch of the book *Zero-Tolerance: Policing in a Free Society* (Dennis, 1997) and was to be addressed by William J. Bratton, the ex-Commissioner of Police in New York City. The audience was a collection of distinguished right wing columnists, a few academics, someone from Conservative Central Office and the odd television journalist. They were looking for something that would quickly and dramatically solve the crime problem, that would set the world alight and reverse the processes of disorder that had beset the cities in the span of their lifetime. Here was a success story, New York City transformed from 'the crime capital of the world' to 'one of the safest big cities in the world': within the space of three years the crime rate dropping by 36% and homicide by over 50%.

On the way to the seminar I armed myself with doubt: had not zero-tolerance in Brixton, South London, led to the riots in 1981? How could Bratton possibly know that it was his policies and police force which had reduced the crime rate? Hadn't precisely the opposite methods been tried in San Diego with just as good results?

But before I turn to the revelations of the seminar, let us look at the concept itself. Zero-tolerance has become a buzz word in community safety in the last few years. Its aim on a policing level is to flag an intolerance of incivilities, to sweep the streets clean of deviance and disorder, to deal with aggressive beggars, squeegee merchants, loiterers, drunks and prostitutes. It intends to reverse the tendency to 'define deviance down' (Moynihan, 1993; Krauthammer, 1993). In penology, it is represented by 'the three strikes and you're out' policy, the war against drugs which has contributed to the steep rise in the US incarceration rate and in the demand for a reversal of the decline in the rates of imprisonment (see Murray, 1997).

The concept of zero-tolerance would seem to have six key components:

1 a lowering of tolerance to crime and deviance;
2 the use of punitive, somewhat drastic measures to achieve this;
3 a return to perceived past levels of respectability, order and civility;
4 the awareness of the continuum between incivilities and crime with both low spectrum 'quality of life' rule breaking and serious crimes being considered problems;
5 the belief that there is a relationship between crime and incivilities in that incivilities unchecked, by various routes, give rise to crime;
6 the key text repeatedly mentioned as the inspiration for this approach: Wilson and Kelling's classic 1982 article in *Atlantic Monthly*, entitled 'Broken Windows'.

But more of this later. Let us return to the seminar where the audience, suitably refreshed with white wine and canapés, were looking forward to hearing something dramatic from the Commissioner: a get tough policy that had worked. William Bratton was a bit of a revelation. He started by totally distancing himself from the concept of zero-tolerance: he thought that the notion was inadmissible in police work, the only exceptions, perhaps, being drug use and corruption within the police force. Discretion was a vital part of policing and this involved working out a joint plan with the communities concerned, taking note of their priorities and preferences. He agreed that action must be taken against the broad spectrum of crime and incivilities, he had read the Wilson and Kelling article in his previous job as Police Chief of Boston and it had confirmed his beliefs. But to deal with crime did not involve a rigid imposition of police control; furthermore, policing itself was only the first step, a holding operation, until the social changes which would engender a more stable society would hopefully be instituted. Finally, he had during his visit (which included a trip to Brixton) been impressed by the tranquil and relatively civil nature of London and warned of the problem of transposing too easily techniques which work in one context to another.

The audience was, to say the least, disappointed: they had come to hear that the simple and the dramatic would work but had heard largely a story of common sense laced with self-congratulation.

False claims and confused categories

It is time we examined the claims and disassembled the categories. The simple equation is that zero-tolerance is based on the philosophy of 'Broken Windows', was tried out in New York City and led to a reduction in crime. All of these links are, in fact, false: they are rhetoric substituting itself for reason, fiction blinding reason. Let us look at the links one by one:

1 *Crime was dramatically reduced in New York City in the period 1993–96.* This is the only part of the equation that is true: it is the bedrock of truth to which the false series of linkages is hitched. The homicide figures which are recognized as the most reliable of criminal statistics reduced by a remarkable 49.5% in this period (the lowest since 1968) and the gunshot wound victims treated by New York City Health and Hospital Corporation data showed a drop of 56.3% over these years (Jacobson, 1997). Both of these figures are extremely unlikely to have been falsified whatever pressures undoubtedly occurred on the NYPD to produce the 'best' statistics during this period of intense departmental and political agitation.

2 *The decrease was due to the specific innovative police practices of the New York Police Department.* Here we encounter the first of the false links. Most obviously such a claim is unreasonable because the decline in crime occurred in 17 of 25 of the largest US cities in the period 1993–96 (see Figure 5.1). It occurred in those cities which had explicitly adopted less aggressive policies (e.g. Los Angeles in the wake of the riots), in cities which utilize community-oriented policing such as Boston and San Diego (Pollard, 1997; Currie, 1997a). It occurred where there had been no change in policing (e.g. Oakland) and indeed in some places where there was a reduction in police officers. Differing police methods seemed to be associated with a drop in serious crime (Shapiro, 1997) and the crime rate in New York City had begun to drop *before* the new policing methods of Commissioner Bratton were instituted. Furthermore, the decline in crime occurred in cities across the industrialized world, long before zero-tolerance had become an international buzz word.

3 *Zero-tolerance was tried out in New York City.* Commissioner Bratton, as we have seen, explicitly denied to our disappointed seminar that he had implemented a zero-tolerance policy. For a blanket no-tolerance policy disallows police discretion and is well nigh impossible to implement in a modern disorderly city. To apply every letter of the law in, say, Harlem day in and day out would stretch the resources of any foreseeable police budget. Indeed, the movement in police focus from minor to more serious crimes (so lamented by Wilson and Kelling in 'Broken Windows') is very largely a function of the rise in crime: *the movement in police tolerance is not merely a function of lowering standards but of the pressure of demand on resources.* What Bratton did was shift the focus so that crimes of disorder would have a greater claim on police resources. He also instituted a series of other policing practices which had nothing whatsoever to do with zero-tolerance, e.g. the use of daily computerized statistics as a guide to results.

Furthermore, not only William Bratton but George Kelling strongly deny that zero-tolerance has any relationship with the philosophy of 'Broken Windows' (see B. Walsh, 1997).

The links between police practice in New York City and zero-tolerance and between the latter and the philosophy of 'Broken Windows' are strongly denied and tenuous.

4 *The 'Broken Windows' approach was tried out in New York City.* If

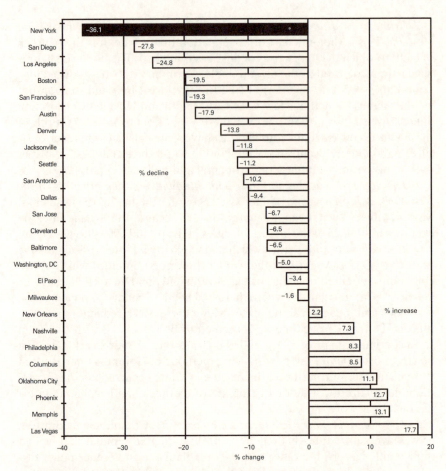

Chicago, Charlotte, Houston and Indianapolis were not included because of incomplete or inconsistent data for the 1993–96 comparison. These cities were replaced by Denver, Cleveland, New Orleans and Oklahoma City for this comparison.

FIGURE 5.1   *Percentage change in total FBI index crimes: 25 largest US cities, 1993–96*

zero-tolerance was not attempted in New York City, was the 'Broken Windows' approach implemented? Commissioner Bratton claims that this is so, indeed that as a police chief in Boston he had come to a realization of the effectiveness of this philosophy, so to speak, before he had read the article. And George Kelling, the co-author, very definitely claims that the ideas he authored with James Q. Wilson were the underlying philosophy. It is such a claim which underscores the triumphalism of his recent book, *Fixing Broken Windows* (Kelling and Coles, 1997).

The reality of 'Broken Windows'

Let us look once again at the classic article published in 1982 in the *Atlantic Monthly* and reprinted, with little change, in Wilson's bestselling book *Thinking about Crime* (1985). It is certainly the most influential article in the field of criminology in recent years. But like many such texts, it is rarely read and its clearly stated policy implications are simply not taken on board.

The background of the article is disillusionment with the efficacy of normal policing methods in part based on George Kelling's pioneer study in Newark, New Jersey and numerous other studies across the United States which suggested that policing had only a limited effect on crime rates (see Wilson, 1985, pp. 61–74; Kinsey et al., 1986, pp. 77–87). Such results were backed up by international research, particularly in Britain under the auspices of the Home Office (Morris and Heal, 1981; Clarke and Hough, 1984). This position represented a sea-change in attitudes to policing and a fundamental undermining of the conventional wisdom of the police as 'the thin blue line' in 'the fight' against crime. 'It may be,' Wilson writes:

> that judging the police solely or even chiefly by their ability to reduce crime is a mistake. Most police work involving crime occurs after the crime is committed and reported. . . . The traditional function of the police . . . was to maintain order in urban neighborhoods. In our concern over crime, we may have mistakenly though understandably turned for help to the most visible and familiar part of the criminal justice system and thereby made the police both the object of our hopes and the target of our frustrations. Perhaps we should stand back and view the police in a broader perspective, one which assigns them an important part, to be sure in crime control, but an even more important part in the maintenance of orderly neighborhoods. (1985, p. 74)

James Q. Wilson explicitly sets himself against what he views as conservative views of policing which believe that old-fashioned, no holds barred tough police tactics will solve the problem of crime. All of this is a far cry from the usual resonance of zero-tolerance. The police can have only a limited purchase on the problem of crime. Wilson is especially clear about this:

> To the extent we have learned anything at all, we have learned that the factors in our lives and history that most powerfully influence the crime rate – our commitment to liberty, our general prosperity, our child rearing methods, our popular values – are precisely the factors that are hardest or riskiest to change. Those things that can more easily and safely be changed – the behavior of the police, the organization of neighborhoods, the management of the criminal justice system, the sentences imposed by courts – are the things that have only limited influence on the crime rate. (ibid., p. 250)

Such a reallocation of the police from central to a more peripheral role in crime control is one which finds ready agreement amongst criminologists of all theoretical persuasions.

Wilson and Kelling's insight was that the control of minor offenders and disorderly behaviour which was not criminal was as important to a community as crime control. Incivilities, 'quality of life' crimes caused a major part of the citizens' feeling of unease in the city. And to this absolutely spot-on insight they added two more contentious propositions. Namely, that the police who were ineffective in the control of serious crime would be easily effective against disorderly behaviour. Indeed that that was their traditional role. And that control of incivilities would, so to speak, kick-start the community out of despair and disintegration and such a revitalized community through informal controls and citizens' vigilance would *in time* reverse the spiral of decay and reduce the incidence of serious crime. I do not want to enter into a critique of this philosophy; my point is that it is scarcely a programme of zero-tolerance against all crime which believes that the police are the key actors in the creation of orderly society and which views the 'sweeping up' of the streets as producing miraculous and immediate results. It is a more subtle theory, it has a more marginal role for the police and it situates the wellspring of social order in more fundamental parts of the social structure. Finally, it talks not of zero-tolerance but of discretion bordering on *realpolitik*. What police chief or politician would subscribe to the following policy nostrum?

> each department must assign its existing officers with great care. Some neighborhoods are so demoralized and crime-ridden as to make foot patrol useless; the best the police can do with limited resources is respond to the enormous number of calls for service. Other neighborhoods are so stable and serene as to make foot patrol unnecessary. The key is to identify neighborhoods at the tipping point – where the public order is deteriorating but not unreclaimable, where the streets are used frequently but by apprehensive people, where a window is likely to be broken at any time and must quickly be fixed if all are not to be shattered.
>
> Most police departments do not have ways of systematically identifying such areas and assigning officers to them. Officers are assigned on the basis of crime rates (meaning that marginally threatened areas are often stripped so that police can investigate crimes in areas where the situation is hopeless)... (ibid., p. 88)

Moral panics and panaceas: folk devils and fairy princesses

Why is it that such miracles are so easily propagated and dispensed across the globe? What is it that makes the notion of the quick fix, the one-off cure so attractive to wide sections of the public? To answer this I want to briefly look at the stance of the mass media, the material predicament of claim-making agencies and the psychological set of people in the pluralistic world of late modernity.

The mass media

The central key to newsworthiness is, as I have emphasized elsewhere, the atypical: that which surprises, which is in contrast to a posited everyday 'normality' (see Young, 1971a; Cohen and Young, 1981). Criminologists and students of deviance have not surprisingly concerned themselves with the negative side of the atypical: villains, serial killers, folk devils and other monsters. But the positive side, stars, heroes, fairy princesses who die in tragic circumstances, are also a site of media focus and the projection of public hopes and anxieties. And exactly the same processes of media selection, accentuation and construction of news occurs here as it does on the dark side of human existence. Thus although crime waves are a staple of news, so are 'miraculous' cures of crime (whether they be nutrition supplements, CCTV, Neighbourhood Watch, DNA testing or zero-tolerance in New York City). Moral panics and moral panaceas go hand in hand, and are the daily stock of news reporting just as are the repeated tragic tales of those inflicted with cancer and the regular 'revolutionary' breakthroughs in its treatment. Over and above this the backcloth of public expectancy in the Western world has been of a regular, somewhat remorseless increase in crime: the sudden decline of crime in of all places New York City, in the violent streets of Scorsese and Lumet, is a miracle indeed!

To this need for and search for miracles and breakthroughs, institutionalized within newsgathering organizations is added a common objective, a drive to generate news in small, simple units which fit the insistent bitty nature of programming. The sound-bite, the fleeting picture that tells it all, combined with an underlying message which winds up the public: 'The solution is simple, why don't *they* try it out here?' is a formula for one-dimensional simplicity and the quick fix.

Claim-making agencies

These make their living from convincing government and public that they have a ready solution to the crime problem. They can be either small independent entrepreneurs (e.g. private drug clinics or crime prevention agencies) or entrepreneurial groups within large organizations (e.g. specialized police drug or burglary units). Their role is to claim and compete for the ownership of social problems (Gusfield, 1989) in contrast with the usually larger organizations that attend to the daily business of social control, which more often than not adopt the role of *disclaiming agencies*. Their concern is more with the processing, administration and warehousing of deviance rather than the rehabilitation or cure of their subjects. It is only when the statistics go remarkably in their direction – as in the case of Commissioner Bratton and New York City – that claim-making is enthusiastically embraced. Such opportunities have been rare in the post-war period. It is scarcely surprising that the Commissioner of Police and the Mayor of New York City should believe in miracles: who after all would look a gift horse in the mouth?

The public

The era of late modernity brings with it a pluralism of value, a world where the embeddedness of the citizen in the setting of occupation, marriage and community becomes precarious and daily threatened. Such ontological insecurity has as one response a need for secure definitions of norms, coupled very often with nostalgia: a desire to redraw the boundaries of behaviour back to an imagined past of civility and predictability. The attraction of zero-tolerance policies is obvious in such a world: they define our tolerance of deviance in terms of a nostalgic past, promising a one-off sweep of the disorder which confronts them. Outside of these immediate pressures, there is a general cultural predisposition to belief in the easy miracle and the instant cure. This lies in two basic fallacies entrenched within conventional wisdom, which I will detail below.

The cosmestic fallacy and the social as simple

The seminar was on the look-out for a quick fix, a simple solution to the problem of crime; its particular politics determined its fixation with zero-tolerance, but panaceas of many varieties are on offer. More liberal audiences, for example, might have preferred the magic of Neighbourhood Watch, or of CCTV, or nutritional supplements or the treatment of offender dyslexia or psychodrama in Grendon Underwood. Take your pick, the fashions come and go – all suffer equally from the two fallacies.

The cosmetic fallacy conceives of crime as a superficial problem of society, skin deep, which can be dealt with using the appropriate ointment, rather than as any chronic ailment of society as a whole. It engenders a cosmetic criminology which views crime as a blemish which suitable treatment can remove from a body which is, itself, otherwise healthy and in little need of reconstruction. Such criminology *distances* itself from the core institutions and proffers technical, piecemeal solutions. It, thus, reverses causality: crime causes problems for society rather than society causes the problem of crime. Although this belief is easily held when crime is a relatively unusual behaviour, the more common it becomes the more difficult it is to hold this belief without suggesting that crime itself is usually trivial in nature and impact. Such a position has its adherents although the vast majority of academic criminologists, whether conservative or liberal in their disposition, do not find this logic satisfactory.

The second fallacy revolves around the remarkably widely accepted idea that the social world is a relatively simple structure in which rates of different social events (e.g. marriage, suicides, strikes, crimes) can be related to narrowly delineated changes in other parts of the structure. In fact the social world is a complex interactive entity in which any particular social intervention can have only a limited effect on other social events and where the calculation of this effect is always difficult. Thus the crime rate is affected by a large number of things: by the level of deterrence exerted by the criminal justice system, to be sure, but also by the levels of informal control in the community, by patterns of employment, by types of child rearing, by the cultural, political and moral climate, by the level of organized crime, by the patterns of illicit drug use, etc., etc. To merely add together all these factors is complicated enough but insufficient, for it does not allow human assessment and reflexivity – the *perceived* injustice of unemployment, for instance, or the *felt* injustices of bad policing or imprisonment. For the social is not only complex, like the natural world (who would ever think that only one factor would explain the weather?). It is even more intricate because each factor can be transformed over time by human interpretation. To take imprisonment, for example, the same sentence can be perceived by the individual as perfectly just ('I had it coming'), or as an unjust and unwarranted reaction to a petty crime which stokes up further resentment, leading to more serious crime in the future, or as a rite of passage which everyone in one's social circle goes through. Strange and distinctly unlinear relationships can occur. Low rates of imprisonment can act as an effective deterrent when the community is in accord as to the venality of the crime and the impartiality of the criminal justice system. In contrast, high rates of imprisonment can be counterproductive where they are seen as grossly unfair with regard to the level of gravity of the offence and the degree to which the system focuses on some sections of the community rather than others.

It is important to stress how both the notion of the cosmetic nature of crime as a problem and its simplicity flies in the face of a consensus across the varied political and theoretical perspectives of modern criminology. James Q. Wilson, as we have seen, views the source of crime as involving basic values of liberty – child rearing, prosperity – which in his estimation we are least likely to wish to change. An impulsive, consumer-oriented society with permissive child rearing habits will produce criminals – policing and prisons can manipulate only the surface of the problem. This is the basis of his 'realism'; whole areas of the city are beyond redemption, his criminology is one of the containment of crime, not of fundamental reduction, let alone elimination. Listen to Wilson, the major architect of the recent war against drugs, talk of the result of this massive and costly intervention:

> Many people ... think, we have lost the war on drugs. ... [but] We did not surrender and we did not lose. We did not win, either. What the nation accomplished then was what most efforts to save people from themselves accomplished, the problem was contained and the number of victims minimized, all at considerable cost in law enforcement and increased crime. (1992, p. 36)

And Wilson, the hard-bitten 'realist' is perhaps the most optimistic of those on the right of the political spectrum. Travis Hirschi, the influential founder of control theory, ends *A General Theory of Crime,* which he co-authored with Michael Gottfredson:

the state is neither the cause of nor the solution to crime. In our view, the origins of criminality of low self-control are to be found in the first six or eight years of life, during which time the child remains under the control and supervision of the family or a familial institution. Apart from the limited benefits that can be achieved by making specific criminal acts more difficult, policies directed toward enhancement of the ability of familial institutions to socialize children are the only realistic long-term state policies with potential for substantial crime reduction. (1990, pp. 272–3)

And in an article in *Society* they lambast American crime policy in the following terms:

Lacking a theory to guide it, crime policy relies on the unexamined slogans and catch phrases of an ostensibly stretched-thin and embattled constabulary, with its emphasis on career criminals, boot camps, drug testing, 'intermediate sanctions,' gang units, and ever-increasing prison terms.

The proper response to these circumstances is to return to social theory and research. Recent events demonstrate too well that nothing is more dangerous than a policy justified only by the ambitions of politicians and bureaucrats. (1995, p. 30)

Even Charles Murray, who advocates the widespread use of zero-tolerance methods together with extensive use of imprisonment, believes that these methods will not tackle the root causes, they will contain 'not win the war' and that 'if you are looking for a return to 1950s crime levels . . . you are going to be disappointed' (1997, p. 20).

The shift into late modernity

Both of these fallacies, the belief in the cosmetic nature of crime and the notion of the social as simple, become even more difficult to sustain as we shift into late modernity.

Let us take the cosmetic fallacy first of all. The movement from an inclusive to an exclusive society involves an unravelling of the labour markets: a creation of large sectors of the population who are either economically precarious or actually excluded. Relative deprivation becomes blatant in the comparisons across such a dislocated social terrain. Meanwhile, the same market forces which transform the labour market generate a new world of lifestyle and consumerism on the back of which emerges an individualism which permeates society (see Currie, 1997a). Crime springs from this combination and becomes a normal feature of everyday life (see Lea and Young, 1993; Garland, 1996). The incidence of crime, although always much more widespread than official figures suggest, spreads palpably and obviously across the map. Criminal areas remain but there are fewer and fewer areas with low rates of conventional crime; serious, repeat offences still occur yet now there are far many more of them and the casual offender is commonplace. We cease to use the word 'criminal' and substitute 'offender'; the belief in the delimited number of distinct criminals beloved by positivism becomes much less sustainable, even within their own ranks, and neo-positivism begins to conflate the rational offender with the rational citizen; indeed the opportunistic thief is cast in the same mould as the impulsive shopper (see Clarke, 1980).

In such a world it is harder to ascribe crime to the individual criminal with a maverick dysfunctional background or to areas which 'progress' left behind. The cosmetic blemish has spread throughout society. Let me give an example. Geoff Pearson and his associates, in their brilliant study of the British heroin epidemic of the early 1980s, note that although heroin addiction is compatible with widely varying lifestyles which contradict the 'junkie' stereotype:

> Research has established over many years that heroin addiction is compatible with widely varying lifestyles – from stable addicts with a more-or-less normal family life and employment record, to those who live a chaotic 'junkie' lifestyle, living by crime and by doses of imprisonment. . . . Nevertheless, it is probably true that a decade ago the 'typical' heroin user would be more likely to have been someone leading a bohemian-type lifestyle, or to have been someone with some form of temperamental instability. However, as the heroin using population has steadily grown in recent years this has undoubtedly become less true, so that although some individuals are psychologically more vulnerable to opiate misuse, attempts to explain heroin use solely in terms of personality factors and psychopathology are nowadays quite inadequate. (1985, p. 8)

Alan, one of their interviewees, an experienced ex-user put it nicely:

> 'Oh you know how it was, like. You used to be able to tell 'em a mile off, well you used to be able to . . . typical junkies, you know, scars up their arms, clapped-out hippies, that kind of thing, the whole works . . . you know what I mean. . . . But now, well, I don't know about you, but I couldn't tell one if I fell over him in the street.' (Alan, 24 years, Manchester). (ibid., p. 9)

The normalization of drug use is paralleled by the normalization of crime. It is no longer possible to talk of the isolated cosmetic blemishes; the spot, if you wish, has become a rash! Furthermore, it is not a great step from the normalization of crime to the normalization of the criminal. Such a shift involves a turning away from the modernist notion of the distinct criminal with his (*sic*) distinctive causality. Such a loss of the fixed locus of offenders is paralleled by the way in which the offence itself, so clear cut in neo-classicism, becomes blurred and continuous with a wide range of behaviours. In modernity positivism provided us with the notion of a small number of distinct criminals with their own individualistic aetiology – maverick characters, the product of dire and atypical situations – whilst neo-classicism delineated the clear-cut legal parameters of the crime. Late modernity loses the precision of both offender and offence; offenders are everywhere, offences blur together with a host of anti-social behaviours.

Let us turn now to the second fallacy: the social as simple. Here, too, the notion that the social world is simple, that intervention verges on the obvious and that measurement is easy, becomes even more stretched and tenuous. If the social world has always been complex and more resilient to change than the material world – this is the more so in the late modern period. The complex becomes more complex, the intransigent more intransigent, its measurement more elusive than ever. If we think of intervention as consisting of two components, input (the variables to be changed) and output (the effect of the intervention and its measurement), it helps to look at the stages of this process in a late modern society. Where there is a markedly greater pluralism of value and a social system which is less inclusive and integrated.

Input

Public priorities   In a modernistic society experts proclaimed public priorities and bestowed, so to speak, problems on the public. In late modernity, experts are less able to successfully designate problems to a receptive public; 'authoritative' sources, whether experts in nuclear power, food hygiene, transport, drugs or crime, are much more readily questioned. Authority is less respected and, furthermore, authority has a stranger and stranger habit of disagreeing amongst itself (Giddens, 1991; Beck, 1992). Expert opinion is less able to present itself as detached from interest groups or, even worse, as the objective singular pronouncement of science: experts speak with many voices and the cacophony of opinion is presented readily and competitively in the mass media. The media, themselves, have become more profligate and extensive, they constantly present a wide array of problems which differ and which change with remarkable speed and alacrity (McRobbie and Thornton, 1995). Meanwhile, the public itself is more heterogeneous: it shares some priorities but it disputes others and it is more frequently unclear and vacillating as to the problems of the community. What, therefore, are the problems to be tackled and which is the desirable outcome become contested and uncertain.

The variables available   The standard inventory of interventions to lessen crime include, in the forefront: the police, the community, the family, the economy, the educational system. All of these variables are weakened in late modernity. The community has become less cohesive, talk of reasserting community values fails to confront how we are to achieve this nostalgic dream, while policies of rehabilitation within the community are either wishful thinking or cynical manoeuvres which leave mental patients roaming the streets or ex-offenders bereft of support and sustenance. The ability to provide jobs with long term futures and security capable of building people into the social order depends on global forces not within the power of central, let alone local, government. Much of the fundamental repertoire of social democracy is enfeebled (see Hofman, 1993) and the standard conservative options of strengthening the family and the criminal justice system are less easy to implement. As we have seen, thoughtful commentators such as James Q. Wilson (1985) readily admit that the factors most effective in the crime rate are hardest to change. And even those reasonably easy to change, such as number of police or prisoners, or the moral stance of the schools, are grossly undermined by the weakened forces of family, community and employment.

The changing values of interventions   As society shifts into late modernity some strange things happen to variables: in a plural society the value and even the charge of a variable changes as it passes from one subset of society to another and changes with increased volatility over time. Let me give two examples: a given sentence of imprisonment, say two years, will differ in meaning and impact whether one is a man or a woman, whether professional or unemployed, whether young or old. For some part of the inner city in the United States the prison sentence amongst young blacks becomes so commonplace (where perhaps one in four young men is in prison at any one time) that doing time becomes 'earning your stripes' and is scarcely a negative status. In the context of the American penal experiment as a whole, the units of penality begin to change valence and in wide swathes of society correctional supervision (probation, parole or prison) is scarcely a stigma but rather a normal fact of life, like having your driving licence endorsed or a minor illness. Or let us take a more positive variable: wages. An extra payment per hour offered in work (say £2 per hour) will vary in attractiveness widely through the structure. Of course it will not be noticed by those in middle incomes upwards, but whereas it will be seen as a welcome inducement to commit oneself to work by those on lower to middling incomes, it may well be regarded as a nonsense by those caught in the well dramatized 'poverty trap'.

Output

Measurement   The problem of measurement in criminology (and indeed the social sciences in general) is that different audiences define the 'same' behaviour differently. What is violence to one person is of little or no consequence to another. The macho-adolescent gang member and the middle class professional will have totally different scales (see Young, 1988; Mooney, 1998). As pluralism increases in late modernity, the scales multiply between subsets of the population and are volatile over time. To take another example, definitions of what is vandalism will vary from one group on the same housing estate to another (particularly by age and gender) and, even more confusingly, definitions of unsightly vandalism may change rapidly over time.

Culture of congratulation   The need to have hard-headed accountancy of

crime control measures is paramount. Yet a culture of congratulation permeates the crime control industry; if, for example, one tenth of the reports
by practitioners working in the field of drug abuse were correct, we would
have solved the drugs problem years ago. Such a problem is particularly
prevalent at a time where there are relatively frequent decreases in crime
rates. The temptation to claim declines for one's own agencies is so attractive as to undermine any professional restraint. We must replace a culture of
congratulation with one of scepticism.

Displacement   Displacement is an inevitable result of any social intervention. It is not a technical problem which, with enough ingenuity, can be
avoided: the question in any society is not whether but when, where and to
what degree displacement occurs. A further question, less frequently asked,
is to whom? 'Benign displacement', as Roger Matthews has argued, should
aim 'to limit the level and impact of victimisation by deflecting crime and
incivilities away from the most vulnerable populations' (1992, p. 46). Late
modernity is characterized by a widening gap between those in the primary
labour market and those in the secondary markets or out of the labour
market altogether. Crime control strategies must be seen in the light of
these social divisions and displacement be judged not as a marginal technical problem. As it is, evidence suggests that the wider social division within
society is exacerbated by increased disparities in criminal victimization (see
Hope, 1996).

The limits of tolerance

In the above discussion, I have analysed zero-tolerance in terms of its effectiveness and its degree of conceptual clarity. We have been concerned with
what it is and does it work? Let us turn, finally, to perhaps the most central
problem of all: the ethical and political question of tolerance. What does
tolerance mean in a liberal democracy? Where should the lines of normality and deviancy be best drawn in a late modern world?

   Until now we have discussed *the criminology of intolerance*. That is the
intolerance forged by an intensive policing which focuses on marginalized
people and minor infractions paralleling the intolerance of the prison
system which regularly increases numbers every year. This recent pattern is
in contrast to a generation of liberal opinion and scholarship whose aim was
to minimize police intervention and lower police numbers. One might even
say that this has been the hidden agenda of academic criminology ever since
the nineteenth century. The implicit assumption being that a liberal democratic state implies minimal penality and, more recently, that the aim is to
create a society tolerant of diversity and difference – the very *reverse* of
zero-tolerance.

   At this juncture the easiest thing would be to close this chapter with a
resounding criticism of zero-tolerance as part and parcel of the new

penology. That is to roundly condemn it as a manoeuvre which aims to sweep the streets clean of human 'debris'; part of the process of exclusion concomitant with the emergence of a society with a large marginalized and impoverished population that has to be suppressed and contained – an actuarial processing concerned more with sanitization than justice (Young, 1998). For the contented shoppers in the mall must not be disturbed by the antics of the dispossessed, drinking strong lager in the middle of the day. All of this is true, but such an easy conclusion is not the answer for the predicament contains a contradiction central to criminology and close to the concerns of realism.

The crux of this matter becomes evident when we turn to the other discourse of zero-tolerance – that of feminism. For the feminist advocacy of campaigns for zero-tolerance of violence against women clearly parallels the policing initiatives of the same name. They have their origins in the Canadian 'Family Violence Initiative' started by the Federal Government in the wake of the 'Montreal Massacre' of 6 December 1989 of 14 young women, mostly engineering students, by a man enraged that they were encroaching on the male preserve (Foley, 1993). The slogan was imported by Edinburgh District Council Women's Committee, who launched their famous campaign for zero-tolerance of violence against women in November 1992 (see Kutzinger and Hunt, 1993) and was taken up by various London boroughs (for an evaluation, see Mooney, 1998). Here we have a campaign which advocates zero-tolerance but who in their right mind would not agree that we should be intolerant of violence against women, sexual attacks and child abuse?

Not only then is there confusion over the term zero-tolerance in relation to policing, but there is another contrasting usage put to good use by the women's movement. There are great differences, of course; feminist zero-tolerance does not suggest that there should be any discretion in standards as do Wilson and Kelling. Violence against women is not tolerated anywhere in society whether amongst the rich or the poor. The same standard must be applied everywhere but there is no nostalgia, no Golden Age of the past in here. For the past for women was never 'golden', violence was always present in patriarchal society. It is not nostalgic, but progressive: it seeks to gain a world, to raise standards not resuscitate the past.

Of course the answer to the contradiction between the two discourses of zero-tolerance is that we could heed one and ignore the other: one can be zero-tolerant of violence against women and tolerant about the activities of the dispossessed. This would not only violate the universalistic prescriptions of the feminist discourse (all violent behaviour against women is proscribed wherever it occurs) but would be an act of bad faith only too common in liberal circles. That is to harbour the sort of mind-set which was criticized in the early realist literature:

> There was a schizophrenia about crime on the left where crimes against women and immigrant groups were quite rightly an object of concern, but other types of crime were regarded as being of little interest, or somehow excusable. Part of this mistake

stems, as we have noted, from the belief that property offences are directed solely against the bourgeoisie and that violence against the person is carried out by amateur Robin Hoods in the course of their righteous attempt to redistribute wealth. All of this is, alas, untrue. Indeed, the irony is that precisely the same kids who break into the next-door neighbour's flat sit around the estates wearing British Movement badges and harassing Asians. (Lea and Young, 1984, p. 262)

Furthermore there are very significant similarities between the two discourses. Both wish, obviously, to reduce tolerance – to, in the phrase, 'define deviancy up'. And both are concerned with the range of infractions: that is they are worried by both what are regarded by all as serious offences and by the more minor 'quality of life' crimes. Feminists, in particular, are concerned about how everyday 'normal' male incivilities such as sexual harassment at work or in the street affect the peace of mind and freedom of women's movement through public space.

This takes us back to 'Broken Windows'. Wilson and Kelling's major insight was that the cumulative effect of minor incivilities poses as much of a problem to the public as crime itself. Their limitation is that they tend to hold incivilities apart from crime at times as if they were two *separate* problems rather than crime and deviancy being part of the same phenomenon with the same causes.[1] An awareness of the continuum nature of crime and incivilities, the importance of their overall impact and their common cause is present in both the left realist and the radical feminist literature. Witness:

Crime is the end-point of a continuum of disorder. It is not separate from other forms of aggravation and breakdown. It is the run-down council estate where music blares out of windows early in the morning; it is the graffiti on the walls; it is aggression in the shops; it is bins that are never emptied; oil stains across the streets; it is kids that show no respect; it is large trucks racing through your roads; it is streets you do not dare walk down at night; it is always being careful; it is a symbol of a world falling apart. It is lack of respect for humanity and for fundamental human decency. . . .

. . . racial harassment . . . ranges from clearly criminal offences to just plain nuisance. But they cannot be separated out: the nuisance boils over into criminal violence. The crime sticks in our mind as the most blatant example of such antisocial behaviour, but it is only the tip of the iceberg. A lot of the more frequent, everyday offences are scarcely criminal – they are 'just' kids fooling around – but they are part and parcel of the same appalling aggression towards defenceless people. It is items like this that rebuff those commentators who maintain that because most crime is 'minor', it is unimportant.

A parallel phenomenon to such racist aggression is the sexual harassment of women. Women have to take a considerable amount of sexual harassment at work and in the streets, which severely restricts their ability to move in public spaces, particularly at night. Rape is the end-point of the continuum of aggressive sexual behaviour. Its comparative rarity does not indicate the absence of antisocial behaviour towards women. On the contrary, it is a real threat which also symbolizes a massive undercurrent of harassment. (Lea and Young, 1984, pp. 55–8)

At approximately the same time feminist academics such as Liz Kelly (1987;

Kelly and Radford, 1987) were developing the work of American activists (e.g. Medea and Thompson, 1974) who emphasized the continuum of violence against women.

Thus the notion of a continuum emerged in the criminological literature in the 1980s in three different theoretical traditions: establishment criminology, radical feminism, and left realism. It is pertinent to ask what events exterior to the academy called up this response in the academy. There are to my mind three main changes which relate to the emergence of a late modern world:

1 The last third of the twentieth century has been characterized not only by an increase in crime and disorder but by crime becoming more disorderly and disorder blurring into crime (an early sighting of this is S. Cohen, 1973). Crime becomes less separate from disorder, and poor neighbourhoods which once had select bands of professional criminals who terrorized targeted members of the public (banks, shops, clubs and each other) became racked by amateurish crime. Market individualism flourishes (see Currie, 1997a), delinquency becomes more internecine and Hobbesian: disorder becomes as much of a problem as crime and is more clearly part of a continuum.

2 The development of pluralistic societies entails widespread conflict between groups over what is orderly and disorderly behaviour. The need for tolerance between groups becomes a major issue whereas the limits of tolerance become increasingly disputed. One person's order is disorder for another, one group's 'normal' behaviour creates intolerable conditions for others.

3 One of the major transformations in the social structure is the changed role of women. The entry of women into the labour market has as a consequence the increased transit of women through public space for purposes both of work and leisure. The growing economic equality with men demands an equality of respect and of freedom to come and go undisturbed and unharmed. Women are less willing to tolerate male impositions on their behaviour and security, they enter more significantly politically and economically into public life and they bring with them much greater intolerance of violence and abuse. The feminization of demands on law and order is a key factor in the transformation of public discourse.

The debate about tolerance and growing demands for law and order – concomitant, with the rise in intolerable behaviour – are thus central to both the public and academic discourses with regard to crime and deviancy. Indicative of this is the famous article by Daniel Patrick Moynihan, 'Defining Deviancy Down' (1993). In this he suggests that a response to the rising tide of crime and disorder is simply to define less disorder, whether criminality, family breakdown or mental illness, as deviant. In a way zero-tolerance is a reaction to this – it is an attempt to roll back the levels of tolerance and in its policing aspect carries with it a criticism of

the liberalism which it is supposed has 'allowed' this to happen. As Bruce
Shapiro puts it:

> Zero-tolerance policing unquestionably makes for effective campaign rhetoric,
> and the original Wilson and Kelling broken window hypothesis is an easy sell to
> any society frightened by seemingly uncontrollable crime. On its deepest level,
> however, it is not about crime at all, but a vision of social order disintegrating
> under glassy-eyed liberal neglect. Much of Wilson and Kelling's original argu-
> ment, and Kelling and Coles' recent book, is devoted not to crime policy but to
> repeated attacks on civil libertarians, advocates for the homeless and social liber-
> als. Disorder, Kelling and Coles (1997) write, 'proliferated with the growth of an
> ethos of individualism and increasing legislative and judicial support for protect-
> ing the fundamental rights of individuals at the expense of community interest'.
> Over and over, Kelling and Coles blame the 1960s for that ethos: 'The expression
> of virtually all forms of non-violent deviance came to be considered synonymous
> with the expression of individual, particularly First Amendment or speech-related
> rights.' Civil libertarians even get the blame for the proliferation of the homeless
> mentally ill in American streets – as if the Reagan administration had not cut their
> community support programmes and eliminated public housing construction, as
> if real estate speculators had not gentrified thousands of formerly affordable
> single-room housing units.
>   The course of violent crime is complex, and inextricable from the fate of cities
> and the poor. Here is the real danger of the zero-tolerance gospel: it severs crime
> from context, and instead of a clear vision of a safe society offers only an illusory
> obsession with order at all costs. (1997, p. 6)

Shapiro underscores my argument: it is the social context, the structural
problems of the system which produce crime rates. It is obvious that the
increased 'tolerance' levels of the criminal justice systems throughout the
Western world were a product of the exceptional growth of pressure upon
them rather than 'liberalism' and that the values of individualism and
immediate gratification which contribute so greatly to our crime problem
are not a product of a free-floating permissiveness but of the market society
which flourished in the last part of the twentieth century (see Currie, 1997a).
Crime rates relate to the material conditions within a society: the criminal
justice system, whether scripted by liberal ideals or by a draconian conservative morality, cannot make more than a marginal impact on the overall
crime rates. It can contain a problem, but the problem, as Ramsey Clark so
eloquently argued long ago in *Crime in America* (1970), will simply recur
unless it is addressed. It is necessary not merely to punish offenders for
breaking windows, but to actually mend the windows. That is to engage in
a thorough programme of social reconstruction in our cities. Zero-tolerance
of crime must mean zero-tolerance of inequality if it is to mean anything.

The American prison experiment

Let us now turn to the second pillar of the criminology of intolerance: the
increased use of imprisonment. The rationale for this is not that of simple

intolerance, as many liberals would suggest, but rather that as crime rates soared in the post-war period the criminal justice system was unable to keep up with the pace, and the risk of going to prison for having committed a crime declined. Thus Charles Murray in *Does Prison Work?* (1997) presents us with the two graphs contrasting England and Wales with the United States. In the former we have a simple decline in imprisonment and a rise in crime whilst in the latter the US prison initiative, the much more active use of prison, has attempted to bring back the risk of imprisonment to that of the 1950s.

The rate of crime is an inverse function of the chances of going to prison. What a simple formula and how easy could be the life of the criminologist if it were true! For the rates are, on the face of it, easily measurable and the nostrum which Charles Murray presents us with has a heavy leavening of common sense. Indeed, Figure 5.2 shows quite clearly that crime rose in England and Wales as risk rates declined, whilst the obverse occurred in the United States. The American experiment is thus seemingly a success story and the prison boat that arrived across the Atlantic, as I write this chapter, to be docked somewhat controversially in Portland Harbour, is a tangible export of American know-how and initiative when faced with the intransigent problem of crime.

Charles Murray is a brilliant polemicist: he has a knack of taking the conventional wisdoms of libertarianism and dramatically 'proving' the converse. He has done this throughout his career: in *Losing Ground* (1984), he lambasted the welfare state for generating 'welfare dependency', in *The Emerging British Underclass* (1990) he argues that such dependency has generated an attendant culture where accountability for behaviour is undermined and the disciplines of the family and community disintegrate, whilst in *The Bell Curve* (1994), written with Richard Herrnstein, he provocatively endorses the existing social structure as increasingly reflecting differences in intelligence between classes and races rather than inadequacies in the meritocracy. How compatible these theories are I am unsure. In the first book he has the poor as rational calculator evaluating the benefits of idleness as against work or crime as against honesty; in the second, in Murray's words, their 'habits of virtue' inculcated as youths are seriously eroded and in the last the poor are the lowest 'cognitive class', incapable of accurate assessment of risks and rewards. I sometimes test my students by calling them Murray I, Murray II and Murray III and ask them to try to draw lines of logic between them. On the face of it, they are not compatible. For example, they employ divergent theories of crime: in the first crime occurs because of rational calculation, in the second it is because of lack of suitable upbringing (because of single mothers and feckless fathers), in the third delinquency occurs out of stupidity. In one the poor are rational calculators just like you or me (only poorer), in the second they actively endorse cultures which flirt with risk, in the last they are congenitally less aware of risk. Human nature may not have 'miraculously changed' in the twentieth century, as he argues in his conclusion, but it seems to change within the

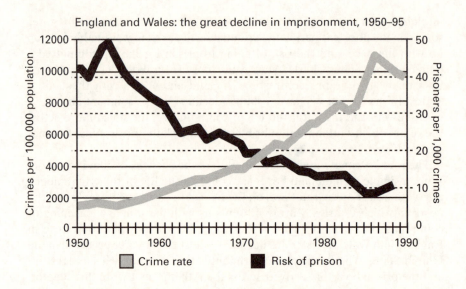

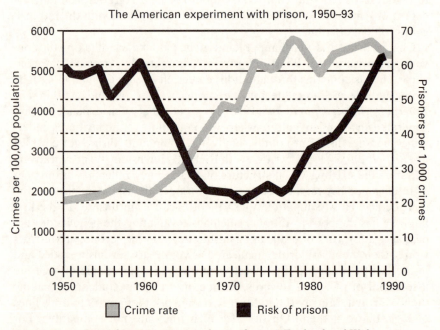

FIGURE 5.2   *Rate of imprisonment and rate of crime: England and Wales and the US*

corpus of his own work. But even more miraculous is his new book *Does Prison Work?* (1997). For here, let us note, he starts off with a very strong statement of the inverse relationship between risk of imprisonment and crime, which is premised on the rational calculator (Murray I) but by the middle of his text his argument crumbles and Murray II emerges. (Murray

III, thankfully, does not set foot in the argument.) For 'habits of virtue' have been irretrievably eroded and the threat of imprisonment, by page 19, is no longer a magic nostrum. It does not affect the root causes of crime, it will never result in a return to 1950s levels of virtue; it is 'a standoff', an amelioration of a dire situation rather than a solution. For it is, he acknowledges, only by tackling the problems at source that crime rates can be substantially reduced.

But let us turn back to the strong version of his thesis, for this is the message that will surely grab the reader: namely, that there is a direct and obvious relationship between high risk of imprisonment and the level of crime. This formula is a classic of common sense, yet it is as incorrect as its opposite, the rather irritating liberal assumption that the crime rate has nothing whatsoever to do with the imprisonment rate. Indeed, the fact that both beliefs exist side by side as self-evident in the public consciousness allows Charles Murray the leverage to dismiss one by appealing to the, just as impossible, mirror opposite. At heart the problem is the recurrent notion that *the social is simple*. Namely, that the social world is a relatively simple structure in which rates of different social events (e.g. marriages, suicides, strikes, crimes) can be related to narrowly delineated changes in other parts of the structure.

So it would be truly remarkable if there were to be found a simple relationship between risk of imprisonment and the rate of crime where there was a one-to-one relationship, with all other factors fading into the background. This is even more so given the timescale (1950–90) which Murray takes to contrast the United States and Britain. This is a period which all social commentators agree has involved a battery of changes, constituting perhaps the most significant structural transformation of industrial societies in the last hundred years. Patterns of employment have changed, family and marriage have altered ineradicably, the role of women has been transformed, youth cultures have flourished, illicit drug use has spread, communities have disintegrated, the mass media have taken on a pivotal role in our lives, and even factors which Murray has himself stressed as relating to crime rates – the changing role of the welfare state and the emergence of an underclass of structurally unemployed – have arisen. And yes, *also* the rate of risk of imprisonment has changed. Surely it would demand a miracle for one factor to override all these others, for all the factors to change exactly in parallel in two very different cultures, and for a simple inverse law to be so easily and unambiguously detected? Yet this is what Charles Murray asks us to believe in the strong version of his thesis: with his dimmer switch theory of crime, turn the risk of imprisonment up and the crime rates fade.

Let us look at some of the evidence. At the very least one might expect countries with high risks of imprisonment to have low crime rates. The international comparison of crime rates is notoriously difficult because of differences in definitions of serious crime and the size of the hidden figure in each country. But homicide figures are reasonably indicative, at least of

levels of violence. What are we to make then of the fact that the imprisonment rate in the United States is over six times that of Britain, and the risk
of imprisonment per recorded crime over 11 times, whilst the homicide rate
is seven times that of Britain, as indeed it is of that of Switzerland which
has an even lower rate of imprisonment than Britain (40% less), and, incidentally, widespread gun ownership. The response to this must, of course,
be to move rapidly to a weak version of the thesis: to say that the high crime
rate of the United States relates to many other factors rather than
imprisonment so that the latter is only one factor out of many.

But perhaps it is wrong to make comparison between countries given the
flaky nature of the data. Isn't it better to look at the impact of changes in
risk of imprisonment over time within countries where the definition of
serious crime remains relatively constant and all the other social factors are
held, over a short time, fairly constant? Alas, such comparisons give even
less credibility to Murray's thesis. For example, between 1987 and 1995 the
United States increased its prison population by 124% and achieved a 2%
increase in crime, whereas Denmark increased its prison population by 7%
and had a 3% increase. Denmark has maintained a very low, stable rate of
incarceration in this period, low risk rate 0.6 per 100 recorded crimes and a
low crime rate, whereas the United States has maintained an extremely high
rate of incarceration, a high risk rate and a high crime rate. At the moment
the United States incarceration rate is just under 20 times that of Denmark.
Why, we might ask, are not hordes of American scientists and senators
going off to Denmark to find out how they got it right, and how the Americans can find means of getting out of the vast and costly prison experiment
which they have got themselves into?

Such examples could be multiplied: the Netherlands, for example,
doubled their rate of imprisonment between 1987 and 1995 and the crime
increase was only 8%. Surely, a success? Not really. Scotland, over the same
period, had a 4% increase in imprisonment and only 4% increase in crime
– half the increase of the Netherlands. Certainly this is a result which satis-
fies the virtues of value for money and efficiency which my countrymen are
well known for!

Finally, let us look at an international comparison of European countries
in the period of 1987–95 in terms of risks of imprisonment and rates of
recorded crime (Table 5.1).

Note first of all there is a built-in tendency for the risk of imprisonment,
when measured in terms of the number of inmates in proportion to the
volume of crime, to decrease with any dramatic increase in the crime rate.
The prison capacity can simply not keep up with the increase and, as Murray
notes, this is particularly true when politicians are unconvinced about the
effectiveness of prison. The causality is, however, the reverse of Murray's:
crime rises because of a host of factors and inevitably reduces the risk of
imprisonment rather than a reduction in the risk of imprisonment bringing
upon us the rise in crime. Such a tendency is especially evident whenever
the rise in crime is considerable, as in the case of England and Wales, the

TABLE 5.1   *Risk of imprisonment* and rate of crime: selected European countries*

1987–95	% Change in risk of imprisonment by 100,000	% Change in recorded crime
England and Wales	−17	+31
Scotland	+1	+4
Ireland	−13	+20
France	−10	+16
Austria	−32	+24
Netherlands	+87	+8
Denmark	+2	+3

*Risk of imprisonment is measured in terms of prisoners per 100,000 recorded crimes.

Republic of Ireland, France and Austria. But where crime rises are small, the failure of Murray's Law can be clearly observed. He focuses on England and Wales where it might seem self-evident, but in neighbouring Scotland the risk remains the same yet crime rises and in Denmark the risk rises and so does the crime rate, whilst in the Netherlands, to finally put the nail in the strong version of the thesis, the risk rate goes up exponentially but the crime rate continues to rise.

Let us begin to reformulate the thesis. Imprisonment and its risk is certainly one factor that determines the crime rate, but it is one factor amongst many. Furthermore, it interacts with other factors: the cohesiveness of the community and the degree of legitimacy of the criminal justice system being obvious examples. Its effect, no doubt, varies by crime and by the subset of the community. Ironically, the white collar criminal is more likely to be deterred by prison than the lower working class youth with nothing to lose, who commits the sort of conventional crimes we send people to prison for. Risk rates, then, are important, but different groups will perceive the same risk differently. The prudent politician will hold such factors in mind just as he or she will be aware that to use one point of interaction as the major source of crime control is bound to have declining marginal returns.

Murray's decision to focus solely on prison as a method of crime control stems possibly from a fascination with the polemical, but it also arises out of a certain fundamentalism. He correctly notes that his present favoured formula fails to touch the root causes of crime: whether it be the left's belief in social inequality as a cause, or his belief in the welfare state and its attendant 'culture of dependency'. It matters not who is correct, he observes, because socialism is scarcely around the corner, nor is the will to dismantle the welfare state as he would wish. I cannot see the logic in this, outside of the belief that without fundamental drastic change, nothing can be achieved. For there are many short term and intermediate goals which can be realized: social inequality is not written in stone, it has decreased in the past and will decrease again in the future. And as for the welfare state, I doubt if advanced industrial societies are feasible without the underpinning of the welfare state, but our experience over the last 20 years has certainly shown that such a bedrock of decency can be undermined by determined forces of the right. What is most paradoxical is Charles Murray's fixation on the prison, given the publication of his recent lengthy personal document *What it Means to be a Libertarian* (1996a). Why, we might ask, is a doughty libertarian like Murray advocating the American penal experiment when he also believes that it is not laws regulating automobile safety which affect the level of accidents, but rather the infrastructure of engineering improvements and that, amongst other things, air traffic control, drug regulating agencies, and anti-discriminatory measures should be taken out of state control? Why should such a staunch opponent of the state put his weight behind the greatest intrusion into the lives of citizens that has occurred in a mature liberal democracy?

Let us look at the vastness of the American experiment. The United States prison population has more than doubled in the 11 years from 1985 to 1996: there are now 1.6 million inmates, a population which, if brought together, would be the size of Philadelphia (Bureau of Justice Statistics, 1996). Furthermore, the imprisoned population is surrounded by a rapidly expanding penumbra of probation and parole. Now, one in 37 of the American adult population is under some form of correctional supervision, a number which, if gathered together, perhaps for some administrative convenience, would make a city of five million adults, and easily be the second largest in the United States (see Currie, 1996). It is not part of the social contract which underpins liberal democracy that it should imprison and oversee so many of its citizens. Nor that it should do so while being so palpably incapable of protecting them. The rates of violence in the United States are exceptional amongst the stable democratic societies: its overall homicide rate is seven times that of England and Wales, its murder rate for young men is a staggering 52 times higher, whilst large tracts of its great cities are no-go areas for its citizens, whether men or women.

The United States crime rate has declined in the last few years, although in terms of violent crime, particularly homicide, it remains at a very high level. Thus the overall crime rate declined by 3% between 1993 and 1996, but as we have seen, the overall rate declined in 12 out of 17 advanced industrial countries during this period. It is certainly nothing to write home about and even if this was due to the unlikely assumption that such a decrease was predominantly due to imprisonment it is difficult to imagine what size of a prison population we would need to achieve Newt Gingrich's dream of bringing the American rate down to European levels. Already some zealots, such as John Dilulio, are talking of doubling the prison population in order to combat crime (see Mauer, 1997). It is hard to see where this would end: a prison population the size of New York City, a correctional population the size of Los Angeles? Already some of our most perceptive critics speak in Zygmunt Bauman's terms of a 'totalitarian solution without a totalitarian state' (1995).

Widespread alarm bells are set off by the extraordinary racial focus of this carceral experiment. Thus, one in nine of African-American males aged 20–29 is in prison at any one point and one in three is either in prison, on probation or parole (Mauer, 1997). These are staggering figures, even more so when we consider that they would increase drastically if we were to look at 'have ever' figures and if we were to focus on poor blacks rather than include the large middle class African-American community (see Simon, 1993). There must be sizeable slices of the ghetto areas of the United States where a young man is regarded as odd if he is not under some form of correctional supervision and any stigmatization would probably be negative; indeed it would be those untouched by the law who were regarded as strange. And yet despite this extraordinary level of risk of imprisonment, violence continues to decimate the black community and even increases. Homicide is the foremost cause of death amongst young black men in America, just as imprisonment is the most likely career move in their lives; can there be any greater indictment of Murray's thesis than this?

Those of us in Europe who are friends of American democracy need to make clear our misgivings rather than import their mistakes. Our politicians, of all complexions, flit across the Atlantic to learn about this gross carceral experiment. But to attempt to learn crime control from the United States is rather like travelling to Saudi Arabia to learn about women's rights. The one lesson to be learnt is not to travel down this path of punishment, to realize that if it takes a gulag to maintain a winner-takes-all society, then it is society that must be changed rather than the prison expanded.

Note

1. I turn my radio on as I write this (29 July 1997), and hear the Home Secretary, Jack Straw, solemnly inform the public that incivilities and crime, anti-social behaviour and 'real' crime, correlate highly. I can hardly believe my ears; for who could have believed otherwise? It is like pronouncing that there is a strong correlation between smoke and fire. Part of this is a result of the legacy of the modernist notion that 'crime' is a separate form of activity committed by 'criminals' and that this professional underworld, small in size, contrasts with a separate sphere of anti-social behaviour, much more widespread and 'amateurish'. Such an idea was given weight by numerous criminological studies which examined this correlation. Perfect correlation was never found. Wes Skogan (1988), for example, in his summary of North American studies reports 0.45 to 0.60, whilst Hope and Hough in their analysis of British Crime Survey data found a higher 0.8, but noted that 'rates of perceived incivilities are more strongly related to levels of fear of crime and neighbourhood satisfaction that the level of [criminal] victimisation itself' (1988, p. 36).

Of course this disparity in evidence of incivilities and crime is bound to occur if one contrasts *actual* crime rates with *perceived* incivility rates, which is why perceptions of incivility and fear (i.e. perceptions) of crime has a much higher concentration. But it is out of such moonshine that criminological conundrums are made!

6 A WORLD HOLDING TOGETHER AND FALLING APART

Both the inclusive society of the 1960s and the exclusive world of recent years have been failures. Inclusion demanded uniformity, a homogeneity of culture and identity. It concealed rank divisions between the sexes, between ethnic groups and between classes. The exclusive world which followed it granted diversity yet it cast difference in an essentialist mould, restricting and stultifying human potential and always liable to demonization and conflict. The gross inequalities of its structure were held together by force, the criminal justice system becoming more and more a part of the everyday life of the citizen. What, then, should we strive for in a new inclusivism: a world which brings together people, distributing wealth in a fair and even fashion whilst granting the freedom of diversity? Let us first of all return once again to fundamentals: the problem of the two spheres – justice and community.

If we wish to understand how a society falls apart we must understand how it holds together. The criminal justice system by itself cannot maintain social cohesion. No society outside of a state of occupation holds together by coercion alone. It is to civil society itself we must turn if we are to locate the sources of both cohesion and disruption in social life. There are two major problems of a liberal democracy. Firstly how are rewards to be distributed fairly in order to gain support for the system and encourage commitment to work and the division of labour? Secondly, how can a society composed of individuals each seeking their own self-interest establish a sense of collective ends and not self-destruct in the proverbial war of all against all? Let us call these two areas the sphere of justice and the sphere of community. These spheres are often confused one with the other, yet they are distinct if interdependent. They both provide the basis in the legitimation of the system and ironically are a prime source of discontent. To achieve a new society which is both just and inclusive demands two things: a meritocratic distribution of rewards and a society which sees itself as a unity whilst respecting diversity.

My argument is that both of these demands are contrary to the prevailing wisdoms of both the left and the right. On the left of the political spectrum much is made of the provision of job opportunities and of income redistribution but this is far from a fully committed meritocracy. In the sphere of community, progressive thinking is dominated by the multicultural: an ideal which is, at heart, essentialist and prey to the problems of cultural nationalism and the demonization of minorities. On the right, the economic argument centres on the virtues of the market place. The market will provide jobs at the rate indicated by supply and demand, it will instil respect and discipline and dispel 'the dependency culture'. That the market place palpably fails to embrace all and is, in fact, a server of rather exclusive markets in labour where rewards are distributed more on the principle of chaos than according to the textbook formulae of microeconomics, makes the market and meritocracy look more like antagonists than natural allies. Further, the substantial existence of inherited wealth undermines the notion that reward in society can possibly be determined by effort in the workplace. In the cultural sphere, Conservatives make much of the family and the community as the solution to creating an orderly society. I will argue that there is nothing inherent in the family that promises social cohesion and that nostalgia for the strong family and community is based on a world that is irretrievably past. Finally, I will focus on the currently fashionable communitarian theories which attempt to bridge both left and right wing positions by stressing multiculturalism and the strong family.

The sphere of justice: the meritocratic society

A meritocratic society is one in which reward is allocated primarily in accordance with effort and ability. In such a society people should have equality of access to the job market whatever their age, class, gender or ethnicity yet their reward should be differentiated by merit. Formal equality of opportunity should be tied to substantive inequalities of reward. There are clear exceptions to these strictures, for example the exception of merit by need. That is, provision must be made in all societies for the sick, the aged, the young, and a basic minimum standard of living must be available to all as a safety net running underneath the hierarchic structure of meritocracy.

In a direct parallel to the pyramid of merit there should be a shadow pyramid of penalty where each person should be equal before the law yet punished proportionally to the offence committed. Once again exclusions of such a principle occur on the lines of age, sickness and the capacity for responsible action. These meritocratic principles entail both rights and obligations. Rights are those of access to the labour market, of equal opportunities both in jobs and in training. The corresponding legal rights are those of equality before the law both in terms of protection and apprehension. Obligations are on the face of it obvious: commitment at work, a responsibility to deliver the goods, to be law-abiding and respect the rights of others.

It is this vision of liberal democracy which is the key to political obligation and citizenship within advanced industrial countries. Yet as sociologists from Durkheim through to Merton have pointed out, such a vision of society, such a European ideal or an American Dream, has within it a deep irony. For the cultural ideal of the meritocracy contradicts the existing structures of inequality of wealth and opportunity. That which legitimizes social order also creates unrest and disequilibrium within it.

Let us return to the metaphor of meritocracy as a racetrack. Ideally, everyone has free access to the race and each individual runs round the track, in competition with others and his or her reward is proportional to effort and ability. Yet it is a strange track, because some seem to start only one metre from the finishing post whilst others start at the very beginning of the track a full 100 metres away. Some people are allowed to run only on a certain part of the track – the high performance areas are not within their reach; some people – usually women – arrive at the track tired after doing a hard day's work and spend only part of their life rather than a lifetime on the track. Some people are excluded from the track altogether; some, on the other hand, do not run, their job is to hand out the prizes. Others own the track. Yet all people are allowed to be spectators, to watch the distribution of glittering prizes in our rich society. And if the first stage of meritocracy is the distribution of reward according to one's performance on the competitive track of life, the second, even more important, is the construction of a track which is set on an even playing field. Meritocracy can never be achieved if a high proportion of reward is inherited. Let me give a concrete example. In the American magazine *Society*, a leader article entitled 'The Myth of Increasing Inequality' noted that

> the share of wealth of the richest 1 percent of households rose from 31.5 percent in 1983 to 36.9 percent in 1989, and then fell to 30.4 percent in 1992. Thus, over the full cycle, inequality decreased slightly; the change is not statistically significant. (1997, p. 2)

It then goes on to argue that the American Dream is not threatened by increasing inequality, as is often suggested! Forget politics: whether one is a social democrat or a libertarian, a conservative or a neo-liberal, this type of differential cannot represent a meritocratic free market in labour. Even a *laissez-faire* liberal might want a more gentle slope of reward in a graph which matched supply of labour to demand.[1]

In such a world, although extremely wealthy by all historical standards, it is not absolute but relative deprivation which engenders discontent. People feel unfairly rewarded in the race either because they have run just as hard as another citizen yet have been rewarded substantially less or simply because they have not been allowed on the track, or on only a short part of it, so they feel deep in their hearts that they could have created a better life for themselves if only the chances had been there. Not all worry so much; some adopt a point of 'realism' – success is a matter of luck, of who you know, of being in the right place. It is probably for this reason that a culture based on merit is so mesmerized by horoscopes, fate and spends so much money on gambling and on lotteries. For what could be a better metaphor for the system than a National Lottery where equality is reduced to the purchase of a ticket and success means being chosen by a random computer?

Without such a culture of cynicism there would undoubtedly be a higher degree of discontent; yet, of course, it is precisely because the system is not random, because effort does result in some reward although far from perfect in meritocratic terms, that relative deprivation occurs. For in a completely static world where rewards were fixed at birth or a completely random one – reminiscent of a novel by Philip Dick – where all rewards were allocated by lottery, relative deprivation would be absent (see Runciman, 1966). The irony of the system is not only that one of its central legitimizing principles generates widespread disaffection but that the mechanism by which it does so is because it *partially works*.

The left and meritocracy

> If the Tories are over-ready to talk of merit yet silent on equality, traditionally socialists have been garrulous about equality but weak on merit. At times this borders on a belief that differentials in income or resource allocation in terms of services are in themselves non-socialist and that there is, in reality, little difference between people. It is almost as if it were believed that we are actually equal in capability and motivation and that all that was missing was equality of opportunities. . . .
>
> Such idealistic notions of equality commit a common fallacy. They confuse substantive equality – all people are equal in ability – with formal equalities of opportunity and reward. The first is palpably untrue, and any process of levelling through social intervention unrealistic; the second is the main aim of an attainable meritocratic socialist policy. (Corrigan, et al., 1988, p. 9)

The provision of jobs for all in the community is not meritocracy. The feudal lords of Europe did this well, providing for themselves as they provided for others. The allocation of jobs in a colour blind fashion is not a meritocracy: the Empire of Rome did this well. The distribution of jobs perfectly reflecting gender and ethnicity is not a meritocracy. This is achieved in some of our major television news channels, it may be perfectly politically desirable, but it has only a contingent relationship to meritocracy: for the individuals allocated may be privileged by class and contact, compared to others of their group. Meritocracy is none of these; it is about the allocation of jobs by merit and the distribution of reward consequent on this. It is the heart of the American Dream, it is the vital centre of the dreams of modern Europe and the ambitions of South East Asia.

Yet the notion of social inclusion is all too often seen in economic terms as merely providing work and achieving equal opportunities throughout the workforce. Neither of these deals with the underlying problems of reward by merit, namely, the creation of a fair gradient of wages throughout and the problem of inherited wealth. Such a meritocratic order was the goal of most left of centre social commentators until recent years. Anthony Crosland, for example – a revisionist to many and scarcely a dangerous Bolshevik – in *The Future of Socialism* (1956) had no problem about recognizing that equality of opportunity alone was not sufficient and that the problem of inherited wealth was paramount. And, of course, the sociological legacy from Durkheim – let alone that from Marx – was clearly concerned with the destabilizing effects of inherited wealth. But if one reads any of the policy statements coming from either the Clinton or the Blair administration one finds that any talk of the problem of inherited wealth is completely absent, while even the restricted notion of meritocracy as reward by merit in terms of one's occupation alone is, strangely, muted. Thus welfare to work schemes would seem to believe that the mere fact of achieving employment at a rate over the minimum wage is an end goal – the colossal differentials in rewards between different jobs and professions and those that occur between the different labour markets is not questioned. The 'winner takes all' society which allows enormous wealth at the top of society and excessive wealth amongst the upper middle classes is not subject to political scrutiny. As the city editor of the *Guardian* puts it in a prolonged cry of indignation:

> Small children confront it in the playground when their BHS trainers meet a pair of Nikes. Secondary school kids come across it when they wear Next and a best friend turns up in DKNY. But it is only the workplace which has the power to thrust home, day after day, the realisation that life really is unfair.
>
> In this arena, justice is way out on a limb. What you do and what you get paid have only the most tangential connection.
>
> Look at Jan Leschly, the former tennis star who is now the highest paid executive in Britain as boss of drugs giant SmithKline Beecham. This Wimbledon player and one time opponent of Ilie Nastasie now earns more in an hour than a teacher in London does in a year.
>
> The futures of millions of people lie in the hands of Mr Leschly whose company is the world's biggest maker of life-saving vaccines and which is prepared to pay him £65 million a year in salary and share windfalls for being at the helm.
>
> It would take the teacher 3,000 years to earn that much. But during an average teaching career more than 1,200 young lives can be shaped. And the cost or benefit to society could be immeasurable.
>
> Footballers can earn anything up to £50,000 a week for entertaining their fans, but for the £22.5 million wage bill paid by Manchester United last year you could probably staff a decent-sized hospital.
>
> The disparities in pay and perks across both the private and public sectors are huge.
>
> The notion that there should be approximate pay parity for similar jobs, or even that one sector should be roughly comparable with another, has long since been regarded as nonsense in the commercial world. (Buckingham, 1998, p. 19)

Indeed, as I have suggested, the problem is not simply that of a palpably unmeritocratic society but of a veritable chaos of reward, where wealth is seemingly distributed willy-nilly without rhyme or reason. It is scarcely surprising that, like a gigantic satire, the national lotteries of the advanced industrial countries create millionaires every week, emulating the arbitrariness of success and the winner takes all structure of reward. Gambling becomes a major growth industry and in the United States involves a turnover of $37 billion a year, purveying what Robert Goodman (1995) called, in a grim phrase, 'the pathology of hope'.

Without a move towards justice in the distribution of reward there will never be a tranquil social order, but meritocracy alone cannot bring about tranquillity. For the incessant competition of one against another, the grading of other human beings in their monetary value in 'the race of life' scarcely promises social tranquillity or human altruism. And the effect on the individuals concerned can be deleterious: to turn themselves into commodities to be priced and marketed. The present obsession with work of the middle classes demonstrates this clearly: the dual family income (supported perhaps by an au pair on a minimum wage or below) where every hour of the day is dedicated to the god of maximizing income and where 'quality' time with the children means, in fact, 'little' time – holidays become short and costly, leisure, that time necessary to get over the stress of work. It would be invidious to blame the individuals alone because there is little doubt that the downsizing of corporations has placed a greater load on those employees who remain and the pressure to take work home becomes greater. The travesty of those with large incomes working all hours that God gives them whilst those at the bottom of the heap are idle and unfulfilled is too obvious to pursue but the redistribution of work as well as of income is a vital political necessity.

Will justice suffice?: the role of the family

The long literature on the basis of political obligation and social cohesion shows a clear demarcation between the two spheres. Writers on the left prioritize justice over community, whereas those on the right grant priority to community over justice. Thus social democrats have always argued that society will never hang together if injustice prevails. Indeed social order follows justice and there is little else needed. The sphere of community becomes a reflection of the sphere of justice. Conservatives, on the other hand, have traditionally reversed this formulation. Community is of paramount importance: nation, tradition, regiment, school – all are evoked as being of greater importance than the individual and his or her rewards. Without such an acceptance of the given order justice is impossible (see van den Haag, 1975). And a related demarcation occurs between the family and the economy. For those on the right the family is the key institution in the generation of law-abiding behaviour. Here discipline is learnt, impulse curbed, respect instilled and the grounding of civilized behaviour laid down in childhood to inform the adult throughout the future exigencies of life. Politicians of the right extol the family, criminologists of that persuasion, whether it is Travis Hirschi, Charles Murray or James Q. Wilson, all pinpoint the early years as formative and predictive of future delinquency or conformity. But for those on the left, in the recent period, focus on the family is seen as a red herring. Indeed with a few honourable exceptions, such as Elliot Currie and William Julius Wilson, to pinpoint vulnerabilities in the family, such as single parentage, is seen as 'blaming the victim'. Furthermore, as Wilson has graphically indicated, in the case of the black family liberals have frequently seen any description of pathological aspects of ghetto life as tantamount to racism:

> Thus earlier arguments which asserted that some aspects of ghetto life were pathological, were rejected and replaced with those that accented the strengths of the black community. Arguments extolling the strengths and virtues of black families replaced those that described the break-up of black families. In fact, aspects of ghetto behaviour described as pathological in studies of the mid-1960s were reinterpreted or re-defined as functional because, it was argued, blacks were demonstrating their ability to survive and even flourish in an economically depressed and racist environment. (1987, pp. 8–9)

Thus it is argued that not only is the type of family irrelevant to the aetiology of crime and delinquency, but that to suggest that alternative types of parenting outside the standard nuclear family are inadequate is tantamount to ethnocentrism. For it is not the family which is the locus of the causes of delinquency but the wider social forces of economic deprivation, racism and other forms of social injustice which are its source. If we wish to reduce crime we must tackle injustice – all else concerned is scapegoating and mistargeting.

So for Conservatives the family is the key to an orderly society whilst for the left, the family is somehow irrelevant: it is social justice, the sphere of economy and employment which is the key. Let us examine the role of the family in the genesis of crime and disorder. A realistic approach would first of all stress the two constituents of the crime equation: motivation (the deviant action) and control (the social reaction). The family is conventionally thought of as a site of control; a building block in the community. For those on the right any weakness in its powers allows the essential selfishness of human nature to spill over. To explain motivation for crime is, therefore, unnecessary: each of us carries the motive within us like Original Sin. Starting from such a position it is difficult to explain variation in crime rates between different groups in society as the result of differences in their levels of family stability. This blanket contention would, certainly if we are talking about conventional crime, be hard to sustain. Why should not our own Royal Family with its growing tendency to live in separate palaces be, under this measure, likely to produce a prodigious crop of delinquents? Or would not the English upper classes, with their institutionalized practice of 'broken' homes where children are separated from their parents at an early stage and sent to the tender mercies of 'prep' and 'public' school, store up many difficulties for the future? Certainly the occurrence of widespread sexual peccadilloes in adulthood is frequently gainsaid although not, as yet, subject to detailed research scrutiny; however, the rate of burglary, mugging and armed robbery amongst such gentlemen is surely extremely low? But let us, in contrast, take the opposite example of close-knit families. Few of us who watched with professional interest the film of the life of the Kray twins could fail to be impressed by their close and supportive family structure with extensive relatives and well buttressed by friends in the warm community of the East End in the 1950s. But these men were living in a world without structure compared to the great Mafia families of organized crime. Here we have it all: the dedicated father, the traditional mother, the extended family, the children entering into the family business, the close sense of community. Was not one attraction of these movies, which enthralled the world, the depiction of the family we have 'lost', or never had? Yet in the case of organized crime, the strong family is almost a *sine qua non* of success.

There is obviously no one-to-one relationship between family stability and crime, nor for that matter between the vitality of the family and the strength of the community. The family can well be atomistic, indeed, as feminists such as Carol Pateman (1988) have pointed out, the family is often seen as the *individual* building block in liberal democratic theory. Was that not the meaning of Margaret Thatcher's famous remark that there is no such thing as society, only individuals and their families? The problem of how you can construct a stable society out of egoistic individuals merely becomes transformed into how can you create it out of a conglomeration of egoistic families? The family can, of course, teach adherence to the values of the wider community, but the presence of a strong family does not magically entail community. Indeed the strong family of the entrepreneur can be the basis for behaviour of altruism at home and gross egoism outside of it, while that of the organized criminal will probably involve a community which stops abruptly at the outer reaches of his ethnic group. Finally, it should not be assumed that the strong family entails harmony in the home. About half of the violence in British society occurs within the home, usually by the male partner in the marital relationship. It is not always a good idea to keep such a family structure together like boxers in a clinch. As Jayne Mooney has pointed out (1998), a dreadful irony is that single mothers have the highest violence rates against them of all groups of women, so to call for a united family would be to ask the perpetrators to return to the home. As Philippe Bourgois puts it:

> The moralistic debates that condemn deficient child-rearing practices in the inner city bemoan the absence of fathers in families. It is assumed that fatherlessness destroys a child's moral fiber, even though the single most overwhelming problems faced by female-headed households is poverty. . . . public policy efforts to coax poor men back into nuclear households are misguided. The problem is just the reverse: Too many abusive fathers are present in the nuclear households terrorizing children and mothers. If anything, women take too long to become single mothers once they have babies. They often tolerate inordinate amounts of abuse. (1996, p. 287)

What we must be aware of is what values the family carries, what behaviour it permits and countenances as well as the strength of its structure. Sometimes, as Carl Nightingale has shown in his Philadelphia study, the emphasis on the weak family misleadingly allows us to ignore the values which the family transmits; and that the family itself as a cockpit of violence creates violent children. The trauma of 'forceful' parenting and the experiencing of violence between parents (often as we have seen in Chapter 1 an attempt by the man to maintain a traditional patriarchal family) are clearly indicated as the root causes of much violent behaviour when the child grows into the adult (see Currie, 1998).

We must look, therefore, at both the values that the family carries as well as at its level of integration into the total society. None of this warrants the reverse proposition, held by many on the left, that the strength of the family is irrelevant or, in its even more ridiculous idealist form, that all families are equally strong. Crime is not just about control, it is about control and motivation. Motivation to commit crime can occur in the most 'exemplary' of families, but it can also occur in families with weak structures. Here, the strength of the family is important because the individual – say an adolescent boy – is more likely to be influenced by outside pressures if the family, although law-abiding and community oriented, is weak. That is, in an area where there is massive deprivation, it is blatantly obvious that the youth who is unsupervised and who is allowed to stay up to all hours is more likely to succumb to the delinquency of his peers than are those whose family have the time, energy and personnel to provide supervision. Furthermore, there is no logical reason why every type of family structure should be equally strong – there must be variation in control between different family forms and to believe otherwise would invite us to engage in a nonsensical relativism whose real agenda is political correctness rather than reasoned argument. But let us not pre-judge the shape of the family which can protect, albeit marginally, from the pressures of delinquency. Thus, although absence of restraints does not explain crime or deviancy, it makes it more likely where and when motivation does exist (cf. Gottfredson and Hirschi, 1990).

The strong family is not a magical bringer of order nor a cure all for crime. The family may be strong but atomistic and carry no collective values, it may carry values which are competitive or indeed violent, it may be a site of crime and it may, by traumatization of its members, cause crime. The weak family, on the other hand, does not guarantee crime but it does nothing to prevent it if the motivation for crime is already present. But perhaps this is the crunch: it is in the families of the poor, where the temptation to conventional crime is greatest, because of blatant inequalities, that a strong family bulwark against crime is necessary.

The unreflexive constraint

There is a sense in which the conservatives are completely correct. If you wish to maintain an orderly society which is in essence unfair and inequitable you must train the individuals within it to accept the world as it is. Deterrence, obedience, respect for tradition, compliance with community norms must be drilled into the individual from birth. Poor families must be the most disciplined because they have the greatest cross of inequities to bear. Few conservatives have the gall to spell this out – one exception is Ernest van den Haag who, for example, quite cheerfully admits this in the case of penal law:

> Since the law quite deliberately restricts the tempted, as well as the untempted, there is a kernel of truth in the belief, held by revolutionaries of various persuasions (most elaborately by Marxists) that the law is a device of the rich and powerful to keep the poor and powerless in check. The threats of the law are meant to restrain those who would do what the law prohibits. Obviously, the poor and powerless are more tempted to take what is not theirs, or to rebel, than the powerful and wealthy, who need not take what they already have.
>
> However, the discovery that the penal law restrains the poor and powerless more than the wealthy and powerful who are less pressed, or tempted, to do what it forbids is about as revealing as the disclosure that the Prohibition laws were meant to restrain drinkers more than the teetotalers who imposed them. Obviously, the law restrains some groups more than others and is violated by some groups more often than by others. . . . So because the temptation to break the laws is unequally distributed, because of different personalities and different living conditions, the laws – and the punishments for violating them – must weigh or fall most heavily on some persons and groups. Those less favored by society are most tempted to violate laws and therefore suffer punishment for doing so more often. (1975, pp. 45–6)

And, of course, the law alone is a crude and insufficient instrument to control 'the tempted': the discipline of early life is essential to maintain an orderly society. Hence the widespread concern about the state of the families of the poor with the almost Victorian attachment (which allows the causal agency of inequality to be conveniently forgotten) that they have brought it upon themselves.

All of this discussion must now be placed in the context of late modernity. For there has been a major shift in the level of demand people make of their lives. In the political sphere this is expressed in terms of rising expectations of citizenship, in the economic sphere in the raised sense of relative deprivation, and in the personal sphere by a demand for a life which is more expressive and which has personal actualization as a major goal. The gross mistake with regard to institutions like the family is to depict it like some vessel which holds together its members and which, because of various reasons, has become leaky. This mechanical metaphor is wrong because it views the individuals as separate from the vessel when in truth the individual members *are* the vessel of the family. It is not the family which has lost coherence and solidity in its containment of the men, women, adolescents and children within it. It is these family members who, for various reasons (some good, some ill), have deconstituted the family. They are less willing to be put upon, less willing to be obedient, less unreflecting in their attitudes to rules, less dependent on its structure and economy. It is women less willing to put up with the control of husbands, it is adolescents less easy about accepting their parents' rules, it is men less ready to accept their commitments. It has both progressive and regressive moments: patriarchal structures dissolve as people begin to commoditize each other to a greater extent.

It is this unravelling of social relations which Eric Hobsbawm stresses is the key to the social changes of the late twentieth century, which simultaneously promises greater freedom and more mutually respectful communities, yet holds the ever-present dangers of divisiveness and oppression.

Let us turn now to Amitai Etzioni's communitarianism, which combines a stress on family and on the community and claims to take a middle path between the social philosophies of the left and the right.

The sphere of the community

When various civic groups discuss new measures that public authorities may be allowed to use to help combat crime, liberals often argue that these will serve, at best, to curb crime, not prevent it. It is suggested that the best way to fight crime is to ensure that everybody has a well-paying job, is treated with dignity and not discriminated against, and is not alienated from society. Although these are worthy goals in their own right, the question of what causes crime is a surprisingly complex one. One of the best authorities on the subject, James Q. Wilson, dedicated more than six hundred pages to the issue in his book *Crime and Human Nature*. Still, no easy conclusions emerged. I cite here, very briefly, major findings that are relevant to our Communitarian approach.

First, while vulnerable members of the society, those who truly cannot help themselves, ought to be helped, and while social justice should be advanced – these and other social goals should be advanced because they are good in themselves, not because they are likely to reduce crime significantly. The fact is that crime is more rampant in the United States than in many countries where the average income per capita is much lower (including Portugal, Chile, Spain, Indonesia and Kenya). Crime has *risen* in the United States as income has *risen* (crime has increased three-to-fourfold since the fifties). And there are as many law abiding citizens among the poor and quite a few lawbreakers among those who are well off.

Second, the level of crime is deeply affected by the total community fabric. It is not enough for families to be strong, or schools to be fine educational institutions, and so on. To minimize crime all of these elements must reinforce one another. Thus, in those parts of the country (and the world) where families are strong, schools teach moral values, communities are well intact, and values command respect. In Utah, for instance, crime is much lower than in places where these factors are absent. The national violent crime rate in 1990 was 730 per 100,000; in Utah it was 284 ... what works in situations such as Utah is that families, schools and communities – all the factors that go into making the moral infrastructure – come together to support moral conduct. In effect, they work not merely or even mainly to fight crime, but to sustain civility and values in general. Prevention of crime is a bonus of a moral and civil society. (Etzioni, 1993, pp. 190–1, emphasis in original).

I have quoted extensively from Amitai Etzioni's *The Spirit of Community* not merely because his communitarianism has a wide audience and the respect of politicians on both sides of the Atlantic but because it clearly illustrates a series of common fallacies with regard to crime. Firstly the caution that the causes of crime are complex is followed quickly by the conclusion that there seems to be no relationship between social justice and crime. High income societies like the United States have high crime rates, low income societies often low rates and, as we saw earlier, increase in wealth seems to have not an inverse but a direct relationship to the rise in crime. Note James Q. Wilson's famous invocation: pursue social justice if you will but do so for its own sake; do not justify it or believe that it has anything to do with reducing crime rates. Such a dislocation between crime and social justice is common amongst all of the neo-positivist, conservative thinkers: Travis Hirschi, Hans Eysenck and, of course, James Q. Wilson himself. This rests on the simple fallacy of confusing absolute with relative deprivation. Human discontent is experienced, by evaluation, by judgement of fairness and just allocation. It is not about simple economic deficit. Social injustice can, of course, be concealed, it can be unknown to the mass of the population. It is only in circumstances where people experience social injustice that discontent will occur and only in those societies where there is no political or perhaps religious outlet for discontent, that crime is likely to occur. Thus the path from social injustice to crime is mediated by human evaluation and the specific possibilities which confront the citizens of a particular society. It is not automatic, it is not law-like and it would be foolish to seek such ahistorical generalizations.

But there is more to this, for the severance of the relationship between justice and crime serves to suggest that crime is simply a result of disorder. This is to admit quite freely that injustice occurs within society – society is after all far from perfect – but that crime is not a symptom of this injustice. Rather, crime is a perennial feature of the human condition: it occurs where people have not been taught to be orderly. Crime is synonymous with disorder, it needs no explanation outside of it; indeed any such 'external' explanation simply rationalizes and attempts to justify its essential impropriety.

The second fallacy reproduces the features of the first. Given that the causes of crime, rooted in injustice, have been ruled out as part of the explanation of crime, then the second half of the crime equation, the level of control, becomes the sole mode of explanation. Note that causes and control are seen as either–or modes of explanation, further, that variations in the level of social control are viewed as mechanistically affecting the behaviour of people. This suggests that levels of social control alone can explain crime rates; that, given injustice is obviated as a cause of crime, the variation in levels of control must in itself constitute an explanation and that such control in a simply mechanistic way is effective to the extent that it impinges upon people. Its quantity not its quality is its measure. Just as injustice is ruled out as a cause of crime because wealth does not automatically correlate with crime, the level of social control is seen as being *the* explanatory variable because it supposedly does. Once again it is not human beings assessing their situation and acting accordingly, it is people propelled by their surroundings of control neither standing back and agreeing with its dictates nor rebelling against it. The conscious reflecting actor is nowhere to be seen in this positivist vision. Yet, in reality, the tight intermeshing control which Etzioni advocates does not always cocoon consensus; often such a stultifying atmosphere can generate discontent. The 1950s United States of small town, high school and conformity was followed by 1960s of wide scale rebellion and discontent. Of course control theories will explain this transition as a crisis of control, where family values were threatened and a hedonistic consumerism undermined the discipline necessary for an orderly life. Yet there was no hint of such an analysis at that time. Indeed the literature was obsessed with conformity, it emphasized the strength of the family and saw the new-found consumerism as creating acquiescence and conformity. Witness the popular commentaries of the time such as Vance Packard's *The Status Seekers* or John K. Galbraith's *The Affluent Society* (see Chapter 1, p. 3). What happened was not that people's demands were moulded by the forces of social control but that they themselves demanded more of life and rejected the restraining templates which they saw as dominating their lives. The revolt of the individual, the cultural revolution of the 1960s which is widely acknowledged as the sea-change of the late twentieth century *preceded* the loosening of the control structures, it was not a result of them. If it had been so there would scarcely have been anything to revolt against.

Social control if it is to be effective has to be seen as just. Strength alone does not guarantee its efficacy although it would be wrong to jump to the opposite conclusion: that the strength of the family, the school, peer group and, indeed, the police is of no importance. Both sides of the crime equation, motivation and control, are essential to understanding crime rates but without motivation control alone is an insufficient explanation (cf. Gottfredson and Hirschi, 1990). It may well be true that Utah, where all the multi-agencies of social control come together in a religious rubric, has a much lower rate of violence than the US national rate. Indeed the murder rate is about one third the national rate, but *there again*, it is almost two and a half times the rate of England and Wales. Even a devout and family-oriented state like Utah greatly outstrips our country with its low rate of religious attendance, high divorce rate and rising proportion of single mothers. Newt Gingrich, in his ambition to bring the US crime rate down to a European level, would need to go much further than to reduce Californian rates to that of Utah. We are not faced here with an eternal constancy of human nature which if not tightly contained will burst through at whatever time and place and produce crime rates. We are dealing with particular configurations of motivation and control which vary remarkably both within and between countries.

The separation of the motivation to commit crime from the forces which control it is too simplistic. The two parts of the crime equation – the motive to commit a crime because of perceived injustice and the system of social control which might prevent it (both informal and formal) – are conceptually distinct but also intimately related. Usually they are seen as distinct, often they are presented as in the quote from Etzioni as either–or but in truth they are closely related. It makes sense to maintain the distinction yet it is wrong to ignore the interaction of the two. Of course, a heated feeling of the injustice of the system – say because of unemployment, or poor wages – is more likely to boil over into crime if the person concerned has little peer pressure to conform and the police are rarely seen in the streets. But the opposite is also true: the presence of an overbearing police force which treats the poor and dispossessed with contempt can be the spark which sets off riots and disorder. The 1992 disturbances in Los Angeles and the history of rioting throughout the century is evidence of this. And the spectacular riots which periodically make the headlines of the world media have the same causes as the slow riots of endemic crime which blight whole areas of our cities. Economic marginalization is a potent source of discontent; 'political' marginalization in the sense of manifest powerlessness in the face of authority is the catalyst that transforms discontent into crime (see Lea and Young, 1993). For it is the very fact of the force of law and order acting illegitimately which snaps the moral bind of the marginalized that is already strained and weakened by economic deprivation and inequality.

All of this takes us back to the study of the Philadelphia ghetto which we discussed in Chapter 3. Economic and social exclusion (social injustice) is compounded by exclusion by the agencies of control. The communities disintegrate *because of* the lack of work and the war of all against all that this engenders. The inhabitants of the Philadelphia ghettos are *not* culturally excluded from the wider community. They are very much part of it: indeed, it is the taking up of the American Dream and their inability to realize it (cultural inclusion, combined with cultural exclusion) that spurs their resentment. It is the values of the wider community that legitimizes their subsequent violence and competitiveness. They are *not* bereft of role models of work, marriage and social stability, as the theorists of the underclass suggest. They are awash with classic stereotypes of the American family and the helpful community, fed by their diet of television, which, given the targeting of audience, precisely presents the successful black middle class of *The Cosby Show* and *Sister, Sister*, to US blacks and, indeed, to the black diaspora both sides of the Atlantic.

Social justice therefore underscores successful social control: it is not separate from it. Yet Amitai Etzioni persists in his most recent book, *The New Golden Rule* (1997), to relegate 'socio-economic factors' to a sideshow and to insist that the main route to producing a good society is the balance between autonomy and community. In this his argument inevitably counterposes the philosophies of libertarianism and conservatism, rugged individualism (neo-liberalism) and the conservatism of tradition and conformity. Social democratic ideas are left at the wayside and two right wing philosophies take centre stage as the debate of our times, with communitarianism happily providing the 'golden' compromise.

Our critique of Etzioni up to now, then, is that firstly he excludes social justice from the problem of order and secondly he stresses the strengthening of institutions such as the family which may or may not generate an orderly society. Above all he is unwilling to acknowledge that the core American values may themselves be a major source of social conflict. Let us, finally, turn to the community, the key basis of his philosophy of communitarianism.

Justice and community

Success in the two spheres – a society where desiderata are distributed fairly and where values are held in common – is necessary to a stable social order. The most meritocratic society would not solve the problem of social order: competition between individuals would proceed apace and although rewards would be distributed more fairly than at present there would be no social peace. The existence of generally agreed values is necessary if people are willing to aid each other in times of trouble, to act honourably towards each other, to avoid cheating, betrayal and general skulduggery but, above all, to value humanity equally whatever their success and skills in life. Nor will the most secure family or the most cohesive community deliver social harmony. Families can become precisely the units which compete against each other and communities likewise. Indeed, as Amitai Etzioni himself recognizes: 'Communitarians hold that unless there is some shared *substantive* core values [between communities], a "thicker" framework, which most people in a community find compelling, social order cannot sustain itself' (1997, p. 198). A society which was meritocratic but not communitarian would not suffice nor would one which was communitarian but not meritocratic. But let us now delve a little deeper into the problems of community. For if we are clear that what is needed is meritocracy in the sphere of justice, what do we need in the complementary sphere of community?

Melting pot, rainbow or mosaic

Etzioni, in *The New Golden Rule*, charts what he calls 'The Fall and Rise of America'. It starts, like our own depiction of the Western world, with the inclusive 1950s and points to the gradual 'erosion' of standards and orderly behaviour. Nowhere, however, is the economy or the market a factor in this change; rather like other commentators on the right, such as James Q. Wilson, Etzioni sees it as a decline in values which somehow mysteriously occurs without rhyme or reason. He then ends in the 1990s with his rather optimistic 'rise' of America with its turn, he hopes, to communitarian values.

His characterization of diversity fits around this frame. Thus he contrasts the assimilationist melting pot of the immediate post-war period with the 'rainbow' of diversity of the 1980s onwards (associated particularly with the politics of Jesse Jackson) which he views as much too heterogeneous, divisive and conflictual with his final communitarian stage:

> As I see it, the image of a mosaic, if properly understood, best serves the search for an intercommunity construction of bounded autonomy suitable to a communitarian society. The mosaic is enriched by a variety of elements of different shapes and colors, but it is held together by a frame and glue. The mosaic symbolizes a society in which various communities maintain their cultural particulars (ranging from religious commitments and language to cuisine and dance), proud and knowledgeable about their specific traditions. At the same time, these distinct communities recognize that they are integral parts of a more encompassing whole. (1997, p. 193)

In a fashion, Etzioni's formulation parallels our concern with the movement from inclusive to exclusive society and then beyond but his communitarianism, which purports to be the basis of a new inclusivism, would seem to merely fudge the issue. For really what he is suggesting is a multiculturalism held together by the glue of basic agreement. In the image of the 'mosaic': the cultures are held separate, their traditions valued and preserved, their separate entities are held together by the contractual glue of mutual respect and a rather basic collection of common values. I wish to argue that this image, fitting to an extent Clinton's America and mooted as the basis of reconciliation in places as diverse as Northern Ireland, Bosnia and the Middle East, is deeply flawed.

In Chapter 5 we discussed how multiculturalism tended to envisage a series of pre-scripted communities which were fixed and, indeed, viewed in a positive light the notion of maintaining and excavating tradition ('back to roots'). Furthermore, that such a series of diverse cultural essences provided ontological security and identity in a rapidly changing era. I argued that first of all this essentialism is a response to the precariousness of identity which is in itself fragile and, secondly, that it held within it the possibility of conflict and mobilization of aggression. But let me now return to the work of Eric Hobsbawm, whose critique of recent multiculturalism, or 'identity politics' as he calls it, has been both trenchant and penetrating.

Eric Hobsbawm and the rise of identity politics

In Eric Hobsbawm's *Age of Extremes* the transition of the late twentieth century is described with a fine sense of irony. The pre-capitalist institutions of trust and honour broke down just as capitalism became supremely successful as a world system. And just such a twist of events informs his understanding of community and identity:

we are living – through a gigantic 'cultural revolution', an 'extraordinary dissolution of traditional social norms, textures and values, which left so many inhabitants of the developed world orphaned and bereft.' If I may go on quoting myself, 'Never was the word "community" used more indiscriminately and emptily than in the decades when communities in the sociological sense became hard to find in real life' (1994, p. 428). Men and women look for groups to which they can belong, certainly and forever, in a world in which all else is moving and shifting, in which nothing else is certain. And they find it in an identity group. Hence the strange paradox, which the brilliant, and incidentally, Caribbean Harvard sociologist Orlando Patterson has identified: people *choose* to belong to an identity group, but 'it is a choice predicated on the strongly held, intensely conceived belief that the individual has absolutely no choice but to belong to that specific group.' That it is a choice can sometimes be demonstrated. The number of Americans reporting themselves as 'American Indian' or 'Native American' almost quadrupled between 1960 and 1990, from about half a million to about two millions, which is far more than could be explained by normal demography; and incidentally, since 70% of 'Native Americans' marry outside their race, exactly who is a 'native American' ethnically, is far from clear. (1996, p. 40, emphasis in original)

Just as community collapses, identity is invented, and note Orlando Patterson's observation of how the choice of identity, as in multiculturalism in general, is predicated on the essentialist notion of no choice. You discover your *correct* identity, your roots: it is an objective procedure with seemingly one answer. Further, Hobsbawm argues that such a politics is not so much a solution to the problem of social breakdown as a symptom:

Identity politics and *fin-de-siècle* nationalism were thus not so much programmes, still less effective programmes for dealing with the problems of the late twentieth century, but rather emotional reactions to these problems. (ibid., p. 430)

Hobsbawm argues that identity politics contains the seeds of disintegration and conflict: identity is always defined exclusively (that is inclusion *demands* exclusion) and alliances between various identity groups ('communities') are fickle: they are temporary alliances which break up.

The contradictory nature of late modernity is captured precisely in this debate about culture and identity. On the one side commentators point to the widespread appeal of essentialism (both in terms of essentializing oneself and essentializing the other). Thus we have the rise of nationalism, the scourge of ethnic cleansing, the emergence of increasingly successful racist political parties across Europe, the strident advance of ethnic identity politics, the emergence of fundamentalist religious groups, the cult of masculinity, the presence of black separatism and the insistent voices of radical feminism. All of these currents undoubtedly occur where human beings define themselves in terms of essences which, by definition and practice, exclude others, and which purposively truncate human choice and creativity with their notions of fixed natures and destinies. But they occur *at the same time* as the wide scale deconstruction and demoralization of these essences. As Les Back puts it in his brilliant book on urban ethnicities:

As we move towards the end of the twentieth century, ideas about nationhood, culture and identity are increasingly seen either as in a state of attrition and fragmentation or as being reified through a language of authenticity and cultural absolutism. The choice is presented pointedly as one between viewing cultures as rooted and fixed and a vision of cultural processes as in a constant state of flux producing creative and promiscuous routeways of identification. What is omitted in the deafening row over 'essentialism' versus 'anti-essentialism' is the complex interplay between these two impulses at the everyday level and how forms of social exclusion and inclusion work through notions of belonging and entitlement in particular times and places. Within Europe's major conurbations, complex and exhilarating forms of transcultural production exist simultaneously with the most extreme forms of violence and racism. . . . (1996, pp. 8–9)

Cultures, in fact, resonate with each other, bricollaging and crossing over in a way in which essences are always undermined and, in fact, changing without the members ever realizing the shifting nature of their 'true' identity. But Hobsbawm takes us one step further. For he sees such essences as a response to the deconstruction of fixed identity and certainty which abounds in the late modern world. The desire to demonize others is based on the ontological uncertainties of those who would site themselves at centre stage. Their very basis is the fact that earlier taken-for-granted cultures and traditions – essences – are dissolving. To expect, then, new essences and certainties to firmly establish themselves goes against the grain of history. Hobsbawm points to a world whose very fluidity brings about the desire for its opposite. Young American Jews searched for their 'roots' precisely at the time when the process of discrimination and segregation which marked them off as different had disintegrated. Quebec's nationalism emerged precisely when Quebec as a distinct society began to disappear. The desire for ethnic identification occurs at a point where out-marriage reaches new heights: 60% of American-born women of all ethnic origins now marry outside of their group. The tragedy is that:

Increasingly one's identity had to be constructed by insisting on the non-identity of others. How otherwise could the neo-Nazi skinheads in Germany, wearing the uniforms, hair-styles and musical tastes of the cosmopolitan youth culture, establish their essential Germanness, except by beating up local Turks and Albanians? How, except by eliminating those who did not 'belong' could the 'essentially' Croat or Serb character of some region be established in which, for most of history, a variety of ethnicities and religions had lived as neighbours? (Hobsbawm, 1994, p. 429)

Yet Hobsbawm notes that such separateness even in the most extreme examples will fail against the forces of globalization:

Even a world divided into theoretically homogenous ethnic territories by genocide, mass expulsion and 'ethnic cleansing' was inevitably heterogenised again by mass movements of people (workers, tourists, businessmen, technicians), of styles and by the tentacles of the global economy. That, after all, is what happened to the countries of Central Europe, 'ethnically cleansed' during and after the Second World War. That is what would inevitably happen again in an increasingly urbanised world. (ibid., p. 430)

At the point where people seek fixed identities, positions which by some miracle of social navigation provide a certainty of longitude and latitude, a precise cartography of difference, the compass fails and the coastlines and headlands of identity blur and become unreliable. None of this will stop the struggle for certainty: of demons being invoked outside of our borders and within the heartlands of our security. But the process loses strength in a global society where identities constantly cross boundaries and forever change. The fundamental irony is that the solidity of identity deteriorates in proportion to its very urgency.

Note

1. The belief then that the United States is something of a classless society is clearly dismissed by these awesome disparities, whereas the notion that Britain, with its social democratic tradition, is somehow more muted in its inegalitarianism is similarly dissipated.

The equivalent figures for the United Kingdom in 1981 are: the marketable wealth of the top 1% (less value of dwellings) was 29% and in 1992 it was similarly 29%. Whilst the top 1% have 29% of the wealth, the bottom 50% have 6% of the wealth (*Social Trends*, 1995, Table 5.23).

Peter Townsend comments on the distribution of wealth:

Riches are not only inherited or made; to be riches they have to be unavailable to the vast majority of the population. A theory of riches depends not only on theories of acquisition – how much wealth is inherited, accumulated by entrepreneurial effort or by the exercise of scarce skills. It depends, also, on theories of denial of access to wealth – through selective succession, testamentary concentration, limitation of entry to the professions, monopolisation of capital and property or at least severe restriction on the opportunity to acquire land and property. (1979, p. 365, cited in Abercrombie and Warde, 1994, Ch. 3)

7 HOLDING CHAOS IN ABEYANCE: THE MAINTENANCE OF ORDER AMONGST LIGHTLY ENGAGED STRANGERS

> The deepest problems of modern life derive from the claim of the individual to preserve the autonomy and individuality of his existence in the face of overwhelming social forces, of historical heritage, of external culture, and of the technique of life. . . .
>
> The psychological basis of the metropolitan type of individuality consists in the *intensification of nervous stimulation* which results from the swift and uninterrupted change of outer and inner stimuli. Man is a differentiating creature. His mind is stimulated by the difference between a momentary impression and the one which preceded it. Lasting impressions, impressions which differ only slightly from one another, impressions which take a regular and habitual course and show regular and habitual contrasts – all these use up, so to speak, less consciousness than does the rapid crowding of changing images, the sharp discontinuity in the grasp of a single glance, and the unexpectedness of onrushing impressions. These are the psychological conditions which the metropolis creates. With each crossing of the street, with the tempo and multiplicity of economic, occupational and social life, the city sets up a deep contrast with small town and rural life with reference to the sensory foundations of psychic life. The metropolis exacts from man as a discriminating creature a different amount of consciousness than does rural life. . . . In order to accommodate to change and to contrast of phenomena, . . . the metropolitan type of man – which, of course, exists in a thousand individual variants – develops an organ protecting him against the threatening currents and discrepancies of his external environment which would uproot him. (Georg Simmel, 1950, p. 273, emphasis in original)

Thus Georg Simmel, in his famous lecture given in 1909 referring to the experience of life in the great metropolises of Berlin and London, charts the need for a changed psyche, a character armour necessary to resist the onrushing impressions of the city. He situates the blasé attitude, the calculative approach to others, the habits of reserve, as defensive mechanisms. All of this fits well with our discussion of the actuarial attitude and the multicultural epoché. All that can be said is that if the metropolis at the beginning of the century posed problems for the individual, then the megalopolises of the late twentieth century set like giant structures in the global village pose problems of a far more acute nature. The *Umwelt*, the little movable bubble settled around us, carries with it an awareness of risk and a wariness, a discreet distancing from the moral mêlée around us. The area of security has shrunk just as the area of apprehension has increased unceasingly. But Simmel went a little further than this and his visionary comments must surely strike a chord in anyone who has spent their life in the city:

> it is this reserve which in the eyes of the small-town people makes us appear to be cold and heartless. Indeed, if I do not deceive myself, the inner aspect of this outer reserve is not only indifference but, more often than we are aware, it is a slight aversion, a mutual strangeness and repulsion, which will break into hatred and fight at the moment of a closer contact, however caused. (p. 275)

The city, then, is a place of endless possibilities and stimulation but it is also a place where there is a social withdrawal and disengagement which can easily boil over into hostility. There is both an acute sense of difference and an indifference in the urban experience.

The Chicago urbanists who followed Georg Simmel made much of the *frisson* of difference in the city. They were, in David Matza's (1969) phrase, 'appreciative' of the wide variety of social worlds co-existing in the city and they encouraged their students to go out in the city and with notebook and sharp eye observe differences. Robert Park talked of 'a mosaic of little worlds which touch but do not interpenetrate' (1916, p. 608). And the neo-Chicagoans, Becker, Lemert and Goffman, revived the interest in direct observation and the underlying excitement of entering 'deviant' worlds. In all of these studies there is, if you want, a reversal of what Simmel sees as the 'ordinary' cognition of the urban dweller, an opening out of perception of the social scientist compared to the everyday protective shutting out of the citizen (cf. the discussion of the phenomenological epoché in Chapter 4).

But at the same time as stressing Simmel's emphasis on the stimulation of the city, the Chicagoans also emphasized his accent on the reserve and standoffish nature of the citizens, the anonymity of the city and its domination by the abstract ties of money.

As Richard Sennett, in *The Conscience of the Eye* puts it:

> For them, as for Baudelaire, the culture of the city was a matter of experiencing differences – differences of class, age, race and taste, outside the familiar territory of oneself, in a street. And as for the poet, urban differences seemed to Park and Louis Wirth provocations of otherness, surprise, and stimulation. Yet these sociologists had a brilliant, counter-intuitive insight; provocation occurs in the very loosening of strong connections between people in a city. (1991, p. 126)

Sennett's account of this development rather peculiarly suggests that this 'counter-intuitive' insight of the Chicagoans was a breakaway from the 'abstractness' of Simmel, which, as we have seen, is far from the case. What is true, however, is that the Chicago School clearly developed Simmel's ideas, transposing them from Berlin to Chicago, and that such insights have clear implications for the present-day debate on difference.

Richard Sennett brings this out in the proposition that 'deviance is the freedom made possible in a crowded city of lightly engaged people' (ibid., pp. 126–7). Difference and indifference, therefore, interrelate closely: difference results in a protective indifference, indifference permits difference. None of this permissiveness is, in these terms, a product of a culture which exhorts difference but rather one in which people simply care too little about each other to prohibit diversity. And to finalize this dystopian dialectic, the situation of indifference tinged with hostility can easily boil over into outright hostility: demonization of cultural others can occur. Thus a scenario of false differences can be imported to vulnerable sections of the population which can, in both its material and its ideological impact, create real differences.

Richard Sennett, the reluctant *flâneur*

Richard Sennett takes us, in *The Conscience of the Eye*, on a walk through the streets of New York City. He transports us from his apartment in Greenwich Village three miles to a favourite French restaurant mid town, on the streets of the Fifties just above the United Nations. We meet cocaine dealers just east of Washington Square, middle aged women and men escaping their families for a while in the blocks around Gramercy Park; polo players and leather fetishists mix in the equestrian stores of the middle Twenties between Third and Lexington, in the Upper Twenties Indian spice dealers enigmatically guard their mysterious bags of spice, whilst on Murray Hill the New York elite, shabbily dressed and permanently rich, talk of children and divorces, and, finally, in the east Forties, between Lexington and First, in an area of junior diplomats and their children, we reach the restaurant itself.

But Sennett is profoundly disappointed: this is not the world of Baudelaire, he does not feel like the *flâneur* who is profoundly engaged by the vivid scenes around him. Here in New York City, the paragon city of differences, something is missing. People are indifferent to each other and Sennett, himself, professes indifference to them. People are turned inward, not outward, by the great city which surrounds them. The leather fetishists and the straight equestrians show no interest in each other, 'saddles and whips are sold by harassed salesmen, wrapped by clerks ostentatiously bored', the spice merchants distance themselves from their clientele, 'the junkies doing business are seldom in the mood to chat', the various races encountered live together in a segregated fashion, mixing but not socializing, the rich at Murray Hill maintain themselves apart from others in 'strategic discretion', and, finally, the restaurant is set in the most neutral area of Manhattan: 'the forest of tall dull apartment blocks . . . blot out the sun on the streets. On the periphery of the city, one can see literally miles of burned-out or abandoned ruins . . . the permissible belt of desolation in so rich a city . . . like a blast of civic indifference' (ibid., p. 131). And to this Sennett adds his own plea of alienation:

Nor are the chameleon virtues of the Chicago urbanists much in evidence: people do not take on the colors of their surroundings, the light-hued colors of otherness. A walk in New York reveals instead that difference from and indifference to others are a related, unhappy pair. The eye sees differences to which it reacts with indifference. I, too, feel no curiosity to know what is problematic in the life of a drug dealer; I am too polite to intrude upon the solitude of a middle-aged woman, or to violate the privacy of another man's sexual obsessions. When I do reach out, harmlessly, the spice merchant pushes me away with his irony. (ibid., p. 129)

I am struck here by how closely Sennett's description comes to other writers who react to the romantic evocation of the diversity of the city. Thus Ken Pryce, in his study of the West Indian area of Bristol, castigates those who confuse social disorganization with the notion of an alternative community:

> The lack of community in St Paul's is often not apparent to strangers visiting the area for the first time, especially students and intellectuals with their tendency to romanticize the deviant and the exotic. Diverse groups with vastly dissimilar backgrounds do mingle freely in close physical interaction in St Paul's. But this is deceptive, for mingling of this kind does not automatically create a sense of conformity, consensus, and vigilance about community standards. The only unity is an external one, in the form of common services utilised by all.
>   Beneath the romantic's illusion of a tight-knit, friendly, organic, warm, harmonious community, the divisions are deep. There is much suspicion between groups. The very fact that in St Paul's people are 'not fussy' (which is what attracts middle-class students and intellectuals), the very fact that there are no constraining community standards, no overriding considerations that people are forced to adhere to, is one reason why St Paul's is a shanty town. The social heterogeneity of the neighbourhood and the suspicion reigning between groups, especially different ethnic groups, gives rise to a sort of 'anything goes' atmosphere, in which one group tends to view members from other groups as easy prey and fair game for exploitation. There is no melting-pot morality combining disparate elements into one. (1979, pp. 29–30)

The 'community' which occurs, Pryce notes, echoing Simmel, is 'bound only by commerce' – social behaviour is united only by the silver threads of the market place. The city of variety is thus the city of indifference; each sub-group treads their wary way actuarially through the city, ducking and diving, keeping themselves to themselves and, then, sometimes turning upon each other.

But there is something strange about Sennett's claim of indifference. Here he has taken us on a trip through one of the exciting cities on the planet; New York like all the other old convergent cities, has as a major industry people from all over the world coming to sample this city of difference. And Sennett, himself, obviously delights in his stroll, yet he claims indifference. In part this is because he is unable to straddle the two aims of the Chicagoans, which they in turn inherited from Simmel. That is, as David Matza put it, to be *appreciative* of the urban phenomenon yet at the same time be aware of the gross *pathos* of urban living (see Matza, 1969, pp. 49–53). Matza's philosophy of 'naturalism', his invocation to be 'faithful' to the phenomenon studied, demands this: that is, to avoid on the one hand the romanticism of urban life and, on the other, casting the city into the wastebin category of disorganization. That is, neither to indulge difference nor to portray difference as mere deviance. Sennett looks for a city of delights, where one learns from the shock of the other and which turns us outwards, yet nourishes us inwards. But he is repulsed by the anonymity, the alienation and the dislocation. He can maintain his interest only providing he keeps his distance. 'The smell of urine,' he writes, 'is perfumed if only I keep walking' (1991, p. 128).

But there is more than simple dislocation. What is missing is community and social cohesion to be sure, but he seeks more than that, he wants a *metanarrative*, a rubric which holds all of these people, situations and things together, providing a shared history, purpose and future. Sennett captures this vividly when he writes:

> A New York street resembles the studio of a painter who has assembled in it all the paints, books of other artists, and sketches he will need for a grand triptych that will crown his career, then the painter has unaccountably left town. (ibid., p. 129)

He wants, in short, the bits of the city to fall into place. He is searching both for community and for integration.

The purification process

It is important to place Richard Sennett's stroll through Manhattan in the context of his work in general. In an earlier book, *Uses of Disorder* written in 1970, Sennett describes how the American suburb is a purified space purposely created by exclusion. *The Conscience of the Eye* (1991) pursues this theme from the suburbs into the city, with his notion of fear of exposure. The ancient Greeks, he believes, could use their eyes in their cities to see the complexities of life. The temples, the statues, the markets, the political meeting places were representations of the inner life of the citizen. In the modern world, he argues, there is a marked divide between our inner selves and the outside world, between self and the city. The city is constructed to cut us off from each other, to create a mental space outside of ourselves:

> The division between inner, subjective experience and outer, physical life expresses in fact a great fear which our civilisation has refused to admit, much less to reckon. The spaces full of people in the modern city are either spaces limited to and carefully orchestrating consumption, like the shopping mall, or spaces limited to and carefully orchestrating the experience of tourism. This reduction and trivialisation of the city . . . is no accident. . . . The way cities look represents a great unreckoned fear of exposure. 'Exposure' more connotes the likelihood of being hurt than of being stimulated. . . . What is characteristic of our city dwelling

is to wall off the differences between people, assuming that these differences are
more likely to be mutually threatening than mutually stimulating. What we make
in the urban realm are therefore bland, neutralising spaces, spaces which remove
the threat of contact: street walls faced in sheets of plate glass, highways to cut off
poor neighborhoods from the rest of the city, dormitory housing developments.
(ibid., p. xii)

He traces, although a little unclearly, two presumably interactive processes:
the way in which the inner world of the self is cut off from the outer world
of the city, and the way in which different groups are separated from each
other. The fear of exposure is very much like the concept of ontological
security and the actuarial attitude which we discussed earlier in this book.
The result is seen as a purification of the city and public blandness. The
other half of Simmel's city, that of stimulation and *frisson*, is given short
shrift by Sennett and it is in this context that his stroll through Manhattan
is given content. For here, surely, in the heart of this great convergent city,
there is great mixing of people, the separation of suburban housing and mall
is absent, and there is great vitality and excitement? Who ever thought the
Big Apple bland? But perhaps this is Sennett's test case, for even here he
suggests that people are indifferent to each other and indeed he (very
unconvincingly!) is indifferent to those he encounters on his stroll. Thus, he
would seem to argue, even where the architectural paraphernalia of separation are absent, people themselves continue on their own tracks through
the city separate from each other, fearing exposure at every turn. This image
of the city is then rather like a protective *Umwelt* where the area of security
has shrunk to the home and where the whole aspect of *Umwelt* as opportunity for excitement and pleasure is sadly adumbrated.

The 'Soft City' revisited

The city is the site of pleasure and danger, of opportunity and threat. It attracts
and repels, and cannot do one thing without doing the other. The city breeds
excitement and fatigue, offering on one tray tidbits of freedom and enemas of dis-
empowerment. The modern promise to purify the crystal of pleasure and drain
off the contaminating impurities failed to materialize, while the zealous attempts
to act on that promise through forcing urban life into a reason-dictated frame, and
prohibiting everything that the design had not made obligatory, only added new,
artificially produced malfunctions to the old, spontaneously emerging blights. It
seems that the ambiguity of city life is here to stay. (Bauman, 1995, p. 137)

For Zygmunt Baumann the city of late modernity retains its contradictory
nature: indeed, it is more so; the process of purification has not worked, the
planners have failed, Raban's *Soft City* exists in all its emporium of delights
and dangers. Sennett generalizes from the suburbs, particularly those of the
United States, to the city just as in another context the various interpretations of Mike Davies' *City of Quartz* generalizes from the dispersed and
divergent city of Los Angeles to the convergent cities of the world.

The city is attractive because it has no metanarrative – or more succinctly because the regulated city of the planners has broken down. It is in the bars and the nightclubs, the restaurants which have sprung up, sometimes in the most unlikely places, in the mixture of people knowing little of each other, in the sheer impersonality of contact, in the lack of responsibility and need to form community, in the absence of a need to stop every minute to give account of oneself to family and neighbour. It is a world of the stroller and of the bricoleur; the accent is on the city dweller drifting around his or her city picking up this and that, peering and learning, rather than on the passive citizen of the planners' drawing board – acting appropriately in designated areas. The inner world is constituted by this diversity outside, it informs the boundaries of one's subculture (as one's subculture does theirs), it involves a cultural crossover where one subculture takes on board ideas and behaviours from another.

At best such a context can be liberating: it gives both the freedom to develop and the cultural materials by which to constitute one's development; an environment which permits diversity and a diversity which feeds upon itself. At worst, it can involve the cultural process of demonization and the material risk of crime and harassment. The city, as Baumann points out, is not open for all to freely stroll around its streets and byways; the behaviour of others threatens and excludes, creating monsters out of strangers, and constructing binaries of normality and deviancy in opposition to others around them. The city is forbidding and disquieting, then, because of the patterns of domination, of lack of social recognition or respect and because also, and often closely intertwined, it presents vistas of injustice: of inequality and unfairness.

To walk those streets must of necessity produce feelings of risk, of ontological insecurity and of disquiet. All of these things may engender detachment and indifference but it is an indifference which is markedly affected by the world of difference around it. The blasé front is an act, part of a character armour of indifference. But the city can also engender fascination, a *frisson* of excitement, a rush of ideas and a constant battering of preconceptions. No Greek *polis* ever provided an external world of such variety and stimulation, no small slave-owning city could ever harbour such ideals of citizenship, however frustrated and bruised by reality.

The idealized community

In the last chapter I detailed the problems of the sphere of justice and those of community. Let us here elaborate those of community.

Liberal democracy has to deal with the problem of how individuals relate to each other and the problem of how diverse communities relate to each other. That is, of how the constituent parts of society hold together in a unity rather than act egoistically or divisively. Such a process involves mutual trust and respect: it is the converse of a Hobbesian war of all against all or of the diminution and demonization of less powerful sections of the population by more powerful. The most common resolution of this is the evocation of the single community posed as the binary opposite of the solitary individual. Thus on one side we have the notion of individualism, separation, selfishness and on the other we have the notion of collectivism, integration and working together. Indeed, much radical criticism of society holds 'the community' as the ideal against which the present competitive and unequal situation is to be judged. Iris Young, in *Justice and the Politics of Difference* (1990a), has produced a scathing critique of the privileging of community in this fashion:

> I shall argue that the ideal of community fails to offer an appropriate alternative vision of polity. . . . this ideal expresses a desire for the fusion of subjects with one another which in practice operates to exclude those with whom the group does not identify. The ideal of community denies and represses social difference, the fact that the polity cannot be thought of as a unity in which all participants share a common experience and common values. In its privileging of face-to-face relations, moreover, the ideal of community denies difference in the form of the temporal and spatial distancing that characterizes social process.
>
> As an alternative to the ideal of community, I develop . . . an ideal of city life as a vision of social relations affirming group difference. As a normative ideal, city life instantiates social relations of difference without exclusion. Different groups dwell in the city alongside one another, of necessity interacting in city spaces. If city politics is to be democratic and not dominated by the point of view of one group, it must be a politics that takes account of and provides voice for the different groups that dwell together in the city without forming a community. (1990a, pp. 226–7)

What community denies is any notion of difference; it threatens to assimilate diversity into the dominant culture and to devalue those outside of it.

> Racism, ethnic chauvinism, and class devaluation, I suggest, grow partly from a desire for community, that is, from the desire to understand others as they understand themselves and from the desire to be understood as I understand myself. Practically speaking, such mutual understanding can be approximated only within a homogeneous group that defines itself by common attributes. Such common identification, however, entails reference also to those excluded. In the dynamics of racism and ethnic chauvinism in the United States today, the positive identification of some groups is often achieved by first defining other groups as the other, the devalued semihuman. I do not claim that appeal to the ideal of community is itself racist. Rather, my claim is that such appeals, within the context of a racist and chauvinistic society, can validate the impulses that reproduce racist and ethnically chauvinistic identification. (Young, 1990b, pp. 311–12)

Iris Young is at pains to situate this process in the context of the United States where, as we saw in Chapter 1, the exclusive ideology is exceptionally virulent but it is, of course, a general aspect of all attempts to create a unitary community. It is also more of a pressing problem as we move from an inclusive society to one which is more diverse and pluralistic. The problem, therefore, is how to construct a community which will facilitate a universe of difference.

Furthermore, and here she makes an exceptionally important point, just as the notion of a unitary community denies difference, so too does it imply the rather Arcadian idea of the community as, of necessity, a place of face-to-face relations between like-minded and well acquainted people. This image, redolent both of the inclusive society with its idealization of small town society and the urban village, or of the exclusive society with its invocation of a necklace of well-knit communities, is to her the very opposite of what is attractive in the urban life experience. For her advocates of community privilege face-to-face relations because of their immediacy, yet it is mediated relations that have allowed the rich growth which links people across space and time.

Echoing Simmel, she celebrates the diversity of the city, its bringing together of strangers, and she actively seeks to circumvent the traditional binary of individualism and community.

> Even for many of those who decry the alienation, bureaucratization, and mass character of capitalist patriarchal society, city life exerts a powerful attraction. Modern literature, art, and film have celebrated city life, its energy, cultural diversity, technological complexity, and the multiplicity of its activities. Even many of the most staunch proponents of decentralized community love to show visiting friends around the Boston or San Francisco or New York in or near which they live, climbing up towers to see the glitter of lights and sampling the fare of the best ethnic restaurants.
>
> I propose to construct a normative ideal of city life as an alternative to both the ideal of community and the liberal individualism it criticizes as asocial. By 'city life' I mean a form of social relations which I define as the being together of strangers. (1990a, p. 237)

We must start from what is possible, from the reality of urban life, rather than hold out an ideal which is a futile attempt to reverse the history of urban development:

> Contemporary political theory must accept urbanity as a material given for those who live in advanced industrial societies. Urban relations define the lives not only of those who live in the suburbs and large towns. Our social life is structured by vast networks of temporal and spatial mediation among persons, so that nearly everyone depends on the activities of seen and unseen strangers who mediate between oneself and one's associates, between oneself and one's objects of desire. . . .
>
> Starting from the given of modern urban life is not simply necessary, moreover; it is desirable. (ibid., pp. 236–7)

The city, then, is a source of variety and offers the possibility of social differentiation without exclusion; it facilitates a wide variety of subcultures. Gay life, for example, would not be possible without urban anonymity whilst the city itself, in its restaurants, shops and sights, has an erotic, pleasurable quality. In this sense, as we have seen, it is in the anonymity and impersonality of the city that a diversity of subcultures is possible. Young therefore does not deny the importance of small group relations, this is the very nature of most subcultures, but rather the privileging of them over the impersonal urban world because, amongst other things, it is in this substratum that they have the room to develop. The truly personal arises in the context of the impersonal.

Iris Young is, of course, well aware of the dark side of the *Soft City* and that her ideal is realized only 'incidentally and intermittently' in some cities. It is after all an ideal, a highlighting of the potential of reality, not a description of the present. In reality, racism, sexism, xenophobia, homophobia, suspicion and mockery 'all darken the possibilities'. Her ideal in contrast is the 'unoppressive city' which she defines as where there is 'an openness to unassimilated others', where 'The public is heterogeneous, plural, and playful, a place where people witness and appreciate diverse cultural expressions that they do not share and do not fully understand' (ibid., p. 241). The unoppressive city does not necessitate the extraordinary, one might suggest almost totalitarian levels of informal control of an idealized urban *Gemeinschaft* or indeed of the television soap opera. Civility is oblique, implicit, laid back – one is reminded of Jane Jacobs' characterization of the successful city in *The Death and Life of Great American Cities*. Indeed Iris Young starts her chapter on 'City Life and Difference' with a quote from this famous text:

> The tolerance, the room for great differences amongst neighbors – differences that often go far deeper than differences in color – which are possible and normal in intensely urban life, but which are so foreign to suburbs and pseudosuburbs, are possible and normal only when streets of great cities have built-in equipment allowing strangers to dwell in peace together on civilized but essentially dignified and reserved terms. (1961, p. 83)

To achieve this aim one needs above all distributive justice. As Young clearly realizes, without fairness in the sphere of justice, tolerance in the sphere of community will not be achieved. This was the mistake which Jacobs herself made: her lightly engaged, tolerant West Village of Manhattan was possible only when each part of the structure of the neighbourhood felt the American Dream was there to be realized. When, as Marshall Berman pointed out, a black and Hispanic underclass emigrated to the city and were palpably economically excluded, then the fragile community broke down. For:

> It was clear by the late 1960s that, amid the class disparities and racial polarities that skewered American city life, no urban neighborhood anywhere, not even the liveliest and healthiest, could be free from crime, random violence, pervasive rage and fear. Jacobs' faith in the benignness of the sounds she heard from the street in the middle of the night was bound to be, at best, a dream. (1983, p. 325)

Where Jacobs was correct, however, was that in the right economic circumstances it was not necessary to have a tight-knit community to control crime and disorder. Indeed, we might note that just as the strong family does not obviate crime (see Chapter 6), the strong community can well support criminal networks and subcultures. Such a finding has occurred throughout the literature on communities and crime control. Most recently Evans, Fraser and Walklate in their study of the 'Oldtown' area of Salford note the irony of how completely their findings fly in the face of communitarian and crime prevention notions of community: 'In Oldtown your *place* in relation to crime *places* you in a community of belonging and exclusion' (1996, p. 379, emphasis in original). In particular, commitment to professional crime meant inclusion, 'grassing' meant exclusion. Many run-down estates have, of course, considerably stronger kinship networks, lack of geographical mobility (because of unemployment) and knowledge of each other than middle class areas which have extremely low crime rates.

The unoppressive city as openness to unassimilated others

Although one might agree wholeheartedly with Iris Young's endorsement of the loosely engaged community as most likely to encourage diversity, especially where there is an underpinning of distributive justice and shared values of tolerance, her rather dramatic notion of difference to be tolerated and learnt from is scarcely sustainable. Unassimilated otherness is a fantasy of Fascists and of their political opposites, multiculturalists. There is no such thing as a hermetically separate otherness in the late modern city – there is always a degree of assimilation, crossover and influence between subcultures. As we have seen in Philadelphia, the stereotype of the black underclass is an example of such shared fantasies. Part of their cultural othering has been to project upon themselves a radical difference. This is, of course, particularly true in the exclusive society: in the earlier period of inclusivism they, their 'other', would be seen as a lack; that is, not difference but merely defective normality. Ironically, as Carl Nightingale shows, as the culture, historically, becomes more 'American' they are widely viewed as less and less American. And the same is true of Philippe Bourgois' Puerto Ricans. In reality, difference in late modernity, because of the extraordinary level of interaction and mediation which Young acknowledges, is a matter of differential emphasis, accentuation and interpretation of a general culture admixed with specific cultural features which have been historically transmuted. Subculture is a useful concept, here, because it captures both the global and the local, and the way in which in late modernity there is a globalization of culture because of the intense influence of the mass media, while at the same time a greater creativity at the local level (the so-called phenomenon of 'glocalization').

Young's problem is that in her attempt to erect a position independent of both egoistic individualism and the 'community', she teeters on the edge of multiculturalism. She is aware, of course, of the dangers of essentialist and absolutist views of group difference where difference is seen 'as sharing no attributes with the defining group, locked in despised bodies and fixed natures' (Young, 1990a, p. 260). But despite this she is, perhaps understandably, so concerned with charges of being assimilationist, of being blind to domination and of paying scant recognition to values of dominated groups, that she is hesitant to go beyond the invitation to be open to unassimilated others. But not only does this disregard the very real changes which have occurred in late modernity, it is scarcely a desirable political outcome.

Difference multiculturalism

Nancy Fraser in *Justice Interruptus* develops an incisive critique of what she calls difference feminism and its multicultural equivalent: pluralist multiculturalism. Her criticisms closely resemble those we discussed in Chapter 4, but have particular purchase on the work of Iris Young. Her accusation is that *Justice and the Politics of Difference* displays an indiscriminatory multiculturalism, a politics of recognition divorced from a politics of justice, which treats all cultures and differences as worthy of recognition:

> Like difference feminism, pluralist multiculturalism tends to substantialize identities, treating them as given positivities instead of as constructed relations. It tends, consequently, to balkanize culture, setting groups apart from one another, ignoring the ways they cut across one another, and inhibiting cross-group interaction and identification. Losing sight of the fact that differences intersect, it regresses to a simple additive model of difference.
>
> Furthermore, both tendencies valorize existing group identities assuming that all that is needed is equality of respect. But, in fact, they may be tied to social relations of domination and would not survive the supplanting of these relations. Many identities are incompatible with others – white supremacism and antiracism, for example. It is impossible to avoid judgement between identities and differences, yet pluralist multiculturalism attempts to remain neutral. (Fraser, 1997, p. 185)

There are many groups who are underprivileged in Young's terms, like neo-Nazi skinheads or working class Orangemen, whom we would certainly not like to recognize or valorize. We must avoid at all costs what Todd Gitlin calls the 'romancing of otherness' (1992; see also Turner, 1994). Fraser's own answer to the question of valorization of difference is to distinguish four positions on difference:

1 Humanism: where difference is seen as a result of oppression, e.g. pathologies and dysfunctions. This is close to the inclusivist strategies we discussed in Chapter 3 which seek to get rid of all difference;

2 Those who see difference as a mark of cultural superiority over dominant groups, e.g. Afro-centrism, or gyno-centrism;
3 Those who see difference as cultural variation. This is Young's position: there are no superiorities or inferiorities, just variations;
4 Fraser's own position which admits *selectively* all of the above three. That is, some differences are pathologies and we should seek to *eliminate* them, some are superiorities (such as female nurturance, for example) and should be *universalized* amongst all groups, and some (but not all) are variations and these should be *enjoyed*.

This is, to my mind, an extremely satisfactory solution to the relationship to cultural others which does not commit the sin of relativism (as for example multiculturalism does), which by admitting the possibility of pathology as well as healthy adaptation does not fall into the errors of theories of social disorganization and by stressing the possibility of learning and universalizing from many others gets out of the notion of some absolute culture against which difference is judged as defect. In short, Fraser suggests the possibility of an approach to others which transforms oneself as well as changing others. It is this last notion of the transformative approach to difference which I will turn to now.

A transformative openness to others

> If we are to think again about the vexed question of multiculturalism it is vital to avoid any slippage into the false comfort of simple cultural archetypes and reify 'minority' and 'host' cultures respectively. Imperialism and the racist discourses that have flourished in its wake insist on what Roland Barthes called the 'simplicity of essences'. However, cultural processes themselves found the idea that cultures exist as hermetically sealed absolute unities. Urban cultures, in particular, are highly promiscuous in their endeavour constantly to re-make and invent traditions in the present. Edward Said attempts to name this process by insisting that one must view the politics of culture within 'overlapping territories' and 'intertwined histories' (Said, 1993). The key question thus becomes how to render explicit the multiple influences that resonate within metropolitan contexts such as London, Amsterdam, Paris, Hamburg and Berlin. (Back, 1996, pp. 7–8)

We must set against the multiculturalist notions of difference what I will call a transformative multiculturalism. I touched upon this notion in the discussion of essentialism in Chapter 4: it has clear resonances in the work of Edward Said, Paul Gilroy and Les Back. This is where one stresses the open nature of cultural exchange, the way in which norms overlap and cross over, and boundaries blur. Furthermore, one must stress in the subculture tradition the constant creation, rejuvenation and transformation of subcultures: they are always in flux, they are never finished. Lastly, each subculture is a context for the others and each changes in response to and is transformed by the others.

Nowhere is this awareness of what one might call a transformative openness to others better displayed than in Paul Gilroy's *The Black Atlantic*. He
starts by trying to disentangle what it means to be black British. He is concerned with the way in which such identities are seen to comprise the collision of two separate ethnic absolutes, finished in their nature and one-sided
in their influence:

> Striving to be both European and black requires some specific forms of double
> consciousness. By saying this I do not mean to suggest that taking on either or
> both of these unfinished identities necessarily exhausts the subjective resources of
> any particular individual. However, where racist, nationalist, or ethnically
> absolutist discourses orchestrate political relationships so that these identities
> appear to be mutually exclusive, occupying the space between them or trying to
> demonstrate their continuity has been viewed as a provocative and even opposi-
> tional act of political insubordination. (1993, p. 1)

But conventional analysis makes no sense even in the most extreme
instances:

> [if] the reflexive cultures and consciousness of the European settlers and those of
> the Africans they enslaved, the 'Indians' they slaughtered, and the Asians they
> indentured were not, even in situations of the most extreme brutality, sealed off
> hermetically from each other, then so be it. This seems as though it ought to be
> an obvious and self-evident observation, but its stark character has been sys-
> tematically obscured by commentators from all sides of political opinion. Regard-
> less of their affiliation to the right, left, or centre, groups have fallen back on the
> idea of cultural nationalism, on the overintegrated concepts of culture which
> present immutable, ethnic differences as an absolute break in the histories and
> experiences of 'black' and 'white' people. Against this choice stands another,
> more difficult option: the theorisation of creolisation, métissage, mesizaje, and
> hybridity. From the viewpoint of ethnic absolutism, this would be a litany of pol-
> lution and impurity. These terms are rather unsatisfactory ways of naming the
> process of cultural mutation and restless (dis)continuity that exceed racial dis-
> course and avoid capture by its agents. (ibid., p. 2)

Low intensity difference

It is not only that difference is a question of crossover and exchange in late
modernity: although there is a greater plurality of groups and values, the
intensity of *significant difference* is to my mind less dramatic than is portrayed by multiculturalists. By significant difference I mean those differences between groups which create dynamic conflicts and hostilities within
society.

You will recall Russell Jacoby's critique of multiculturalism. It was a
myth, he maintained, a confusion of different superficial patterns of taste in
the overall American rubric of consumption and dreams of success. In
seeing America as a level cultural playing field he went too far; by insisting

that 'difference' implied almost anthropological contrasts he was using the yardstick set up by multiculturalists. That is, one which insists that the various indigenous cultures of a society are *essentially* different. This is not on the whole true: they cross over as I have argued and have, as Nancy Fraser points out, many cross-cutting links (e.g. men with men *between* subcultures, young people with *all* youth, rich people with rich despite ethnicity, gender or age). Furthermore, there are general agreements (e.g. over reward by merit as a prime value or of equality before the law) as well as variations in the particular traditions and interpretation of values. Hence my preference for subculture as a key to the notion of difference.

Thus Robert Park's picture of a 'mosaic of little worlds which touch but do not interpenetrate' may have been true of areas where immigration is of recent origin, but scarcely corresponds to the usual late modern world of transposition, globalization, hybridization and crossover, where norms overlap, boundaries blur and transformations occur in all directions. It is tempting to portray Amitai Etzioni's mosaic ideal where the cultures are independent and the surround is in common as is almost a contemporary manifestation of Park's picture where different immigrant cultures change little but the total city has reached some measure of communality. Or, indeed, Iris Young's universe of difference where she too upholds the notion of isolation and sharp contrast.

I am not denying that cultures of dramatic difference can occur, but that they do so by great effort of isolation (e.g. the Hasidic Jews, and the Amish) or that they are a product of fairly recent immigration where the culture places great stress on its distinctiveness *because* it is in great danger of subsequent assimilation (e.g. some examples of religious fundamentalism). In the latter instance such high intensity difference is often seen as evidence of a dramatic multiculturalism when it is in fact the sign of the reverse, the ever-eroding presence of assimilation. Instead, my stress is on the pluralism of subcultures which are constantly created, transformed and recreated throughout our society. Furthermore, my argument is that such low intensity variation is a key to the dynamics of inter-group relationships. I have already touched upon this in relation to problems of distributive justice, in particular how relative deprivation is generated. This demands some degree of moral proximity, some sense of identity as well as difference. Thus the sense of deprivation and anguish increases as Nightingale's black underclass becomes more integrated into American society; the Puerto Ricans of Bourgois' *barrio* become more committed to the American Dream as they assimilate. In our own work, levels of discontent displayed by the wave of immigrants entering Britain in the 1950s and 1960s were closely related to levels of integration (see Lea and Young, 1982, 1984). Thus the crime rate amongst African-Caribbeans was lower than average in the first generation but higher in the second generation whilst the immigrants from South Asia, who were much less integrated than the African-Caribbeans, maintained an extremely low crime rate until recently.

Relative deprivation occurs when one compares oneself with people who one would expect to earn similar wages – it occurs between women and men, for example, when women are seen as more equal, not when they are consigned to a totally different social category. Similarly, it occurs when workers on various levels compare themselves with their equivalents (and those immediately above and immediately below them where appropriate differentials should be expected). People do not feel relatively deprived compared to the Royal Family or Mick Jagger, but to the man or woman next door.

I would like to argue that discontent in the sphere of community is similar in pattern to that in distributive justice. Ontological insecurity about others is much more likely to occur where there is a basis of similarity and when people seem to exist in some universe of possibility. Thus in my own neighbourhood it is not the woman dressed in full hijab, the man attired in the fur hat and accoutrements of an eighteenth-century Polish nobleman, the activist with a picture of Joe Stalin on his wall talking about the armed struggle in Kurdistan, the Jehovah's Witnesses on the doorstep with their fundamentalist litany. If anything, these cultural dinosaurs make one feel more ontologically secure, not less so. Rather, it is those people nearer to one, whom one sees as assuringly like oneself and who have made different choices. This is why it is the bisexual, not the transsexual, who generates the greatest insecurity amongst heterosexuals and it is the gay person who is almost straight who generates more insecurity than the person who is decidedly camp in his behaviour.

Low intensity community and transformative multiculturalism

Let us now tabulate those distinctions made between the idealized community and the low intensity community and between the notion of dramatic difference and low intensity difference (see Tables 7.1 and 7.2). Note that I am arguing that there is a close affinity between the two concepts: a low intensity community facilitates the development of difference but it also has no clear demarcations of membership, values and boundary, which sits well with a transformative multiculturalism. Further, I am arguing that there has been transformation across time: there has been a breakdown of the traditional 'organic' communities set around places of work, the sense of identity before late modernity was more clear cut and fixed.

I want to conclude this chapter by looking at the sort of politics which can set about tackling the problems of relative deprivation and ontological insecurity: that is in the sphere of distributive justice and recognition within the community.

Redistribution and recognition, affirmation and transformation

Nancy Fraser in *Justice Interruptus* sketches the outline of a radical politics which will facilitate the sort of social transformation which meshes well with

TABLE 7.1 *Ideal and low intensity communities*

	Ideal community	Low intensity community
Mode of access	Organic: around place of work, birth	Mobility
Admission	Ascriptive	Achievement
Interaction	Face to face	Face to face/mediated
Membership	Fixed	Fluid
Locus	Spatial	Cultural
Intensity	High intensity	Low intensity
Culture	Tradition	Creation

TABLE 7.2 *Difference and transformative multiculturalism*

	Difference multiculturalism	Transformative multiculturalism
Interface	Hermetic	Open
Domination	Inequality ignored	Equality insisted
Valorization	Indiscriminate	Discrimination
Time frame	Stasis/finished	Flux/unfinished
Discovery	In past/roots	In future
Norms	Separate	Overlap and crossover
Boundaries	Distinct	Blurred
Interaction	As tourist	As *flâneur*
Degree	Dramatic difference	Low intensity difference

our concerns. First of all she separates two areas of injustice: redistribution and recognition. Redistribution concerns injustice in terms of the material world, recognition concerns equality or valorization of cultural difference. One is concerned with socio-economic inequalities and the other cultural injustices. These two categories fit nicely with the two spheres of justice and community which I outlined in earlier chapters: the first is identical with redistribution, the second can quite easily be accommodated with it if one widens out the concept from the valorization of different cultures to include the valorization of individuals. That is, by acknowledging that the two basic problematics of liberal democracy are the equitable distribution of goods concomitant with work and merit and the reconciliation of the interests of individuals and – in a multiculturalist society – groups, the apocryphal 'war of all against all' does not occur.

Fraser distinguishes affirmative and transformative remedies for injustice (see Table 7.3). Affirmative remedies correct the inequitable outcomes of social arrangements without changing the underlying structures that produce them. Transformative remedies correct inequitable outcomes because they restructure their underlying framework, the causal mechanisms which produce them.

TABLE 7.3   *Fraser's typology of social intervention*

	Affirmation	Transformation
Redistribution	*Welfare state* • Surface, band-aid remedies to inequality • Maintains group differences • Liable to generate misrecognition	*Socialism* • Changes in deep structures: elimination of causes of inequality • Blurs group differences • May remedy misrecognition
Recognition	*Multiculturalism* • Equalization of respect to existing identities • Maintains group differences	*Deconstruction* • Breakdown of existing classifications of identity, dereification of binaries • Sustains multiple and shifting identities

Let us look at the contrast between these remedies in each of the two realms of injustice: redistribution and recognition.

Redistribution

Affirmative remedies are those characterized by the liberal welfare state. Typically, members of the primary labour market are taxed to provide means-tested aid for those low in the secondary labour market and the unemployed. This does not restructure class differentials but, in fact, re-affirms them; it solves nothing but necessitates reallocation of resources again and again. Furthermore, by marking the disadvantaged class as 'inherently deficient and insatiable' they result in injustices of recognition. The underclass comes to be seen as a more or less permanent class who are culturally as well as economically inadequate and are prime targets for resentment. For, as we have seen in our discussion of the black underclass, affirmative distribution through the limited welfare support provided, far from abolishing class differences, merely reaffirms and strengthens the existing structure.

Transformative methods, in contrast, involve:

> Universalist social-welfare programs, steeply progressive taxes, a large non-market sector, significant public and/or collective ownership, and democratic decision-making about basic socio-economic priorities. They try to assure access to employment for all, whilst also tending to delimit basic consumption shares from unemployment. Transformative methods reduce social inequality without, however, creating stigmatized classes of people perceived as beneficiaries of special largesse . . . thus, an approach aimed at redressing injustices of distribution can help redress (some) injustices of recognition as well. (Fraser 1997, p. 26)

Fraser's transformative policies are not apocalyptic but gradual. She is at pains to make clear that by transformation she is not referring, here, to any necessary abolition of class exploitation but to a robust social democracy, in the tradition of T.H. Marshall, with a developed sense of social citizenship which would suffice and would contrast dramatically with the merely affirmative policies of liberal democracy.

Recognition

Affirmative recognition is the programme of mainstream multiculturalism: this seeks to redress lack of respect and recognition by valorizing groups whose identities are undervalued. It attempts through a historical discovery of roots, by subsidy to support and develop existing cultures, widespread and educational devices to propagate a positive image of the group to affirm the value of each culture. Transformative remedies, in contrast, attempt to deconstruct the cultural dichotomies, to go beyond them. Thus:

> Affirmative remedies ... [leave] identities ... intact, both the contents of those identities and the group differentiations that underlie them. Transformative remedies, by contrast, are currently associated with deconstruction. They would redress disrespect by transforming the underlying cultural-valuational structure. By destabilizing existing group identities and differentiations, these remedies would not only raise the self-esteem of members of currently disrespected groups; they would change *everyone's* sense of self. (Fraser, 1997, p. 24)

The example which Nancy Fraser develops is that of gay identity politics which, by pursuing affirmative remedies, attempts to grant value to gays and lesbians as entities, rather like the conventional notion of ethnic groups. On the contrary, transformative remedies and the queer politics that go with them, attempt to deconstruct the binary homo–hetero itself. That is, homosexuality and heterosexuality are regarded as a fake dualism: a reification of sexual ambiguity. Transformation insists, not on solidifying gay identity, but on dissolving the homo–hetero dichotomy, so as to sustain multiple and shifting sexual identities. The goal is not to enhance existing sexual group differentiations but to destablize them.

Fraser's analysis is, to my mind, extremely productive but I would now like to critically adjust some of the distinctions, bringing them more in line with the argument that we have developed so far.

Sphere of justice: the meritocratic society

Fraser's reasoning as to the justice of a situation tends to be phrased, quite understandably, on the level of the social philosopher judging the fairness of a form of redistribution rather than sociologically from the point of view of the social actors themselves. I have argued in this book that one of the most persuasive ideologies in advanced industrial society is that of the meritocracy. Furthermore, that there is, as famously noted by Merton, a widespread disjunction between this cultural goal and the actual opportunities presented to people. Such a feeling of frustration is experienced not as a general discontent but as relative deprivation – as a comparison of one's material position with that of others who one would expect to earn similar wages and have similar lifestyles.

Affirmative remedies, therefore, which provide relief ('benefits') for those low in the secondary labour market and the unemployed, not only mark a section of the population out as different and liable to stigmatization as an underclass, as Fraser points out, but are also experienced by them as social exclusion: that is, in the case of the structurally unemployed, barriers to them entering on to the meritocratic racetrack and, in the instance of those low in the secondary labour market, permission for them to enter only a part of the track which has low rewards, does not go very far and from which one is ever liable to be called off. In either case chronic relative deprivation is experienced, a gross denial of the full rights of citizenship is sensed and, of course, the result is frequently crime and disorder. Affirmative remedies do not only unsettle the contented, as Fraser has pointed out, they very distinctly unsettle the poor.

We may move this argument a little further if we touch upon the affirmative policies of left of centre administrations like those of Clinton and Blair. These include affirmative methods such as the dragooning of the unemployed into the lower parts of the secondary labour market and a 'tertiary' market of chronic short term work, low pay at – or below – the level of the statutory minimum wage, without any chance of career development or personal job satisfaction. In our terms, far from being genuinely inclusive, these measures merely redraw the lines of social exclusion and are experienced in this way by those who are forced into work. Social inclusion is not simply achieved by being included in the economy, as so many left of centre politicians would seem to believe. The point I have stressed throughout this book is that many of the people who feel most excluded from society (and the most relatively deprived) *are* in work. Indeed the resistance of many of the unemployed to work is based on a very realistic sense of the unmeritocratic unfairness of these policies.

Let us turn now to transformative remedies for distributive injustices. If one looks at Fraser's necessarily brief list of interventions one is struck by their rather conventional nature. They are all the old stalwart measures suggested by social democrats and tried – throughout most of Northern Europe at least – by numerous left of centre administrations. They are in the present decade contentious, to say the least, each and every one has come under considerable criticism and, indeed, the modernization programmes embarked upon by the majority of social democratic and labour parties have been directed at dealing with the manifest problems which occurred over the years. Universalistic social welfare programmes creak under the huge rise in budgets that they have generated, progressive taxation has fallen contentiously on many middle income wage earners who often feel uninspired to take up responsibility in their organizations given the low level of net incentives whilst public ownership has proved cumbersome, inefficient and unresponsive to the demands of a new consumer public. Fierce arguments have occurred in social democratic circles with talk of a 'third way' frequently mooted, and harsh reforms have been implemented worldwide. Yet Nancy Fraser writes as if the debates of the past ten years have scarcely taken place. At the very least one might question the ability of these measures to tackle the mechanisms which lead to the perpetuation of a class society. This is not the place to enter into extensive critiques of the welfare state but it is important to note that there is significant contemporary criticism even from those who are sympathetic to social democracy. Thus:

1 Universalistic measures do not seem to promote equality but are of greater benefit to the middle class. That is, public provision would seem to have least impact on those in greatest need (see Le Grand, 1982).
2 Taxation and welfare benefits often involve a horizontal reshuffling of resources *within* classes (e.g. between earners and dependants, the sick and the healthy) rather than *between* classes (see Westergaard and Resler, 1976).
3 The general efficiency of delivery of the public services has been widely and regularly criticized (see Corrigan et al., 1988).
4 The level of resistance of the status quo, of the existing class structure tinged with resentment of egalitarian measures, is grossly underestimated (see Goldthorpe, 1980).
5 The personnel manning the public bureaucracies are only half-heartedly committed to egalitarianism (see Hindess, 1987).

In various ways, therefore – through the inefficiency of the public bureaucracies concerned, their displacement of goals and the resistance and resentment throughout in the class structure – egalitarian measures are subverted. The 'strategy of equality', in Julian Le Grand's phrase, is inadequate for the immense task facing it. This widespread failure of social democracy to achieve the level of social equality which it aimed for has to be taken on board if we are to talk of transformative rather than affirmative remedies in the area of distributive justice.

In the last chapter I talked of the left's problem with meritocracy. It is as if they confused substantive and formal equality, believing that all people would be literally equal if only given equal opportunities. Reward by merit is seen to be a concept of the market, a rather unpleasant ideal of the political right. Thus Iris Young talks of 'the myth of merit', believing merit extremely difficult to measure and inevitably culturally biased (see 1990a, pp. 192–225), while John Rawls (1971) argues that using natural talents as criteria of reward is just as arbitrary as using sex or race because a person has as little responsibility for his or her talent as for sex or race. And note too how Nancy Fraser, in her list of transformative responses (p. 236), stresses the need 'to delink basic consumption shares from employment'.

Indeed, with respect to the latter, the 'decommodification' of work is seen as a major criterion of a developed social democracy (see Twine, 1994; Epsing-Anderson, 1990). And, quite explicitly, meritocratic and egalitarian policies are seen as opposites. A recent article in the excellent journal *The Chartist* castigates New Labour for being

> meritocratic rather than egalitarian, its aim the creation of a more open and mobile society rather than a more equitable one. It seeks to ensure that all have an opportunity to climb the ladder of success, rather than diminishing the distance between the rungs. What matters is not how resources are distributed but whether all people have the opportunity to better themselves by dint of effort, ability and enterprise. (Shaw, 1998, p. 9)

I wish to argue that the polarities here are simply not opposites, that, far from it, they are integrally related. In an earlier piece (Corrigan et al., 1988), my colleagues and I maintained that meritocracy is a key component of a transformative politics; indeed that it is only by arguing for merit that arguments for equality can be sustained: 'The imperative of equality must be met with the imperative of merit or it will fail to convince' (ibid., p. 8). Reward by merit is not only a widespread and popular value in our society, it provides the incentives necessary to create a dynamic economy and responsive public bureaucracies. The problem is not that society is too meritocratic but the opposite: the economically powerful attempt to control markets, not widen them; educational and job opportunities are severely restricted by class background (see Reay, 1998), and the rewards themselves are grossly distorted by the impact of inherited wealth:

> Two criteria downgraded either explicitly, or by neglect, by the left over the past decade need to be rescued. Without their use, a programme which stresses equity and community can never be delivered. . . .
>   People should receive rewards on a measure which recognises what they put into society, while institutions, public and private, should be judged according to their efficiency in carrying out agreed tasks. (ibid., p. 5)

Indeed, the problem of the ineffectiveness of public bureaucracies necessitates meritocratic criteria of reward, the plethora of performance indicators which have become part of the world, as well as public institutions and officials should surely be criticized when their measures are inappropriate but should be welcomed overall. As to the unfairness of rewarding talent which is supposedly distributed so randomly and unfairly, it should be noted that talent usually requires a large amount of effort and application whether it be in the concert hall or the operating room; it is scarcely a fixed quality bestowed upon the individual.

  The notion of a radical meritocracy, advocated here, whilst falling far short of a fundamental transformation in the ownership of capital, would by insisting on opening up the work sphere to all, by restricting inherited wealth, and by ensuring that payment reflects merit, begin to change the mechanisms which reproduce class differentials. It would tackle the problems of resentment which occur where egalitarian policies ignore effort. This is particularly true in the zone of employment of those in low pay just above those who are not in work. Here hours are long and work is most alienating and here is the most likely social basis of moral indignation (see the discussion of Luttwak in Chapter 1, pp. 8–9). For, ironically, Fraser's notion of a transformative politics of distribution would without meritocracy create precisely the problems of stigmatization and discontent which she recognizes in affirmative politics.

Sphere of community: the transformative other

Let us turn now to Nancy Fraser's notions of politics of recognition. Her transformative remedies which destabilize the sense of fixed identity of both majority and minority groups fit well with the advocacy of a transformative multiculturalism which I have outlined in this chapter. Fraser has been criticized, here, as coming close to being assimilationist (Phillips, 1996); because, whereas Iris Young is keen to maintain cultural difference once shorn of the stigma of misrecognition, Fraser is only too ready to advocate a melting-pot solution to multiculturalism.

I think if we take Fraser's argument a little further we can see that such criticism of a deconstructionist approach to the injustice of recognition is wrong for the following two reasons:

1 Multiculturalism just like inclusivist notions of a dominant culture, inevitably results in a division of the world in an essentialist fashion. Such essentialism provides the prerequisite base for demonization. For as writers as diverse as Bauman, Hobsbawm and Hughes have argued, difference multiculturalism is no protection against social conflict, indeed it facilitates it.
2 Social reality itself in the late modern period is hopelessly interwoven: both majority and minority cultures already share much of each other. Assimilation *and* differentiation is a constant process of interaction which is facilitated in Nancy Fraser's politics rather than hindered as in that of Iris Young.

The search for a non-oppressive city which provides opportunity and celebrates diversity takes us on a path towards meritocratic policies in the sphere of justice and transformative policies in the sphere of community. The terrain over which we must travel in order to reach these goals poses many problems yet the changes engendered in late modernity have much to offer. It is to this I will turn in the final chapter.

8 THE CONTRADICTORY WORLD OF LATE MODERNITY

There is a tendency amongst social critics, particularly those on the left of the political spectrum, to celebrate the detection and announcement of dystopia. Each new development is seen as tightening the ratchet of control, and as the forerunner of some new and technologically sophisticated totalitarianism. Once upon a time, in a not too distant past, such sightings were seen as proof of the inevitable slide into social barbarism which would galvanize the population into making structural changes in the social order. I have no doubt that such fundamental change is necessary but the dystopians seem to have given up on the transformation of the future and all they are left with is a gloomy reflex about the present.

Of course there is much to be apprehensive about. The great penal gulag being constructed in the United States has taken liberal democracy to its limits; the incarceration of the majority of young black men at some time in their life is an indictment which is as obscene as it is unbelievable, whilst the carceral archipelago has stretched throughout the US population. Not only is violence a common currency of American culture, whether it be in cartoon or feature film, and violent crime has become a normal part of everyday life, but, also, the criminal justice system in the form of prison, parole and probation has become normalized. The creation of such an excluded population, its size that of Philadelphia, with a penumbra the size of New York City, is as significant an event of the latter part of the twentieth century as are the astonishing scientific achievements of space and biology – and surely some day some American dissident will chart the American gulag as did Solzhenitsyn the Russian gulag before him. Indeed the American prison gulag represents as much the crisis of late modernity as the Russian gulag represented a clear sign to the world of the crisis of Soviet modernity.

We should also be fully apprehensive about the forces of technology which will without doubt transform our lives for good and for ill. We live in a society where, as Frank Webster (1995) has astutely noted, information about each other has declined yet information available to political, commercial and criminal justice elites has increased exponentially. Data bases generated in economic transactions in supermarkets, in encounters with the police, in mail order shopping, in health checks, in a myriad activities but, above all, in the generation of credit ratings (the ultimate basis of actuarialism) build up, intermesh and interface. The possibility of smart cards which will contain a wealth of our personal data is with us. Computer technology allows the massing of such data bases and their ready access – other new technologies, such as genetic profiling, will further add to this package. Thus an individual's profile in terms of trustworthiness, creditworthiness and physical vulnerability will be easily available. As we move to late modernity, information gathering shifts from harvesting general and sparse information with regard to the behaviour of groups (men, women; old, young; AB compared to C1, C2, etc.) to precise and plentiful information on individuals (cf. Simon, 1987). This is a risk quotient for each of us. And to this modern panopticon is added visual surveillance. The cameras invade our corner shops, our shopping malls, the city centre, the residential estate, our factories and, finally, the home itself. The cameras move from surveying outside the home to inside the home so that the activities of babysitters, cleaners (and perhaps our partners!) can be surveyed and checked upon. The technology becomes more adept and inexpensive as the months approach the millennium.

Such a burgeoning of ever more sophisticated technology facilitates the actuarial sifting of the population. In an article written in 1975 I pointed, using the phrase of William Burroughs, 'to the soft machine' of social control, the major locus being the workplace with its 'judicial distribution of rewards tied into a thousand pinpricks of punishment', contrasting this with the criminal justice system which was 'the ultimate arsenal, at the terminus of social control' whose 'hard edge was directed as those who are "disorganized", "unproductive" and "idle"' (p. 83). The soft machine of modernity is still with us, although by late modernity the 'hard edge' has sharpened considerably. It has also, as I have argued, developed a littoral aspect: the gradient of acceptability has stretched throughout the population. And if the criminal justice system has grown and grown in its orbit (to encompass, as we have seen, 1 in 37 of the US adult population), the actuarial assessment of the rest has developed a control aspect. For as credit becomes a central *modus vivendi* of the late modern citizen, it also becomes a form of social control. As Jonathan Simon put it:

> We have looked at the modern rationality of risk as a means of providing security. But the risk principle, and the techniques of aggregation and security that constitute it, are also a form of social control. These techniques operate to regulate the access each of us has to the commodities and opportunities that exist in society. The control works two ways. First, methods of risk assessment assure that the access people have is controlled. Second, people alter their behaviour in order to receive access. (1987, p. 76)

People alter their behaviour because regular payments and a high credit rating allow them access to the most amazing array of choice, from clothes and restaurants to travel around the globe. Social control becomes located not only in performance at work, but in financial status; the soft machine moves its locus from the workplace to the counting house.

Apprehension is also justified with regard to the public itself – not merely the agencies of the state and civil society. The downsizing of industry, the shrinking of the primary labour market – the creation of widespread economic insecurity – is accompanied by a world of moral diversity, of greater choice, of less embeddedness and greater disjointedness which makes for ontological insecurity. The two uncertainties rub shoulders and are a perfect recipe for projection of fears upon others and the phoney embellishment and shoring up of one's own position. As we have seen, essentialism both bestowed upon deviant others and conferred upon ourselves is one outcome of this situation. The demonization of others, the creation of folk devils and moral panics, is thus an ever-present possibility.

All in all, I have seemingly made a case for dystopia. The forces that would create an exclusive society are widespread and well founded, yet they are far from pushing in one direction: they have both positive and negative moments.

Let us first clear up the problem of the technology of social control. Technology is not necessarily dystopian, it is only so if one believes the old 1960s libertarian illusion that *all* social control is repressive. But gates and barriers not only exclude the dispossessed, they are also used by the vulnerable to protect themselves. The gated city in an aggressive world can be either an island of privilege or a sanctuary; it depends which way the gates are turned. The development of technologies can scarcely be arrested but it can be, in the right political situation, harnessed and controlled. Even the unintended consequences of the commodification of news by the mass media and the insatiable market for the controversial and the startling can be progressive in its impact. To take a famous example, in 1992 a black man, Rodney King, was caught on video camera in Los Angeles being beaten by three white LAPD officers and this image was relayed by television. The single beating was repeated a million times around the globe, each blow to Rodney King resonating across the black diaspora of the Western world. In the cafés of La Corneuve in Paris, in the pubs of Stoke Newington, London, in the bars of Kingston, Jamaica, the message was clear: 'police racism is endemic, whatever lies the officials tell you'. The globalization of news creates commodities which are shared by the world and which enter into the historical accounts of a particular place and time. They are viewed not only everywhere now, but may, as in this instance, be viewed repeatedly in the future.

It is in this context that we must view the new technology. CCTV, for example, is undoubtedly one of the most invidious of inventions. In the wrong hands it can police factories in a minute and draconian fashion ('the boss is everywhere'), it can generate a web of surveillance which far exceeds anything that is historically known, it can invade privacy and make Orwell's 1984 a reality. But it can also, in a different political context, be liberating and protective. The kids who hound the elderly on sink estates can be documented and traced, the 'neighbours from hell' can be brought to book, and many more innovative uses could be designed. CCTV can log police racism on the streets, it can produce pictures of a violent raid upon a club, it can show up overzealous officials and spotlight corruption. The cameras can be turned around; their context and control can be changed. Similarly, the use of electronic tagging does not carry with it a necessarily repressive implication. The extremely difficult problems of providing 24-hour protection for women threatened by their violent partners can be facilitated by tags which register and announce their entry into delineated exclusion zones. And the same can be true of stalkers, paedophiles, fascist thugs and a whole host of predatory individuals. To create an inclusionary society of civility does not mean that intrusions which threaten the lifestyles of others should be tolerated. An inclusive society, of the future, which prizes human diversity will make a central virtue of tolerance – but tolerance by its very nature must be guarded by intolerance of predation.

The contradictory nature of late modernity

> Our past, whatever it was, was a past in the process of disintegration; we yearn to grasp it, but it is baseless and elusive; we look for something solid to lean on, only to find ourselves embracing ghosts. . . .
>
> The process of modernization, even as it exploits and torments us, brings our energies and imaginations to life, drives us to grasp and confront the world that modernization makes, and to strive to make it our own. I believe that we and those who come after us will go on fighting to make ourselves at home in this world, even as the homes we have made, the modern street, the modern spirit, go on melting into air. (Berman, 1983, pp. 333, 348)

The movement into late modernity is like a ship which has broken from its moorings. Many of the crew cry to return to the familiar sanctuary of the harbour but to their alarm the compass spins, the ship continues on its way and, looking back, the quay is no longer so secure: at times it seems to be falling apart, its structure fading and disintegrating. The siren voices which forlornly, seriously, soberly try to convince them that going back is possible are mistaken. It must be clear by now that I believe there is no going back and that there is little that would be gained if it were, indeed, possible. Yet politicians argue as if they can reconstitute the nuclear family for life, bring back full male employment as we once knew it, engineer communities which are as caring and densely structured as a soap opera, reinstate respect for authority, eliminate crime by zero-tolerance and regulate the lives of teenagers by curfew, CCTV and truancy squads. They are trying to move against the most massive current of economic, social and technological change which we have experienced in this century. It would be like expecting in 1950 that you could reconstruct the post-war world so that 1980 would be like 1950 only richer – which, of course, is precisely what many people thought possible. Yet the changes which occur are inherently contradictory, they bring forth opportunities as well as restrictions and dangers.

Marshall Berman talks of a world disappearing, of, in the words of the *Communist Manifesto*, 'all that is solid melting into air', and to this Eric

Hobsbawm adds a touch of historic irony – that capitalism depends on all the pre-capitalist virtues of trust, honour and respect, that at the time of its seeming triumph, the very oxygen on which it was dependent becomes more dissipated and rarefied. Let us add to this that these virtues included defer-ence to authority, stoic acceptance of unfairness, sacrifice to the will of others, unthinking obedience both in wider society and in the family. To the extent that these values are disappearing, it is no bad thing. The stoic char-acter armour of self-denial and restraint, of blinkered acceptance and rigid-ity, which so many of our parents and our parents' parents wore through their lifetimes is falling away. The market, as Paul Willis indicated, is sub-versive to the Protestant ethic, it undermines deferred gratification and denial. James Q. Wilson talks of a shift from a culture of self-control to one which celebrates self-expression:

> We have become a nation that takes democracy to mean maximum self-expres-sion, though it never meant that originally, and to be suspicious of anything that looks like an effort to state or enforce a common morality. Democracy has become an end, though it originally was embraced as a means to other ends – a way (to quote the Constitution) of forming a more perfect union, establishing justice, insuring domestic tranquillity, providing for the common defense, pro-moting the general welfare, and securing the blessings of liberty. In the hands of reasonable, decent people, a devotion to self-actualization is at best artistic or inspiring and at worst banal or trivial. In the hands of persons of weak character, with a taste for risk and an impatience for gratification, that ethos is a license to steal and mug. (1985, pp. 248–9)

It is an axiom of conservative social commentators that the unravelling of the rigours and disciplines of culture and everyday life will automatically release the dangerous anti-social creature that exists just beneath the patina of civiliz-ation. In this instance to celebrate self-expression makes matters even worse: first you weaken the culture then you actually exhort the individuals to do their own thing! In this book I have argued the reverse of this: *true*, deferen-tial, unreflecting discipline is necessary if order is to be maintained in an unequal world; *true,* the rise of individualism helps the cataracts of con-formity fall away and the individual is likely to be mightily discontented with what he or she sees; *very true,* that this may well cause a rise in crime, dis-order and disagreement; but *false* that this is a product of human nature and the only thing to do is 'realistically' put up with the world ('we have made our society and we must live with it', Wilson notes gloomily: p. 249). For the growth of individualism and the greater reflexivity of the human actor offers great promises as well as the pitfalls and perils of late modernity.

Behind all of this rising discontent is the motor of the market place. First of all the greater and greater globalization of the economy lumps together people into a wider congress and exchange, allowing and encouraging them to make comparison with regard to distributive rewards. The fundamental systemic contradiction in capitalism, noted so well by Merton, between a culture of meritocracy and a structure of inequality, becomes all the more evident both in the unfairness of the comparative rewards of those included and the injustice of those excluded from the market place. Secondly, on the back of the consumer revolution, is a demand for the self-actualized individual. Here the desire for personal fulfilment is thwarted by the actual nature of work and the possibilities of fulfilment. Listen to John K. Galbraith at his most acerbic, as he describes the relationships between the 'work' of the poor and that of the rich:

> Work, in the conventional view, is pleasant and rewarding; it is something in which all favored by occupation rejoice to a varying degree. A normal person is proud of his or her work.
>
> In practical fact, much work is repetitive, tedious, painfully fatiguing, mentally boring or socially demeaning. This is true of diverse consumer and household services, and the harvesting of farm crops, and is equally true in those industries that deploy workers on assembly lines, where labor cost is a major factor in the price of what is finally produced. (1992, p. 32)

And there is a surprising/unsurprising relationship between work and payment:

> It is a basic but rarely articulated feature of the modern economic system that the highest pay is given for the work that is most prestigious and most agreeable. This is at the opposite extreme from those occupations that are inherently invidious, those that place the individual directly under the command of another, as in the case of the doorman or the household servant, and those involving a vast range of tasks – street cleaning, garbage collection, janitorial services, elevator operation – that have an obtrusive connotation of social inferiority.
>
> There is no greater modern illusion, even fraud, than the use of the single term *work* to cover what for some is, as noted, dreary, painful or socially demeaning and what for others is enjoyable, socially reputable and economically rewarding. Those who spend pleasant, well-compensated days say with emphasis that they have been 'hard at work', thereby suppressing the notion that they are a favored class. They are, of course, allowed to say that they enjoy their work, but it is presumed that such enjoyment is shared by any *good* worker. (ibid., pp. 32–3)

At heart, he suggests, there is a hidden fact which even the most sophisticated economic and social commentators are reticent about:

> From the foregoing comes one of the basic facts of modern economic society: the poor in our economy are needed to do the work that the more fortunate do not do and would find manifestly distasteful, even distressing. (ibid., p. 33)

Perhaps this was always so, but the fact of the modern world is that citizenship entails expectations of reasonable payment (meritocracy) and of job satisfaction (self-fulfilment). We have seen how the separation of the labour markets ensures that meritocracy is much more evident on the primary level (where you have career structure and ample rewards) but Galbraith adds that this is true also of self-fulfilment.

The American Dream of the middle of the century of success through hard work has been extended to that of self-fulfilment. The very concept of citizenship is widened so that the First World Dream of late modernity is concerned with meritocracy and identity rather than simply material comfort in the absolute sense. Yet the system promises meritocracy but delivers a 'fixed' racetrack where the prizes are distributed with blatant unfairness; it promises self-actualization but it relegates a large proportion of its members to the role of service providers to the egos of the super-rich and the successful. It embodies a stark winner takes all distribution of wealth and a sharp spotlight on stardom and celebrity. The positive moment of this is a rising and expanding concept of citizenship, people demand more of life, they are both more frustrated with the system and more demanding of it. The negative moment of this is a bitterness which can lead to treating people like commodities, as things and as essences. Let me, now, pause to recapitulate the arguments against an inevitable dystopian outcome.

The case against dystopia

1 **The ambivalence of technology**
   I have argued that there is nothing in the new technologies which is inherently repressive: the possibilities depend entirely on the political context rather than on the techniques *per se*. Indeed with sufficient public awareness and vigilance all of these techniques could be turned to advantage.

2 **Discarding tradition**
   The demise of the traditions which provided the civilities necessary to underwrite capitalism is not something that should be lamented, as Hobsbawm himself comes close to doing. Habits of deference, humilities of class, structures of patriarchy all contaminated the old-fashioned virtues of trust. These stand in the way of progress towards an inclusive society of trust between equal citizens. The Hobbesian war of all against all is not an inevitable corollary of their absence; rather their breakdown is a necessary prelude to any possible realization of a more equitable inclusive society.

3 **On the back of the market**
   The demands of social citizenship engendered by the market include both meritocracy and self-fulfilment. These have the potentiality, as Willis has indicated, to be subversive of the existing structures of capitalism. In the right circumstances they are the seeds of transformation, in others they can generate frustrations which are individualistic and internecine. In neither instance can they be considered a *deficit*, more an 'upping of the ante', a raising of demands rather than an experience of loss. The system then contains at its core a source of great instability: the motor for change occurs within the very engine room of capitalism.

4 **The elusive other**
   The unfairness, chaos and uncertainty of the market creates a world of

material insecurity; the diverse, transitory, reflexive world of late modern society generates a world of ontological insecurities. The uncertainties and frustrations in the sphere of justice and community generate feelings of both resentment and precariousness. There is a desperate need for identity and there is a pervasive desire to blame. Essentialism provides a seemingly hard core identity and an other from which to distinguish oneself, to assign guilt to and on to which to project negativities. Yet this essentialism, however dangerous and precarious in its impact, is at base flawed. This is because the circumstances necessary for the construction of deviant others, for their successful demonization, their blaming for the ills of society and for the achievement of ontological certainty amongst the 'normal' population become extremely tenuous in late modernity. The paradox is that at the moment of its greatest need such essentialism is most frequently invoked but less and less likely to work. The blaming of the single mother occurs when single parenthood becomes widespread, the war against drugs is accompanied by the normalization of drug use, the underclass becomes more and more like the core population, the stigmatization of the 'workshy' occurs at a time when a larger and larger percentage of the population are only too aware of the arbitrary and precarious nature of employment, etc. When I say 'doesn't work' I do not mean, of course, that such beliefs have no impact, far from it: the war against drugs has helped fill the American prisons, the vendetta against single mothers can be crippling for the most vulnerable, the fixation on dependency cultures is not only stigmatizing but further impoverishes the unemployed. But they do not work in terms of either being a believable ideology or nostalgically bringing back the inclusivist world of the post-war period.

The social contract of late modernity

The social contract of modernity has broken down in part because it was ill conceived, in part because the world has changed. Let us look at the transition to late modernity in terms of three areas: goals, *modus operandi*, and terrain. If the goal of modernity was the elimination of absolute deprivation and the creation of opportunities within a society of consensus, that of late modernity must be the distinctly different tasks of tackling relative deprivation and moving towards a more meritocratic and diverse society which provides both fulfilment and identity. The social contract, then, of the inclusive society of the post-war period, was to provide employment and, where this was absent, benefits so that the person could live as a civilized person in society:

> By the social element I mean the whole range from the right to a modicum of economic welfare and security to the right to share to the full in the social heritage and to live the life of a civilised being according to the standards prevailing in the society. (Marshall, 1996 [1950], p. 8)

Thus T.H. Marshall in his classic statement of citizenship describes the third social part, after the legal and political elements. I have argued that this social constituent has been dramatically expanded in the last half of the twentieth century. The social contract of late modernity must not simply provide employment but must insist on a meritocracy, it must not only seek to provide leisure facilities but must set its sights on meaningful work and leisure which gives a person a sense of purpose and identity.

We live in a society which is grotesquely unmeritocratic. By this I do not mean the inequalities of inherited wealth *which surely is the problem at core* but the way that from the top to the bottom desiderata are distributed with the logic of merit entering as only one of a series of entirely contingent factors in the calculation of reward. At times one confronts blatant unfairness; at other times, a *chaos of reward,* where there seems no rhyme nor reason to distributive justice. Indeed, such a process is widely recognized by the population as the *key* principle of distributive justice: 'the luck of the draw' – an extremely unmeritocratic concept. Unfairness is blatant and unapologetic. Let me cite just a few examples. We are privileged in British society to have at the very top of our social hierarchy a family, large and hospitable, whose principal reason for receiving large sums of public funds is genetic. And this gold filling exists in a mouthful of decay. There has recently in Britain been great controversy over a wide range of top people's remuneration and perks: the salaries of the heads of privatized utility companies, the extraordinary fees of top lawyers, the refurbishment of the homes of high-ranking army officers, the costs of maintaining circuit judges in the style to which they have been accustomed while travelling around the country. Yet it is not only such examples of unfairness at the top but the chaos of reward throughout the system. For many middle aged people, for example, in the middle income range, the largest source of income has been the completely arbitrary rise of house prices which occurred during the 1980s. It is as if fortune had placed them on an escalator where their worldly goods increased manifold without any effort on their part. And in the lower part of the class structure: the allocation of public largesse and the distribution of benefits often appears, not as the rational activity of a bureaucracy geared to the 'merit of need' but as arbitrary, flawed and, very frequently, corrupt. Lastly and most obviously, the allocation of individuals in the labour market, whether to the primary or secondary sector or to the ranks of those excluded from long-term employment, has only a partial relationship to merit. Too often the barriers of class, race, gender and age are self-evidently influential over those of merit and talent. The destructive effect on society of such widely perceived unfairness, uncertainty, and even arbitrary good fortune readily fuels relative deprivation and discontent.

In terms of methods of operation we must construct a new contract of citizenship which emphasizes diversity rather than absolute values, and which sees such diversity not as a catalogue of fixed features but as a plethora of cultures, ever changing, ever developing, transforming themselves and each other. It must be a contract which does not permit the state and its experts to bestow problems but involves and encourages intense democratic debate and evaluation, which is not a citizenship of rights but one of reciprocity between all citizens and which fully recognizes the necessity of reciprocity between citizen and state in the enactment of social goals and institutional change.

Finally, the terrain in which modernism flourished has fundamentally changed. It is not possible to go back to the world of the 1950s. We must work on the terrain which we are now given. We cannot go back to full employment in the sense of puberty to grave, nine till five and for men only. We cannot go back to the Kellogg's Cornflakes image of the nuclear family with its patriarchal structures and lifetime permanence. We cannot go back, outside of the soap operas anyway, to the community of perpetual interference, observation and meddling. We cannot go back to the thin blue line that protects us against crime and a welfare state which decides our priorities and bestows our problems. We cannot go back to monoculture, moral certainty and absolute values. We cannot return to the uncontested, the unambiguous, the unequivocal and the undebated.

The switchback of modernity takes us ever forward, closing down accustomed paths and offering us new panoramas and possibilities. 'All that is solid melts into air' but it must be remembered that all that was solid was often oppressive, unthinking and unexamined. Reason takes apart the old basis of trust but enjoins us to form new and more rational bases of order. Crime and intolerance occur when citizenship is thwarted; their causes lie in injustice, yet their effect is, inevitably, further injustice and violation of citizenship. The solution is to be found not in the resurrection of past stabilities, based on nostalgia and a world that will never return, but on a new citizenship, a reflexive modernity which will tackle the problems of justice and community, of reward and individualism, which dwell at the heart of liberal democracy.

REFERENCES

Abercrombie, N. and Warde, A. (1994) *British Society*, 2nd edn. Cambridge: Polity.

Anderson, S., Kinsey, R., Loader, I. and Smith, C. (1994) *Cautionary Tales*. Aldershot: Gower.

Anthias, F. (1995) 'Cultural Racism or Racist Culture? Rethinking Racist Exclusions', *Economy and Society* 24(2), pp. 279–301.

Archer, D. and Gartner, R. (1984) *Violence and Crime in Cross-National Perspective*. New Haven: Yale University Press.

Auld, J., Dorn, N. and South, N. (1986) 'Irregular Work, Irregular Pleasures' in R. Matthews and J. Young (eds) *Confronting Crime*. London: Sage.

Back, L. (1996) *New Ethnicities and Urban Culture*. London: UCL Press.

Baer, J. and Chambliss, W. (1997) 'Generating Fear: The Politics of Crime Reporting', *Crime, Law and Social Change* 27, pp. 87–107.

Bauman, Z. (1989) *Modernity and the Holocaust*. Oxford: Basil Blackwell.

Bauman, Z. (1995) *Life in Fragments*. Oxford: Blackwell.

Beck, U. (1992) *Risk Society*. London: Sage.

Beirne, P. (1993) *Inventing Criminology*. New York: State University of New York.

Berger, P. and Luckmann, T. (1967) *The Social Construction of Reality*. Harmondsworth: Penguin.

Berk, R (1990) 'Thinking about Hate-Motivated Crimes', *Journal of Interpersonal Violence* 5, pp. 316–333.

Berman, M. (1983) *All That Is Solid Melts Into Air*. London: Verso.

Blumstein, A. (1982) 'On Racial Disproportionality of the United States Prison Population', *Journal of Criminal Law and Criminology*, 73, pp. 1259–1281.

Bourgois, P. (1995) *In Search of Respect*. Cambridge: Cambridge University Press.

Bottoms, A. and Stevenson, S. (1992) 'What Went Wrong? Criminal Justice Policy in England and Wales' in D. Downes (ed.) *Unravelling Juvenile Justice*. Basingstoke: Macmillan.

Bowling, B. (1996) 'Zero Tolerance', *Criminal Justice Matters* 25 (Autumn), pp. 11–12.

Boyes, R. (1997) 'Heroin Subsidy Pushes Addicts off the Streets', *The Times*, 1 December, p. 14.

Braithwaite, J. (1998) 'Reducing the Crime Problem: A Not So Dismal Criminology' in P. Walton and J. Young (eds) *The New Criminology Revisited*. London: Macmillan.

Brannigan, A. (1998) 'Criminology and the Holocaust: Xenophobia, Evolution and Genocide', *Crime and Delinquency* 44(2), pp. 257–276.

Buckingham, L. (1998) 'Analysis: Salaries', *The Guardian*, 17 April, p. 19.

Bureau of Justice Statistics (1995) *Correctional Populations in the United States*. Washington: US Department of Justice.

Bureau of Justice Statistics (1996) *Correctional Populations in the United States 1994*. Washington: US Department of Justice.

Campbell, B. (1998) *Diana: Princess of Wales*. London: The Women's Press.

Campbell, C. (1987) *The Romantic Ethic and the Spirit of Modern Consumerism*. Oxford: Blackwell.

Cavadino, M. and Dignan, J. (1997) *The Penal System*, 2nd edn. London: Sage.

Chambers, I. (1986) *Popular Culture: The Metropolitan Experience*. London: Methuen.

Chambliss, W. (1994a) 'Profiling the Ghetto Underclass: The Politics of Law and Order Enforcement', *Social Problems* 41(2), pp. 177–194.

Chambliss, W. (1994b) 'Don't Confuse Me With Facts – "Clinton Just Say No"', *New Left Review* 204, pp. 113–128.

Chapman, D. (1968) *Society and the Stereotype of the Criminal*. London: Tavistock.

Chein, I., Gerard, D., Lee, R. and Rosenfeld, E. (1964) *Narcotics, Delinquency and Social Policy*. London: Tavistock.

Christie, N. (1993) *Crime Control as Industry*. London: Routledge.

Christie, N. and Bruun, K. (1985) *Den Gode Fiende*. Oslo: Norwegian University Press.

Christopherson, S. (1994) 'The Fortress City: Privatized Spaces, Consumer Citizenship' in A. Amin (ed.) *Post-Fordism*. Oxford: Blackwell.

Clark, R. (1970) *Crime in America*. London: Cassell.

Clarke, R. (1980) 'Situational Crime Prevention', *British Journal of Criminology* 20(2), pp. 136–147.

Clarke, R. and Hough, M. (1984) *Crime and Police Effectiveness*. London: HMSO.

Cohen, A. (1955) *Delinquent Boys*. New York: The Free Press.

Cohen, S. (1972) *Folk Devils and Moral Panics*. London: Paladin.

Cohen, S. (1973) 'Protest, Unrest and Delinquency: Convergencies in Labels and Behaviour', *International Journal of Criminology and Penology* 1, pp. 117–128.

Cohen, S. (1985) *Visions of Social Control*. Cambridge: Polity Press.

Cohen, S. (1995) *Denial and Acknowledgement: The Impact of Information about Human Rights Violations*. Jerusalem: Center for Human Rights.

Cohen, S. (1997) 'Intellectual Scepticism and Political Commitment' in P. Walton and J. Young (eds) *The New Criminology Revisited*. London: Macmillan.

Cohen, S. and Young, J. (eds) (1981) *The Manufacture of News*. (Revised edn.) London: Constable.

Cooper, A., Hetherington, R., Baistow, K., Pitts, J. and Spriggs, A. (1995) *Positive Child Protection: A View from Abroad*. Lyme Regis: Russell House.

Cooper, D. (1967) *Psychiatry and Anti-Psychiatry*. London: Tavistock.

Corrigan, P., Jones, T., Lloyd, J. and Young, J. (1988) *Socialism, Merit and Equality*. London: Fabian Society.

Council of Europe (1995) *Penological Information Bulletin* 19–20. Brussels: Council of Europe.

Crosland, A. (1956) *The Future of Socialism*. London: Jonathan Cape.

Currie, E. (1985) *Confronting Crime: An American Challenge*. New York: Pantheon.

Currie, E. (1996) *Is America Really Winning the War on Crime and Should Britain Follow its Example?* London: NACRO.

Currie, E. (1997a) 'Market, Crime and Community', *Theoretical Criminology* 1(2), pp. 147–172.

Currie, E. (1997b) 'Zero Tolerance and its Alternatives'. Paper presented at the ESRC/University of Salford Colloquium The Quality of Life and the Policing of Incivility, September.

Currie, E. (1998) *Crime and Punishment in America*. New York: Metropolitan Books.

Dearing, A. (1998) *No Boundaries: New Travellers on the Road*. Lyme Regis: Enabler Publications.

deMause, L. (1991) *The Untold Story of Child Abuse*. London: Bellow Publishing.

Dennis, N. (1993) *Rising Crime and the Dismembered Family*. London: Institute of Economic Affairs.

Dennis, N. (ed.) (1997) *Zero-Tolerance: Policing in a Free Society*. London: Institute of Economic Affairs.

Dennis, N. and Erdos, G. (1992) *Families without Fatherhood*. London: Institute of Economic Affairs.

Downes, D. (1966) *The Delinquent Solution*. London: Routledge & Kegan Paul.

Downes, D. and Rock, P. (1982) *Understanding Deviance*. Oxford: Clarendon Press.

Dworkin, A. (1980) 'Taking Action' in L. Lederer (ed.) *Taking Back the Night*. New York: William Morrow.

Engels, F. (1969) [1844] *The Conditions of the Working Class in England in 1844*. London: Panther.

Epsing-Anderson, G. (1990) *The Three Worlds of Welfare Capitalism*. Cambridge: Polity.

Ericson, R. and Carriere, K. (1994) 'The Fragmentation of Criminology' in D. Nelken (ed.) *The Futures of Criminology*. London: Sage.

Erikson, K. (1966) *Wayward Puritans*. New York: Wiley.

Etzioni, A. (1993) *The Spirit of Community*. New York: Crown Publishers.

Etzioni, A. (1997) *The New Golden Rule*. London: Profile Books.

Evans, K., Fraser, P. and Walklate, S. (1996) 'Whom Can You Trust? The Politics of "Grassing" in an Inner City Housing Estate', *Sociological Review* 44, pp. 361–379.

Eysenck, H. (1970) *Crime and Personality*. London: Paladin.

Fallows, J. (1996) 'In Gates' Net', *The New York Review of Books* 43(3), 15 February, pp. 14–18.

Featherstone, M. (1985) 'Lifestyle and Consumer Culture', *Theory, Culture and Society* 4, pp. 57–70.

Feeley, M. and Simon, J. (1992) 'The New Penology: Notes on the Emerging Strategy of Corrections and its Implications', *Criminology* 30(4), pp. 449–474.

Feeley, M. and Simon, J. (1994) 'Actuarial Justice: The Emerging New Criminal Law' in D. Nelken (ed.) *The Futures of Criminology*. London: Sage.

Felson, M. (1994) *Crime and Everyday Life*. Thousand Oaks, CA: Pine Forge Press.

Fernbach, D. (1998) 'Biology and Gay Identity', *New Left Review* 228, pp. 47–66.

Ferraro, K. (1995) *Fear of Crime: Interpreting Victimization Risk*. New York: SUNY Press.

Ferrell, J. and Sanders, C. (eds) (1995) *Cultural Criminology*. Boston: Northeastern University Press.

Feys, J. (1996) 'Social Exclusion and Identity Politics'. Paper presented at the ERASMUS Common Study Programme, Critical Criminology and the Criminal Justice System, University of Gent, 5 November.

Fletcher, R. (1962) *Britain in the Sixties: The Family and Marriage*. London: Penguin.

Foley, R. (1993) 'Zero-Tolerance', *Trouble and Strife* 27 (Winter), pp. 16–20.

Foucault, M. (1965) *Madness and Civilisation*. London: Tavistock.

Frank, R. and Cook, P. (1996) *Winner Takes All Society*. London: Routledge.

Fraser, N. (1995) 'From Redistribution to Recognition? Dilemmas of Justice in a Post-Socialist Age', *New Left Review* 212, pp. 68–94.

Fraser, N. (1997) *Justice Interruptus: Critical Reflections on the 'Post Socialist' Condition*. New York: Routledge.

Friedan, B. (1960) *The Feminine Mystique*. Harmondsworth: Penguin.

Furedi, F. (1997) *The Culture of Fear*. London: Cassell.

Galbraith, J.K. (1962) *The Affluent Society*. Harmondsworth: Penguin.

Galbraith, J.K. (1992) *The Culture of Contentment*. London: Sinclair-Stevenson.

Garland, D. (1985) *Punishment and Welfare*. Aldershot: Gower.

Garland, D. (1990) *Punishment and Modern Society*. Chicago: University of Chicago Press.

Garland, D. (1995) 'Penal Modernism and Postmodernism' in T. Blomberg and S. Cohen (eds) *Punishment and Social Control*. New York: Aldine de Gruyter.

Garland, D. (1996) 'The Limits of the Sovereign State', *British Journal of Criminology* 36(4), pp. 445–471.

Garland, D. (1997) 'Governmentality and the Problem of Crime', *Theoretical Criminology* 1(2), pp. 17–27.

Giddens, A. (1991) *Modernity and Self-Identity*. Cambridge: Polity.

Giddens, A. (1992) *The Transformation of Intimacy*. Cambridge: Polity.

Gilroy, P. (1986) *There Ain't No Black in the Union Jack*. London: Hutchinson.

Gilroy, P. (1993) *The Black Atlantic*. London: Verso.

Gitlin, T. (1992) 'On the Virtues of a Loose Canon', in P. Aufderheide (ed.) *Beyond PC: Towards a Politics of Understanding*. St Paul, MN: Grey Wolf Press.

Gitlin, T. (1995) *The Twilight of Common Dreams*. New York: Henry Holt.

Goffman, E. (1971) *Relations in Public*. London: Allen Lane.

Goldberg, D. (ed.) (1994) *Multiculturalism: A Critical Reader*. Oxford: Blackwell.

Goldthorpe, J. (1980) *Social Mobility and Class Structure in Modern Britain*. Oxford: Blackwell.

Goodman, R. (1995) *The Luck Business; The Devastating Consequences of the American Gambling Explosion*. New York: The Free Press.

Gorer, G. (1955) *Exploring English Character*. London: Cresset Press.

Gottfredson, M. and Hirschi, T. (1990) *A General Theory of Crime*. Stanford, CA: Stanford University Press.

Gottfredson, M. and Hirschi, T. (1995) 'National Crime Control Policies', *Society* January–February, pp. 30–36.

Gouldner, A. (1971) *The Coming Crisis of Western Sociology*. London: Heinemann.

Greenwood, V. and Young, J. (1980) 'Ghettos of Freedom' in National Deviancy Conference (ed.) *Permissiveness and Control*. London: Macmillan.

Gusfield, J. (1989) 'Constructing the Ownership of Social Problems', *Social Problems* 36, pp. 432–441.

Hall, S. and Jefferson, T. (1976) *Resistance through Rituals*. London: Hutchinson.

Hall, S. and Whannel, P. (1964) *The Popular Arts*. London: Hutchinson.

Hall, S., Chritcher, C., Jefferson, T., Clarke, J. and Roberts, B. (1978) *Policing the Crisis*. London: Macmillan.

Harper, P., Pollak, M., Mooney, J., Whelan, E. and Young, J. (1995) *The Islington Street Crime Survey*. London: London Borough of Islington.

Harvey, D. (1989) *The Condition of Postmodernity*. Oxford: Blackwell.

Havel, V. (1996) 'The Hope for Europe', *New York Review of Books* 43(8), 20 June, pp. 38–41.

Head, S. (1996) 'The New Ruthless Economy', *New York Review of Books* 43(4), 29 February, pp. 47–52.

Herek, G. and Berrill, K. (1992) *Hate Crimes*. Beverley Hills, CA: Sage.

Herrnstein, R. and Murray, C. (1994) *The Bell Curve*. New York: The Free Press.

Hills, J. (1996) *New Inequalities: the Changing Distribution of Income and Wealth in the United Kingdom*. Cambridge: Cambridge University Press.

Hindess, B. (1987) *Freedom, Equality and the Market*. London: Tavistock.

HMSO (1968) *Children in Trouble*. Cmnd 3601. London: HMSO.

Hobsbawm, E. (1994) *The Age of Extremes*. London: Michael Joseph.

Hobsbawm, E. (1996) 'The Cult of Identity Politics', *New Left Review* 217, pp. 38–47.

Hobsbawm, E. and Ranger, T. (eds) (1983) *The Invention of Tradition*. Cambridge: Cambridge University Press.

Hofman, H. (1993) 'Some Stories of Crime Prevention'. Paper given to the Common Study Programme in Criminal Justice and Critical Criminology, University of Gent, 2 November.

Hofman, H. (1996) 'Kritische Criminologie en Preventie in het Licht van een Postmoderne Conditie', *Tijdschrift voor Sociale Wetenschappen* 41(2), pp. 192–205.

Holloway, W. and Jefferson, T. (1997) 'The Risk Society in an Age of Anxiety: Situating Fear of Crime', *British Journal of Sociology* 48(2), pp. 255–266.

Home Office (1996) *Criminal Statistics: England & Wales 1995*. London: HMSO.

Hope, T. (1995) 'The Flux of Victimisation', *British Journal of Criminology* 35, pp. 327–342.

Hope, T. (1996) 'Inequality and the Future of Crime Prevention', in S. Lab (ed.) *Crime Prevention at a Crossroads*. Cincinnati: Anderson Publishing.

Hope, T. and Foster, J. (1992) 'Conflicting Forces: Changing the Dynamics of Crime and Community on a "Problem" Estate', *British Journal of Criminology* 32, pp. 488–504.

Hope, T. and Hough, M. (1988) 'Area, Crime and Incivility', in T. Hope and M. Shaw (eds) *Communities and Crime Reduction*. London: HMSO.

Hughes, R. (1993) *The Culture of Complaint: The Fraying of America*. London: Harvill Press.

Hulsman, L. (1986) 'Critical Criminology and the Concept of Crime', *Contemporary Crises* 10, pp. 63–80.

Hutton, W. (1995) *The State We're In*. London: Jonathan Cape.

Jacobs, J. (1961) *The Death and Life of Great American Cities*. New York: Random House.

Jacobson, M (1997) 'New York City: An Overview of Corrections, Probation and Other Criminal Justice Trends' Paper presented at the Symposium on Crime and Prisons in the City, London, Middlesex University Centre for Criminology, 19 September.

Jacoby, R. (1994) 'The Myth of Multiculturalism', *New Left Review* 208, pp. 121–126.

Jamieson, R. (1998) 'Towards a Criminology of War in Europe' in V. Ruggiero, N. South and I. Taylor (eds) *The New European Criminology*. London: Routledge.

Jamieson, R. (forthcoming) 'Genocide and the Social Production of Immorality', *Theoretical Criminology*.

Jones, T., MacLean, B. and Young, J. (1986) *The Islington Crime Survey*. Aldershot: Gower.

Joseph Rowntree Foundation (1995) *JRF Inquiry into Wealth and Income*, Vols 1 and 2. York: Joseph Rowntree Foundation.

Karydis, V. (1992) 'The Fear of Crime in Athens and the Construction of the "Dangerous" Albanian Stereotype', *Chronicles* 5, pp. 123–147.

Karydis, V. (1996) 'Criminality of Migrants in Greece', *Chronicles* 9, pp. 169–175.

Katz, J. (1988) *The Seductions of Crime*. New York: Basic Books.

Kelling, G. and Coles, C. (1997) *Fixing Broken Windows*. New York: Free Press.

Kelly, L. (1987) 'The Continuum of Sexual Violence' in J. Hanmer and M. Maynard (eds) *Women, Violence and Social Control*. London: Macmillan.

Kelly, L. and Radford, J. (1987) 'The Problem of Men: Feminist Perspectives on Sexual Violence' in P. Scraton (ed.) *Law, Order and the Authoritarian State*. Milton Keynes: Open University Press.

Kinsey, R., Lea, J. and Young, J. (1986) *Losing the Fight against Crime*. Oxford: Blackwell.

Kitsuse, J. and Spector, M. (1973) 'Towards a Sociology of Social Problems', *Social Problems* 20, pp. 407–419.

Kraska, B. and Kappeler, V. (1997) 'Militarizing American Police: The Rise and Normalization of Paramilitary Units', *Social Problems* 44(1), pp. 1–18.

Krauthammer, C. (1993) 'Defining Deviancy Up', *The New Republic*, 22 November, pp. 20–25.

Kristeva, J. (1991) *Strangers to Ourselves*. New York: Harvester Wheatsheaf.

Kutzinger, J. and Hunt, K. (1993) *Evaluation of Edinburgh District Council's Zero Tolerance Campaign*. Edinburgh: District Council Women's Committee.

Lardner, J. (1997) 'Can You Believe the New York Miracle?', *New York Review of Books* 44(13), 14 August, pp. 54–58.

Lea, J. (1992) 'The Analysis of Crime' in J. Young and R. Matthews (eds) *Rethinking Criminology*. London: Sage.

Lea, J. (1997) 'Post-Fordism and Criminality' in N. Jewson and S. MacGregor (eds) *Transforming the City*. London: Routledge.

Lea, J. and Young, J. (1982) 'Policing and Marginal Groups' in D. Cowell, T. Jones and J. Young (eds) *Policing the Riots*. London: Junction Books.

Lea. J. and Young, J. (1984) *What Is To Be Done About Law and Order?* 1st edn. Harmondsworth: Penguin.

Lea, J. and Young J. (1993) *What Is To Be Done about Law and Order?* 2nd edn. London: Pluto.

Lees, S. (1997) 'Naggers, Whores and Libbers: Provoking Men to Kill' in S. Lees (ed.) *Ruling Passions: Sexual Violence, Reputation and Law*. Buckingham: Open University Press.

Le Grand, J. (1982) *The Strategy of Equality*. London: Allen & Unwin.

Lemert, E. (1967) *Human Deviance, Social Problems and Social Control*. Englewood Cliffs, NJ: Prentice-Hall.

Leonard, E. (1984) *Women, Crime and Society*. New York: Longman.

Lévi-Strauss, C. (1992) [1955] *Tristes Tropiques*. New York: Penguin.

Liebow, E. (1967) *Tally's Corner*. Boston: Little, Brown.

Lippens, R. (1994) 'Critical Criminologies and the Reconstruction of Utopia. Some Residual Thoughts from the Good Old Days'. Paper presented at the ERASMUS Common Study Programme, Critical Criminology and the Criminal Justice System, University of Bari, May.

Lippens, R. (1996) 'Hypermodern Progressive Social Policy: A View from Belgium'. Paper presented at the Conference on Crime and Social Order in Europe, Manchester, 7–10 September.

Lull, J. (1991) *China Turned ON: Television, Reform and Resistance*. London: Routledge.

Luttwak, E. (1995) 'Turbo-Charged Capitalism and Its Consequences', *London Review of Books* 17(21), 2 November, pp. 6–7.

Lynch, J.P. (1988) 'A Comparison of Prison Use in England, Canada, West Germany and the United States: A Limited Test of the Punitive Hypothesis', *Journal of Criminal Law and Criminology* 79(1), pp. 180–217.

Maguire, K. and Pastore, A. (eds) (1995) *Bureau of Justice Statistics Sourcebook 1994*. Washington, DC: US Department of Justice.

Marshall, T.H. (1996) [1950] *Citizenship and Social Class*. London: Pluto.

Matthews, R. (1988) 'Review of *Confronting Crime*', *Contemporary Crisis* 12, pp. 81–83.

Matthews, R. (1992) 'Replacing Broken Windows: Crime, Incivilities and Urban Change' in R. Matthews and J. Young (eds) *Issues in Realist Criminology*. London: Sage.

Matthews, R. and Young, J. (eds) (1986) *Confronting Crime*. London: Sage.

Matthews, R. and Young, J. (eds) (1992) *Issues in Realist Criminology*. London: Sage.

Matza, D. (1969) *Becoming Deviant*. Englewood Cliffs, NJ: Prentice-Hall.

Mauer, M. (1997) *Intended and Unintended Consequences: State Racial Disparities in Imprisonment*. Washington, DC: The Sentencing Project.

Mayhew, H. (1861) *London Labour and the London Poor*, Vol. 1. London: Griffin, Bohn.

McRobbie, A. and Thornton, S. (1995) 'Rethinking Moral Panic for Multimediated Social Worlds', *British Journal of Sociology* 46(4), pp. 559–574.

Medea, A. and Thompson, K. (1974) *Against Rape*. New York: Farrar, Strauss & Giroux.

Melossi, D. (1996) 'Social Control in the New Europe'. Paper presented at the Conference on Crime and Social Order in Europe, Manchester, 7–10 September.

Merton, R.K. (1938) 'Social Structure and Anomie', *American Sociological Review* 3, pp. 672–682.

Messerschmidt, J. (1986) *Capitalism, Patriarchy and Crime*. Lanham, MD: Rowman & Littlefield.

Messerschmidt, J. (1993) *Masculinities and Crime*. Lanham, MD: Rowman & Littlefield.

Metropolitan Police (1986) *Strategy Plan*. London: Metropolitan Police.

Mills, C. Wright (1955) *White Collar*. New York: Oxford University Press.

Mishra, R. (1981) *Society and Social Policy*, 2nd edn. London: Macmillan.

Mooney, J. (1993) *The Hidden Figure: Domestic Violence in North London*. London: Middlesex University Centre for Criminology.

Mooney, J. (1996) 'Violence, Space and Gender', in N. Jewson and S. MacGregor (eds) *Transforming Cities*. London: Routledge.

Mooney, J. (1997) 'Moral Panics and the New Right' in P. Walton and J. Young (eds) *The New Criminology Revisited*. London: Macmillan.

Mooney, J. (1998) 'Single Mothers and Feckless Fathers: Is This the Solution to the Crime Problem?' in P. Walton and J. Young (eds) *The New Criminology Revisited*. London: Macmillan.

Mooney, J. (1999) *Gender, Violence and Social Order*. London: Macmillan.

Morley, D. and Robins, K. (1995) *Spaces of Identity*. London: Routledge.

Morris, P. and Heal, K. (1981) *Crime Control and the Police*. London: HMSO.

Mort, F. (1994) 'Essentialism Revisited?' in J. Weeks (ed.) *The Lesser Evil and the Greater Good*. London: Rivers Oram.

Moynihan, D.P. (1993) 'Defining Deviancy Down', *American Scholar* 62 (Winter), pp. 17–30.

Mugford, M. and O'Malley, P. (1991) 'Heroin Policy and Deficit Models', *Crime, Law and Social Change* 15, pp. 19–37.

Murray, C. (1984) *Losing Ground*. New York: Basic Books.

Murray, C. (1990) *The Emerging British Underclass*. London: Institute for Economic Affairs.

Murray, C. (1994) *Underclass: The Crisis Deepens*. London: Institute for Economic Affairs.

Murray, C. (1996a) *What it Means to be a Libertarian*. New York: Boundary Books.

Murray, C. (1996b) 'The Ruthless Truth: Prison Works', *The Sunday Times*, 12 January, p. 2.

Murray, C. (1997) *Does Prison Work?* London: Institute for Economic Affairs.

Newman, K. (1985) *Report of the Commissioner of Police of the Metropolis*. London: HMSO.

Nightingale, C. (1993) *On the Edge*. New York: Basic Books.

Offe, C. (1984) *Contradictions of the Welfare State*. London: Hutchinson.

O'Malley, P. and Mugford, S. (1991) 'The Demand for Intoxicating Commodities', *Social Justice* 18(4), pp. 49–74.

Packard, V. (1960) *The Status Seekers*. London: Longman.

Painter, K., Lea, J., Woodhouse, T. and Young, J. (1989) *The Hammersmith and Fulham Crime Survey*. Middlesex University: Centre for Criminology.

Park, R. (1916) 'The City: Suggestions for the Investigation of Human Behaviour in an Urban Environment', *American Journal of Sociology* 20, pp. 608–620.

Parsons, T. (1947) 'Patterns of Aggression in the Social Structure of the Western World', *Psychiatry* 10, pp. 167–181.

Pateman, C. (1988) *The Sexual Contract*. Cambridge: Polity.

Pawson, R. and Tilley, N. (1994) 'Evaluation Research and Crime: a Scientific Realist Approach'. Mimeo.

Pearce, F. (1976) *Crimes of the Powerful*. London: Pluto.

Pearson, G., Gilman, M. and McIver, S. (1985) *Young People and Heroin Use in the North of England*. London: Health Education Council.

Pfohl, S. (1985) 'Towards a Sociological Deconstruction of Social Problems', *Social Problems* 32(3), pp. 228–232.

Phillips, A. (1996) 'Inequality and Difference', *New Left Review* 224, pp. 143–153.

Pitts, J. (1988) *The Politics of Juvenile Crime*. London: HMSO.

Pitts, J. (1994) 'What Can We Learn in Europe?', *Social Work in Europe* 1(1), pp. 48–53.

Pitts, J. (1997) 'The Politics and Practice of Youth Justice' in E. McLaughlin and J. Muncie (eds) *Controlling Crime*. London: Sage.

Platt, A. (1996) 'The Politics of Law and Order', *Social Justice* 21(3), pp. 3–13.

Plummer, K. (1995) *Telling Sexual Stories*. London: Routledge.

Pollard, C. (1997) 'Zero-Tolerance: Short Term Fix, Long Term Liability?' in N. Dennis (ed.) *Zero-Tolerance: Policing in a Free Society*. London: Institute of Economic Affairs.

Potter, K. (1997) 'Zero-Tolerance Time Bomb', *Police Review*, 18 April, pp. 24–26.

President's Commission on Law Enforcement and the Administration of Justice (1967) *The Challenge of Crime in a Free Society*. Washington, DC: US Government Printing House.

Pryce, K. (1979) *Endless Pressure*. Harmondsworth: Penguin.

Raban, J. (1974) *Soft City*. London: Hamilton.

Rawls, J. (1971) *A Theory of Justice*. Cambridge, MA: Harvard University Press.

Reay, D. (1998) 'Rethinking Social Class', *Sociology* 32(2), pp. 259–275.

Riesman, D. (1950) *The Lonely Crowd: A Study of Changing American Character*. Newhaven, CT: Yale University Press.

Ritzer, G. (1993) *The McDonaldization of Society: An Investigation into the Changing Character of Contemporary Social Life*. Thousand Oaks, CA: Pine Forge Press.

Rock, P. (ed.) (1994) *The History of Criminology*. Aldershot: Gower.

Rose, S., Lewontin, R. and Kamin, L. (1990) *Not in Our Genes*. Harmondsworth: Penguin.

Roshier, B. (1989) *Controlling Crime*. Milton Keynes: Open University Press.

Ruggiero, V. (1993) 'Organised Crime in Italy', *Social and Legal Studies* 2, pp. 131–148.

Ruggiero, V. (1996) *Organized and Corporate Crime in Europe*. Aldershot: Dartmouth.

Ruggiero, V. and South, N. (1995) *Eurodrugs, Drug Use, Markets and Trafficking in Europe*. London: UCL Press.

Ruggiero, V. and South, N. (1997) 'The Late-Modern City as Bazaar', *British Journal of Sociology* 48, pp. 55–71.

Runciman, W. (1966) *Relative Deprivation and Social Justice*. London: Routledge & Kegan Paul.

Rushton, P. (1995) *Race, Evolution and Behaviour*. New Jersey: Transaction.

Rustin, M. (1994) 'Incomplete Modernity: Ulrich Beck's Risk Society', *Radical Philosophy* 67, pp. 3–12.

Said, E. (1993) *Culture and Imperialism*. London: Chatto & Windus.

Sampson, R. and Wilson, W.J. (1995) 'Towards a Theory of Race, Crime and Urban Inequality' in J. Hagan and R. Peterson (eds) *Crime and Inequality*. Stanford, CA: Stanford University Press.

Sartre, J.P. (1964) *Saint Genet*. New York: Mentor Books.

Sayer, A. (1984) *Method in Social Science: A Realist Approach*. London: Hutchinson.

Schelsky, H. (1957) 'Ist die Dauerreflektion Institutionalisierbar?', *Zeitschrift für Evangelische Ethik* 1, pp. 153–174.

Schiller, H. (1992) [1969] *Mass Communications and American Empire*. New York: Augustus Kelley.

Schutz, A. (1967) *Collected Papers*, Vol. I, ed. M. Natanson: *The Problem of Social Reality*. The Hague: Martinus Nijhoff.

Seabrook, J. (1978) *What Went Wrong?* London: Gollancz.

Segal, L. (1987) *Is the Future Female?* London: Virago.

Sennett, R. (1970) *The Uses of Disorder*. Harmondsworth: Penguin.

Sennett, R. (1991) *The Conscience of the Eye*. London: Faber & Faber.

Shapiro, B. (1997) 'Zero-Tolerance Gospel'. http: www.oneworld.org index oc/issue 497/shapiro.html.

Shaw, E. (1998) 'Labour and Post-revisionism', *The Chartist* 173 (July/August), pp. 8–9.

Sibley, D. (1995) *The Geographies of Exclusion*. London: Routledge.

Simmel, G. (1950) 'The Metropolis and Mental Life' in *The Sociology of Georg Simmel*, trans. K.H. Wolff. New York: The Free Press.

Simon, J. (1987) 'The Emergence of a Risk Society: Insurance, Law and the State', *Socialist Review* 97, pp. 61–89.

Simon, J. (1993) *Poor Discipline*. Chicago: University of Chicago Press.

Simon, J. and Feeley, M. (1995) 'True Crime: The New Penology and Public Discourse on Crime' in T. Blomberg and S. Cohen (eds) *Punishment and Social Control*. New York: Aldine de Gruyter.

Skogan, W. (1988) 'Disorder, Crime and Community Decline' in T. Home and M. Shaw *Communities and Crime Reduction*. London: HMSO.

Smart, C. (1990) 'Feminist Approaches to Criminology', in L. Gelsthorpe and A. Morris (eds) *Feminist Perspectives in Criminology*. Milton Keynes: Open University Press.

Social Trends (1995) *Social Trends 25*. London: HMSO.

South, N. (1994) 'Privatising Policing in the European Market: Some Issues for Theory, Policy and Research', *European Sociological Review* 10(3), pp. 219–227.

Sparks, R. (1996) 'Masculinity and Heroism in the Hollywood Blockbuster', *British Journal of Criminology* 36, pp. 348–360.

Spinellis, C., Dermati, S., Koulouris, N., Tavoulari, M. and Vidali, S. (1996) 'Recent Immigration and Protection of Migrants' Human Rights in Greece', *Chronicles* 9, pp. 119–154.

Steinert, H. (1998) 'Ideologies with Victims' in V. Ruggiero, N. South and I. Taylor (eds) *The New European Criminology*. London: Routledge.

Stewart, M. (1967) *Keynes and After*. Harmondsworth: Penguin.

Sumner, C. (1981) 'Race, Crime and Hegemony', *Contemporary Crisis* 6, pp. 277–291.

Sumner, C. (ed.) (1990) *Censure, Politics and Criminal Justice*. Milton Keynes: Open University Press.

Sumner, C. (1994) *The Sociology of Deviance*. Milton Keynes: Open University Press.

Sutherland, E.H. (1940) 'White Collar Criminality', *American Sociological Review* 5(1), pp. 2–10.

Sutherland, E. and Cressey, D. (1966) *Principles of Criminology*, 7th edn. Philadelphia: J.P. Lippincott.

Tax, M. (1970) 'The Woman and Her Mind: The Story of Everyday Life' in A. Koedt and S. Firestone (eds) *Women's Liberation: Notes from the Second Year*. New York: Justice Books.

Taylor, I. (1999) *Crime in Context*. Oxford: Polity.

Taylor, I., Walton, P. and Young, J. (1973) *The New Criminology*. London: Routledge and Kegan Paul.

Thompson, J. (1995) *The Media and Modernity*. Cambridge: Polity.

Townsend, P. (1979) *Poverty in the United Kingdom*. Harmondsworth: Penguin.

Trickett, A., Ellingworth, D., Hope, T. and Pease, K. (1995) 'Crime Victimisation in the Eighties', *British Journal of Criminology* 35, pp. 343–359.

Turner, T. (1994) 'Anthropology and Multiculturalism' in D. Goldberg (ed.) *Multiculturalism*. Oxford: Blackwell.

Twine, F. (1994) *Citizenship and Social Rights*. London: Sage.

van den Haag, E. (1975) *Punishing Criminals*. New York: Basic Books.

van Swaaningen, R. (1997) *Critical Criminology: Visions from Europe*. London: Sage.

Vidali, S. (1996) 'Selectivity, Police Activity and Internal Enemies in Greece'. Paper given at the ERASMUS Common Study Programme: Critical Criminology and Criminal Justice, University of Gent, November.

Wacquant, L. (1996) 'The Comparative Structure and Experience of Urban

Exclusion: "Race", Class and Space in Chicago and Paris' in K. McFate, R. Lawson and W.J. Wilson (eds) *Poverty, Inequality and the Future of Social Policy*. New York: Russell Sage Foundation.

Waddington, P. (1986) 'Mugging as a Moral Panic', *British Journal of Sociology* 37, pp. 250–256.

Walklate, S. (1995) *Gender and Crime*. Hemel Hempstead: Prentice-Hall.

Walkowitz, J. (1992) *City of Dreadful Delight*. Chicago: University of Chicago Press.

Walsh, B. (1997) 'Can Fixing Windows Help Mend Cities?', *Urban Environment Today* 23, pp. 8–9.

Walton, P. and Young, J. (eds) (1998) *The New Criminology Revisited*. London: Macmillan.

Webster, F. (1995) *Theories of the Information Society*. London: Routledge.

Weeks, J. (ed.) (1994) *The Lesser Evil and the Greater Good*. London: Rivers Oram.

Westergaard, J. and Resler, H. (1976) *Class in a Capitalist Society*. Harmondsworth: Penguin.

Wilkins, L. (1964) *Social Deviance*. London: Tavistock.

Willis, P. (1977) *Learning to Labour*. Aldershot: Gower.

Willis, P. (1990) *Common Culture*. Milton Keynes: Open University Press.

Wilson, J.Q. (1985) *Thinking about Crime*, 2nd edn. New York: Vintage Books.

Wilson, J.Q. (1987) 'Crime and Punishment in England' in R. Tyrell (ed.) *The Future that Doesn't Work*. New York: Doubleday.

Wilson, J.Q. (1991) *On Character*. Washington, DC: AEI Press.

Wilson, J.Q. (1992) 'Against the Legalization of Drugs' in R. Evans and I. Berent (eds) *Drug Legalization: For and Against*. LaSalle, IL: Open Court.

Wilson, J.Q. (1993) *The Moral Sense*. New York: The Free Press.

Wilson, J.Q. and Herrnstein, R. (1985) *Crime and Human Nature*. New York: Simon and Schuster.

Wilson, J.Q. and Kelling, G. (1982) 'Broken Windows', *Atlantic Monthly*, March, pp. 29–38.

Wilson, W.J. (1987) *The Truly Disadvantaged*. Chicago: University of Chicago Press.

Wilson, W.J. (1996) *When Work Disappears*. New York: Knopf.

Woolf, J. (1985) 'The Invisible Flâneuse', *Theory, Culture and Society* 2(3), pp. 37–46.

Yonnet, P. (1993) *Voyage au centre du malaise français*. Paris: Gallimard.

Young, I. (1990a) *Justice and the Politics of Difference*. Princeton: Princeton University Press.

Young, I. (1990b) 'The Ideal of Community and the Politics of Difference' in L. Nicholson (ed.) *Feminism/Postmodernism*. New York: Routledge.

Young, J. (1971a) 'The Police as Amplifiers of Deviance, Negotiators of Reality and Translators of Fantasy' in S. Cohen (ed.) *Images of Deviance*. Harmondsworth: Penguin.

Young, J. (1971b) *The Drugtakers*. London: Paladin.

Young, J. (1972) 'The Hippie Solution: An Essay in the Politics of Leisure' in I. Taylor and L. Taylor (eds) *Politics and Deviance*. Harmondsworth: Penguin.

Young, J. (1975) 'Working Class Criminology' in I. Taylor, P. Walton and J. Young (eds) *Critical Criminology*. London: Routledge and Kegan Paul.

Young, J. (1981) 'Beyond the Consensual Paradigm' in S. Cohen and J. Young (eds) *The Manufacture of News*. London: Constable.

Young, J. (1987) 'The Tasks of a Realist Criminology', *Contemporary Crisis* 2, pp. 337–356.

Young, J. (1988) 'Risk of Crime and Fear of Crime' in M. Maguire and J. Pointing (eds) *Victims of Crime: A New Deal*. Milton Keynes: Open University Press.

Young, J. (1992) 'Ten Points of Realism' in J. Young and R. Matthews (eds) *Rethinking Criminology*. London: Sage.

Young, J. (1995a) *Policing the Streets*. London: Islington Council.

Young, J. (1995b) 'Incessant Chatter: Recent Paradigms in Criminology' in M. Maguire, R. Morgan and R. Reiner (eds) *The Oxford Handbook of Criminology*. Oxford: Clarendon Press.

Young, J. (1997) 'Left Realist Criminology: Radical in its Analysis, Realist in its Policy' in M. Maguire, R. Morgan and R. Reiner (eds) *The Oxford Handbook of Criminology*, 2nd edn. Oxford: Clarendon Press.

Young, J. (1998) 'Breaking Windows: Situating the New Criminology' in P. Walton and J. Young, *The New Criminology Revisited*. London: Macmillan.

Young, J. and Matthews, R. (1992) *Rethinking Criminology: The Realist Debate*. London: Sage.

INDEX